The Woman Who Works, The Parent Who Cares

Books by Sirgay Sanger, M.D., and John Kelly

You and Your Baby's First Year
The Woman Who Works, The Parent Who Cares

The Woman Who Works, The Parent Who Cares

A Revolutionary Program for Raising Your Child

SIRGAY SANGER, M.D.,
and JOHN KELLY

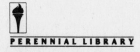

Harper & Row, Publishers, New York
Cambridge, Philadelphia, San Francisco, Washington
London, Mexico City, São Paulo, Singapore, Sydney

Most of the names in this book have been changed, for reasons of privacy.

A hardcover edition of this book is published by Little, Brown and Company. It is here reprinted by arrangement with Little, Brown and Company.

First PERENNIAL LIBRARY edition published 1988.

Library of Congress Cataloging-in-Publication Data
Sanger, Sirgay, 1935–
    The woman who works, the parent who cares.
    Includes index.
    1. Working mothers—United States. 2. Parenting—United States.
I. Kelly, John, 1945–   . II. Title.
HQ759.48.S26   1988   649'.1   87–46170
ISBN 0-06-097159-2 (pbk.)

88 89 90 91 92 FG 10 9 8 7 6 5 4 3 2 1

This book is dedicated to working mothers.
They are the heroines of this last decade
and a quarter of the twentieth century.
And they are raising — with love and
depth and guts — a generation of children
who, as adults, will be able to take on
the twenty-first.

Acknowledgments

FIRST, we would like to thank Sheila Weller and Jane Woznick, whose editorial skills, critical insights, and general supportiveness were invaluable.

Second, we would like to thank our editor, Fredrica S. Friedman; her counsel and assistance — at every stage of the editorial process — were vital in helping us to realize our hopes for this book.

Third, we are grateful to the staff of the Early Care Center, without whom the translation from theory to practice of all the research and ideas in this book would not have been possible.

Finally, and foremost, we are indebted to all the women in the REAP program, who experienced, experimented with, altered, and added to this first developmental program for working mothers and their children. They are the heart of the program, and they are pioneers in a new lifestyle, a new developmental equation of mother and child.

Contents

1 Why Work Has Changed the Rules of Development   3

2 The New Child   12

3 The Work-Shaped Family   24

4 Themes: How to Read Your Child   42

5 The Most Important Points in a Working Mother's Day   66

6 Active Guidance: The Three Developmental Milestones
      Every Working Mother Needs to Know About   90

7 Discipline Without the "No":
      Setting Limits in a New Developmental Age   118

8 The Optimist, the Worrier, the Achiever:
      Three Maternal Styles   135

9 The Single Working Mother   160

10 Thirteen Reasons Why You Shouldn't Feel Guilty
      about Working   174

11 Fathers: Your Support Team   190

12 Caregivers: Your Other Support Team   208

13 The New Developmental Guide to the Preschool Child   217

14 A Final Word   236

     Index   239

The Woman Who Works, The Parent Who Cares

1

Why Work Has Changed the Rules of Development

MOST books about working mothers are, in one way or another, really about guilt. And you will find guilt and its consequences discussed at length later in *this* book because it is a problem for many working mothers. But you also know that your concerns about work and about its effects on your child and on your relationship with him* arise from more than guilt. Firsthand experience has taught you that maternal employment creates real challenges for an infant or toddler and real challenges for his mother — and your concerns are shared by millions of other women.

It isn't that you regret the decision to go to work or doubt the degree of success your generation has achieved in combining a career with motherhood. Indeed, in light of this success, the notion that women with children in the developmentally sensitive period of ages four and under couldn't and shouldn't work suddenly looks as antiquated as the idea that women shouldn't be given the vote. Still, with your success has come a sense of uneasiness. Looking around, you see that through your choices you have created a new developmental world for your child. And you

---

* Here and throughout the book the child is referred to as masculine merely to distinguish him from the mother.

wonder about the effects of this world. What will it be like now that three out of four children born today are going to have a mother who works full time during some period of their first four years, and now that nine out of ten infants or toddlers will spend some portion of those critical first years in a day-care center or with a surrogate caregiver?

Will these boys and girls — will your boy or girl — be more or less secure, happy, and competent than they otherwise might have been? And what about the influence of the figures who people this world? What kind of shadow will your youngster's baby nurse, day-care worker, or nursery school teacher throw across his developmental course? And how will that person's relationship with him affect his relationship with you?

On park benches, around watercoolers, at luncheon counters, at bus stops, wherever working women congregate, these are the questions that are being asked. And as a working mother yourself, you know that they are now being asked with a new urgency and openness.

In the pages that follow, you will find answers to these and the other questions that most concern you and other working women with young children. For example, you will find:

- How to assess your child's adjustment to your work.
- How to help him overcome the challenges and problems it may be posing for him.
- How to make yourself a vivid, felt presence in your child's life even when you are away.
- How both of you can get the most out of your shared time together (and why that does not involve what is currently known as "quality time").
- How to liberate yourself from the debilitating consequences of guilt.
- In short, how to make the work a positive developmental force in the life of your child.

This book also will provide you with the first in-depth look at the new world that is emerging from your hopes and dreams and ambitions and those of millions of other working mothers like you. You will see, for example, why recent research indicates that maternal employment:

- Changes the rules of attachment, that bond between mother and child.
- Alters a woman's maternal style without her being aware of it.
- Changes the developmental timetable for the first four years of a child's life.
- Produces a new set of values and attributes among infants and toddlers.
- Creates emotional and cognitive challenges that test young children in new ways.

Most important of all, you will be introduced to the remarkable child—your child—who is emerging from these new dynamics. You can catch glimpses of him in the pages of a dozen recent studies that show the working mother's infant or toddler is more socially skilled, emotionally mature, self-sufficient, intellectually adventurous, and independent than children whose mothers don't work. Without quite intending it, then, you and other working women have done something at once audacious and deeply validating. You have raised a new kind of child: one who displays strengths not usually seen in the first four years of life and who possesses values that suggest that American society in the twenty-first century will be a more understanding, open, tolerant—*better*—place to live.

The reason experts like Dr. Urie Bronfenbrenner, professor of human development at Cornell University, describe this child as being the product of a new balance is that, as Dr. Bronfenbrenner put it recently, "in light of the new data on maternal employment, work has to be seen . . . as entailing significant benefits [for a child], but also some costs." In other words, along with the advantages, the new research also shows that maternal employment creates developmental risks and vulnerabilities.

This is the first book to explore the new balance—or more accurately, the new developmental equation. Simply put, its goal is to show you and other working women how to shape this new equation so that your child develops only the positive strengths and competencies work can promote. Its starting point is the assumption that because work is also important to you, you want (and, in many cases, need) both to mother and to work. And it is based on two foundations: the important new body of research on maternal employment that has emerged over the past decades; and the clinical insights and practical experiences my staff and I have gained in conducting the first program tailored specifically to the working mother and her child.

What the book does *not* do is show you how to mother the way you would if you stayed at home. All the remarkable skills, values, and attributes associated with your child are a direct result of the developmental rule changes that you and other working mothers have wrought. Not only are you rewriting the rules of attachment and redefining the meaning of a nurturing maternal style, you are changing these important developmental touchstones for the better. What this book *is* designed to do is help you respond more sensitively to those rule changes. Most of the troubling effects that have been laid at the doorstep of maternal employment have arisen not because there are aspects of it that are inherently threatening to a young child but because women are uncertain about how they should respond to the most fundamental rule change work has created: it introduces a child to the real world at a much earlier point in his developmental cycle.

For a boy or girl, this real world can be defined as a place where a large portion of each day is spent in the care of another adult and in the company of other children, and where daily separations from mother are routine. Up until very recently, a child didn't enter it until the start of formal school at five or six. But today, thanks to the lifestyle maternal employment has created, that introduction occurs at three, two, one, even six months or earlier.

This landmark change is the source of both the unique benefits and the risks work poses. An experience like day care provides a case in point. It can teach your infant or toddler lessons about cooperation, independence, self-sufficiency, and even friendship he wouldn't learn if he were home with you. But the day-care experience challenges him in ways that also are unique for an infant and toddler.

All the strategies and techniques in the chapters that follow are designed to show you how to help him not just to meet but to learn and grow from the challenges posed by his work-shaped lifestyle. And each has been adapted from a unique program that I and my staff at the Early Care Center in New York City have been conducting since 1982 for working mothers with children in the developmentally sensitive first four years of life. The program is called Reality Attuned Parenting, or REAP. And while in the largest sense REAP might be said to have evolved out of my nearly two decades of work with mothers and children—first at Harvard Medical School and Massachusetts General Hospital and later as director of the Parent-Child Interaction Program at St. Luke's Roosevelt Hospital in New York—it also has a more specific starting point.

Over the past fifteen years, interactional research has revolutionized our understanding of how children grow and how parents help them grow; I founded the Early Care Center with the aim of making this important new research available to parents generally. It quickly became apparent to me and to my staff, however, that in our at-home mothers and their children and in our working mothers and *their* youngsters we had two different populations with very different needs. REAP arose out of that realization. And its name, Reality Attuned Parenting, is meant to reflect what we believe to be the defining characteristic of the working mother's child: the real world enters his life earlier.

The parenting strategies we have devised to facilitate this introduction to the real world derive from two sources. Some represent a reshaping of general developmental principles to the specific needs of the working mother and her child; others have grown directly out of our experience guiding, counseling, and working with mothers much like you in weekly discussion groups (which are conducted by me or by one of the other developmental specialists on our staff).

Listening to our REAP mothers talk, we find it impossible not to be impressed by their pride, humor, courage, pluck, physical stamina, and intelligence. Many of them have already thought through the issue of work to the point where they have specific

ideas about the kinds of help and support they want from profes-
sionals. And we have been successful in providing that help and
support because we have incorporated the hopes, dreams, fears,
and doubts we have heard over the years into a program for
the working woman with a young child that is unique in five
respects.

1. *The program is shaped to fit a working mother's priorities.* It ac-
   knowledges and respects her desire (and often her need) to
   work and so provides her with tools that allow her to continue
   pursuing her career while being the deeply attached parent she
   wants to be.
2. *The program allows a woman to remain an active presence in her
   child's life, even when she is away at work.* No aspect of work
   troubles a mother more than the daily separations. No aspect
   of our program pleases mothers more than the discovery that
   shared activities like playing and reading can be transformed
   into emotional surrogates that allow a woman to bridge the
   daily separations work entails.
3. *The program offers the working mother solutions she can implement on her own.* Business and government should be doing
   more to help her, but the reality of the situation is that, at
   present, they are not. So the strategies we have devised are ones
   that a woman can implement by herself, without having to rely
   on her company or on the government.
4. *The program takes a realistic view of family life.* Studies show
   that when a woman returns to work, her husband's level of
   involvement in household and child-care chores increases
   marginally if at all. Thus, although the program shows her
   how to get her husband more deeply involved in what should
   be joint responsibilities, its strategies and techniques are based
   on the fact that in most families, the working mother is and
   will remain the primary parent.
5. *Most important of all, the program shows a woman how to make
   work a positive developmental force in her child's life.* This point
   takes us to the heart of the program. Your work and the family
   life you've built around it have given your child a greater

opportunity to learn about personal and social skills by expos-
ing him earlier and more frequently to new faces and places, to
novel situations, and even to complex emotions. But these
experiences also change a young child's needs in important
ways.

Think of the ten- or eleven-month-old in day care. Although he
is in an environment that can teach him a great deal about cooperation, empathy, and even friendship and responsibility, his ability
to begin learning those lessons will depend on whether he first
develops a means of feeling comfortable in a day-care environment. REAP's strategies are designed to provide that means by
providing a young child with the security, self-confidence, flexibility, sense of personal competence, and capacity to cope with stress
and frustration that he needs to operate effectively and benefi-
cially outside his immediate family circle.

To illustrate one way a strategy does this, let me briefly tell you
about a young friend of mine named Jeremy Rensselear and how a
REAP strategy his mother, Isabelle, learned helped put him at ease
when meeting new people and thus helped him to begin using
those meetings as occasions for social learning. Between day care,
play groups, nursery school, and the visits of both a parent's and a
caregiver's friends, meetings with strangers have become almost
routine for even four- and five-month-olds with working mothers.
And like most of the other experiences that grow out of an earlier
contact with the world, this situation has both potentially positive
and negative developmental effects for a young child.

The nature of both is apparent in a videotape I made of Jeremy
and Isabelle. It consists of two meetings mother and son have with
a stranger, who is played in both instances by Joan Simcox, one of
my graduate students. The first encounter occurred a week before
Jeremy and Isabelle entered the program. Jeremy's distress during
the meeting is almost palpable. When Joan first appears in the
doorway, Jeremy, who was fifteen months old when the tape was
made, ignores her warm greeting smile and buries his head firmly
in Isabelle's lap. Joan's offering of a toy only deepens his distress.
As she approaches, toy in hand, Jeremy tightens his grip on Isa-

belle and begins whimpering, "Mommy, Mommy." At this moment, Jeremy is a very distressed little boy.

The video of the second meeting was made two months later, and the reason Jeremy now appears to be an altogether different child is that Isabelle displays a new sensitivity in introducing Joan. Instead of trying to put Jeremy at ease by first offering Joan a warm smile and big hello, as she did during her first encounter, this time Isabelle momentarily ignores Joan and turns first to Jeremy, smiles, and murmurs a few words to him. This seemingly small change makes all the difference in the world because Isabelle is now speaking a language Jeremy understands.

Not until the second year does a child develop the cognitive skill to decipher *how* his mother is responding — friendly or unfriendly — to another person. So Isabelle's attempt to put Jeremy at ease in Joan's presence by offering Joan a warm greeting goes over his head. What an infant or toddler does understand, however, is maternal behavior that is directed at him. And like the rest of us, when that behavior makes him feel loved and secure, he wants to reach out and share his good feeling with others, whether those others be a new day-care worker, a parent's friend, or in this case, Joan. When she smiles this time, Jeremy beams back at her and is full of curiosity and enthusiasm when she offers him a toy. He even feels comfortable enough in her presence to evidence some curiosity about the watch on her wrist. And typically, these are the ways a young child is able to turn meetings with new people to his advantage when his needs have been answered sensitively.

Jeremy's experience is not unusual. Follow-up studies show that as a group the infants and toddlers who have passed through our REAP program display the independence, the social and self-comforting skills, the freedom from traditional male and female sex role stereotypes — all of the strengths that can be associated with maternal employment but few of the vulnerabilities.

Another important but somewhat different measure of the program's success has been the response we have seen it produce in our parents. Guilt has become a byword in discussions of the working mother, but we find that the mothers in our program enjoy a special sense of optimism. You can see it in their faces.

Gone is the look of preoccupation, vulnerability, and guilt so many working mothers wear.

At bottom, these feelings really are expressions of uneasiness and anxiety. Many women now feel uncertain about how to help their children meet the new opportunities and challenges produced by their working. I think the reason REAP and its strategies have proved such a powerful antidote to guilt and vulnerability is that its view of growth and development is shaped to the special needs and concerns work creates in an infant or toddler, and that we provide women with the knowledge to respond to those needs.

Our experience has shown that this knowledge, and the ability and confidence to apply it, represents the truest and most meaningful form of reassurance. Thus, in translating the REAP program from our playrooms and video studios at the center onto the printed page, our goal has been to provide advice and guidance that, as well as being shaped to the new rules that work has created, allow a working woman to be an active, involved, constant presence in her child's new life.

2

The New Child

Zooooom . . .

Traveling at what seems the speed of light, two-and-a-half-year-old Adam Hafferkamp streaks through my office doorway on his Big Wheel and banks a sharp left at the corner of the desk. Screeching to a halt in front of the parson's bench next to the window, Adam turns around and introduces us to the passenger strapped to the back of his vehicle. It is a doll. Spotting it, his mother, Marta, who is perched on the edge of the parson's bench, claps her hands in delight and announces, "I just know any little boy who bombs around with a baby doll on his Big Wheel is going to do just fine, Dr. Sanger."

Of all the ways her work has influenced Adam, Marta Hafferkamp says none pleases her more or gives her a greater sense of validation than this capacity of Adam's for unself-consciously combining boys' and girls' forms of play. Those of us who have studied youngsters like Adam also have been impressed and intrigued by this remarkable quality. The sons and daughters of working mothers really do seem to have arrived at a new way of integrating masculine and feminine traits. And, as in Adam's case, this achievement often announces itself in the most unexpected and delightful ways.

Dr. Kyle Pruett of Yale found himself so enchanted by one such example he encountered that he took the unusual step of including it in a research paper. Asked to identify a test flash card that had a picture of a man's sports jacket on it, Dr. Pruett's three-year-old subject looked thoughtfully at the picture of the jacket for a moment and then loyally pronounced it a "dress" in homage to his businesswoman mother.

Marta believes such egalitarian attitudes are as important to Adam's future as more traditional developmental benchmarks like verbal and problem-solving skills. I agree. As an adult, Adam will live and work in a world where equality is an accomplished fact, and his ability to function successfully in that world will depend on what he is learning now at home from Marta and her husband, Keith.

"Once Keith pointed to a shirt he was ironing and said, 'Look, Adam — man's work!' but that's been about the extent of our indoctrination," says Marta, laughing at the incident and proud that Adam is absorbing the lessons about sex roles in a natural and unself-conscious way. "If his ideas about how little boys behave are different from Keith's or my brother Sam's at that age, it is because he has a mommy who works and does the chores and a daddy who also works and does chores. So Adam doesn't associate either of these roles with one sex or the other."

Later, walking to the playroom, Marta talks about another aspect of her work. And as she does, you can almost see her finger slide from the positive to the negative side of the ledger on work's effects that she keeps in her mind. "During my pregnancy," she says, "I decided that if I was going to keep my job, Adam would need to have three or four loving figures to attach to, not just one. But now I wonder if I haven't been so successful that I have undermined my own importance. It is almost as if Keith and our caregiver, Joyce, have become my rivals." The depth of Marta's concern and doubt about this rivalry is evident in an incident she describes to me as we watch Adam and two playmates build a castle.

It occurred on the bright spring morning that ended Marta's six-month maternity leave. "I'd been having Joyce, whom we had hired a month earlier, come in two days a week so I could observe her with Adam, and she turned out to be everything I'd hoped she would be: loving, responsible, imaginative, and patient. As the weeks passed, it was clear that she and Adam were developing their own relationship and, rationally, that should have pleased me — and of course usually it did. But on this particular morning when Joyce came in and said, 'Good morning, Adam!' in that wonderful, lilting Caribbean voice of hers, I felt awful. There I was, standing at the door, ready to leave for work in my 'Dress for Success' gray suit, and there the two of them were, gurgling at one another with this whole lovely spring day laid out in front of them like a magic carpet.

"You know, my head tells me that what matters is how many hugs and kisses Adam gets a day — not how many I am able to give him. But at moments like that, my heart isn't so sure."

The combination of insight and uncertainty in Marta's observation is characteristic. Just by being the patient, loving, and careful observers of their children that they are, working mothers have arrived at a very good intuitive grasp of maternal employment's benefits and risks. The reason for their uncertainty is that, like Marta, many working women are unsure of how to make the new equation these benefits and risks have formed serve their children. That is why the new research is of such importance. It has given us our first detailed picture of the changes that maternal employment has created, as well as our first look at the remarkable children, like Adam, who are emerging from these changes.

In describing these youngsters, the word investigators most often use is "more." You find it several times, for instance, in a new study by Dr. Dolores Gold of Concordia University in Montreal, who found that compared to an age-matched group of peers, the three- and four-year-olds in her study were demonstrably more socially skilled. While this finding has been echoed in many other reports, what makes Dr. Gold's especially noteworthy is the depth of her analysis. Over the course of the study, she singled out a half dozen individual indices of social behavior for examination. On each one, her young subjects with working mothers rated "more." They were, for example, more skilled at playing with other children; more friendly toward new faces, whether a child's or an adult's; more comfortable in and better at cooperating in group situations; more willing to initiate and better at initiating activities for themselves and their playmates; and more capable of taking direction from others.

These qualities usually are described as by-products of the more stimulating social lifestyle a mother's work creates for a child. And while that is true, what may be the most remarkable social skill boys and girls with working mothers display has its origins not in the way work has changed their lifestyle, but in the way it *changes their perceptions* of their working mothers, and the way that, in turn, influences their feelings toward people generally.

Ask a woman how her work has benefited her child, and often the first benefit she cites is freedom from "stranger anxiety." Laura Crane, a young attorney who spoke to me after a talk I had given to her parents' group, mentioned this characteristic with special pride. Even at eight or nine months, when stranger anxiety is at its most intense, she said her son, Will, felt comfortable around unfamiliar adults. "He's always been interested in people — as long as they seemed friendly. I think he really is a people person."

A recent study by Dr. Pruett is among the first to document this common maternal perception. Instead of shying away from unfamiliar adults, he reports, his study children with working mothers approached a new person in the same way that Laura says Will does — eagerly and full of curiosity. Dr. Pruett's report is also among the first to document the reason for this openness and receptivity. "Because her work transforms her to a coming-and-going parent," says Dr. Pruett, "a woman becomes a source of immense curiosity to her child. He wonders, 'Where does Mommy go and what does she do?' And because working mothers usually answer this question in the most interesting and reassuring ways, their children develop an expectation. Like mother, they expect that people generally will satisfy their curiosity in exciting and imaginative ways and so they approach new faces eagerly and with great interest."

You also find the word "more" in a new report by Dr. Jeanne

Brooks-Gunn, a Columbia University pediatrician. In this instance, though, the "more" refers to the more self-reliant attitude displayed by the two- and three-year-olds of working mothers in her study group. Analyzing why these youngsters scored so much higher on self-reliance than the toddlers with stay-at-home parents against whom they were matched, Dr. Brooks-Gunn suggested that two factors were especially important: first, work makes a woman more likely to encourage and support self-reliance in her boy or girl; and second, through her own daily demonstrations of self-reliance in combining the roles of breadwinner and homemaker, a working mother sets a standard her child strives to emulate.

Everyone who has studied the boys and girls of working mothers, however, agrees that the most exciting and heartening "more" to be applied to them involves the way they have reinvented the meaning of masculinity and femininity. Evidence of this reinvention can be seen in Dr. Brooks-Gunn's study where the "masculine" trait of self-reliance was as evident among the daughters of working women as among the sons, and in Dr. Pruett's report where another "masculine" trait, independence, showed up with equal frequency in the behavior of boys and girls. These are examples of attitudinal changes; and while it is significant that maternal employment is altering them, more significant still is the way it is altering the nature of the hopes and dreams today's youngsters are forming for themselves.

You can catch glimpses of this change in the replies Dr. Gold received to what might be called her "moon question." Wanting to see how maternal employment affected her young subjects' expectations and ambitions for themselves as grown-ups, she asked her study boys and girls to imagine that they were visited by the Man in the Moon. How would they describe the roles men and women play on Earth?

The most suggestive answers to the question came from the daughters of working mothers, whose descriptions of such activities, although slightly askew by today's standards, are fascinating for the glimpse of the future they provide. Leaving their homes, Dr. Gold's extraterrestrial visitor not only would have the impression that work was as integral a part of a woman's life as a man's (an impression that is almost a reality now), but would also believe that the doctor who cared for him, the lawyer who defended him, the carpenter who built his house, the scientist who expanded his knowledge of the universe, and the pilot whose plane carried him from continent to continent was as likely to be a woman as a man. In other words, Dr. Gold's E.T. would depart from these girls' homes with a picture of the world as it is likely to be in the year 2000, when they, along with the daughters of millions of other working mothers, will be entering the labor force.

It isn't necessary to wait that long, however, to see behavioral evidence of the change you are producing in your child's expectations. It is already evident in the way a youngster acts at school, in the games he plays, even in the way children decorate their rooms —as the results of a recent University of Georgia study show. Strictly speaking, it might be said that what Dr. Carol E. MacKinnon and her coworkers found in their report was less evidence of sexual stereotyping in the rooms of boys and girls with working mothers. But the toys and games, the pictures and stuffed animals, the baseball bats and hockey sticks that litter children's rooms, are also emblematic of how they see themselves; thus the data that Dr. MacKinnon collected suggest that maternal employment enriches and expands a youngster's vision of who he or she might be. One sign of this was the way truck collections had joined doll collections in the rooms of little girls. Another was how many of the little boys felt free to express their love of flowers; in the form of real bouquets or pictures, flowers were encountered as often in their rooms as in girls'. Hockey sticks, baseball bats, and gloves, on the other hand, were encountered nearly as frequently in girls' rooms as in boys'.

At the center, we have noticed this same crossover trend among our own boys and girls. And like a number of other investigators, we also have noticed that although this trend has produced many important changes, one thing it hasn't changed is gender identification. Boys in two-career families still identify with and take their fathers as their primary sex role models; girls their mothers. Maternal employment's effect is simply to encourage a child to define these roles more broadly than they otherwise might. Thus boys are put more in touch with their nurturing, caring sides and girls with their capacities for competence, assertiveness, and independence.

You don't have to look any farther than yourself to understand why your children are responding to work in such a unique and exciting way. Observing how you have redefined the role of working mother so that it is broad enough to encompass both your maternal and problem-solving, challenge-seeking sides, they have been inspired to a redefinition of their own — one that shines through everything they do, from the way they decorate their rooms to the passengers they carry on their Big Wheels to the world they imagine themselves living in as adults.

Their unusual social skills also are a tribute to you and your unique vision. They grow directly out of your belief that for a three-, two-, even one-year-old, meaningful, well-rounded personal growth requires the contribution not only of family members but also of other significant adults, and even of the youngster's peers.

The reasons why not every child enjoys the benefits work can create are complex, but in one way or another all of them touch on the issue of *attachment*. This is the rather austere clinical term used to describe the special bond that grows between a mother and her child. While a strong and secure attachment is important, first and foremost, for the human reason that it makes a child feel loved, recent research shows that such an attachment is uniquely important to a child with a working mother because it promotes the growth of a quality we call "stretchability."

A mother's daily absences, the noise and tumult of the day-care center, the arrival of a new caregiver, a business trip that takes a mother away from home for several days, and many other aspects of a work-shaped lifestyle can produce anxiety, frustration, upset, and uncertainty in a small child. Stretchability is what allows a one-, two-, three-, or four-year-old to cope effectively with these feelings. And in the largest sense, the way attachment contributes to it is by creating a global sense of security. A two-, three-, or four-year-old who feels loved and understood feels secure in a way that makes him much more resistant to doubts and anxieties of all kinds.

We have always known this, but until recently, we assumed that what produced a youngster's resistance was the general sense of well-being that security conferred. New research by Dr. Daniel Stern of New York – Cornell Medical Center, however, shows that there is a much more immediate, direct, and concrete reason. It takes the form of what Dr. Stern calls an "evoked companion." In a strong attachment, an infant's or toddler's mental image of his mother — the picture he carries of her in his mind — becomes so palpable and vivid that it acquires lifelike properties. Quite literally, the reason a secure child feels secure no matter where he is and what he is doing is because mother, in the form of this evoked companion, is always there right beside him holding his hand.

No, this doesn't mean such a child will never be made anxious by a maternal leave-taking and never be made upset by an especially stressful morning at his day-care center, or that he will never feel lonely if he is left alone for a few minutes by his caregiver or day-care worker. It does mean, however, that he will find it much easier to make the emotional stretches these experiences demand because mother, in the form of the evoked companion, will be there to comfort and reassure him. In the consulting we do for nursery schools and day-care centers, we see the enormous difference the presence of this evoked companion makes in a young child's ability to benefit from his earlier introduction to the larger world.

Take Perry, twenty-seven months old, and Jared, twenty-eight months, two boys who attend one of the day-care centers we work with in an advisory capacity. In terms of IQ, the boys are in approximately the same range. Perry, however, has been much quicker to absorb the important lessons about cooperation and independence day care can teach because his ability to focus is largely undiluted by anxieties and stresses. His mother's leave-takings do sometimes upset Perry, of course, and so occasionally do the center's noise levels. But because Rachel, his mother, in the form of his evoked companion, is always available to soothe him, Perry doesn't become overwhelmed by his upsets in ways that interfere with his ability to focus and learn for the rest of the day. Jared, being less securely attached, does become overwhelmed by such upset. Because he lacks a strong and vivid maternal image to soothe him, often he stays overwhelmed for the day. So, unlike Perry, he can't focus on or learn from what is happening around him.

You can also see the difference the presence of an evoked companion makes in the boys' social performances. Because this companion puts Rachel next to him, Perry shows few of Jared's anxieties when he encounters a new face. If one suddenly materializes in his life in the form of a substitute day-care worker or new sitter, Perry will feel twinges of anxiety, of course. Usually, however, he is able to quickly put this anxiety behind him. And because this ability makes him especially responsive and engaging in first encounters, very often the new person will extend him- or herself to please Perry. Lacking the stretching power an evoked companion provides, Jared does become greatly upset by new people. And because he tends to act out his upsets, often he quickly becomes labeled "a problem." Last summer, in fact, his mother, Tina, had to take him out of day camp. Jared was so upset by all the new adult and toddler faces around him that he became raucous and unmanageable. The camp's director, fearing that Jared would be what the director called "a disruptive influence," asked Tina to withdraw him.

If you were to examine children like Perry—those who have derived the most out of their work-shaped lifestyle—not only in terms of social and self-comforting skills and cognitive performance, but also in terms of self-reliance and gender identification, you would find that they all have one thing in common. Like Perry, each carries a mental image of his mother with him, in the form of a soothing, comforting evoked companion, wherever he goes. This companion is the greatest benefit a strong, secure attachment confers on a young child, which is why the greatest challenge facing every working mother is how to create the experiences that foster it. Developmental texts describe a secure attachment—quite accurately—as the by-product of a sensitive maternal environment. The qualities that produce such an envi-

ronment were described very well several years ago by Dr. Mary
Ainsworth of the University of Virginia in a book called *The Origins of Social Relations:*

> The sensitive mother is tuned in to . . . her child's needs; she
> interprets them correctly and responds to them promptly and ap-
> propriately. Although she nearly always gives her child what he
> wants, when she does not she is tactful in acknowledging his com-
> munication and in offering an acceptable alternative. . . .

The reason for the doubt that Adam's mother, Marta Hafferkamp, voiced earlier is that like most working mothers, Marta is
uncertain about how Dr. Ainsworth's rules of sensitivity apply to
the new developmental world work has created. Take Dr. Ainsworth's emphasis on the need to interpret accurately and respond
promptly to a child's signals. At the center, we call this the capacity
to "read" a child. It is a key building block of attachment because
seeing mother respond correctly to his thoughts and feelings
makes a two- or three-year-old feel that she understands him in a
way no one else does. Although such reading poses little difficulty
for an at-home mother, who is able to track her youngster's preoccupations on an almost minute-by-minute basis, work puts a
woman in a different position. Having been away for eight to ten
hours, often she won't know what her child means by this or that
statement or question or behavior when she walks in the door at
night. How is she to maintain a sensitive persona in the face of this
knowledge gap?

Another of Dr. Ainsworth's rules of sensitivity — responding to
a child's wants — raises the same question. While it, too, is an
important building block of attachment, how does a working
mother maintain a sensitive persona given that often she won't be
able to grant her child's request that she stay home this morning or
that he be allowed to skip day care because he is tired? There is also
the even more fundamental question of how she can respond
sensitively to the new wants and needs work creates. Which innate
competencies does he need and want most? And how does a working mother provide him with earlier access to them?

Implicit but unstated in Dr. Ainsworth's rules of sensitivity is also another quality that is central to attachment — one that might be called the capacity to focus. An infant or toddler expects (because of the way he is biologically programmed) that when mother is with him she will offer him her undivided attention. He also expects that if, for whatever reason, he is too distracted to focus on her she will know how to pull him out of his distraction. But how is a working mother to respond sensitively to this expectation when she is preoccupied by a meeting that didn't go right or by groceries that have to be picked up, or when she is simply exhausted? And how is she to help soothe her distracted child when she has no way of knowing which, of all the things that happened to him today, is at the root of his inability to focus?

The trouble working mothers have in answering these difficult and complex questions is reflected in the results of a recent review of the attachment literature by Dr. Michael Lamb of the University of Utah. Dr. Lamb is among our leading theorists of attachment, and the several studies he examined in his review are among the most comprehensive and searching ever to probe the relationship between attachment and work. Therefore his conclusions carry a special weight. Examining the findings from the studies, Dr. Lamb concluded that maternal employment raises the risk of attachment disruption by 15 percent.

Our clinical impressions tally with Dr. Lamb's conclusions. We find that the working mothers and children who visit us at the center do have a higher rate of attachment disruption. Like Dr. Lamb, we have found that these disruptions are of a special kind. In his review he noted that no correlation was evident between maternal employment and avoidant attachments. This is the most serious form of attachment disruption, and it is so named because the child, feeling the maternal environment is either insensitive to or doesn't care about his needs, begins consciously to avoid that environment.

The disruption working mothers and their children are prone to is what is technically known as an insecure attachment. The most frequent source of this disruption is the child's feeling that while the maternal environment wants to respond sensitively to him, often it doesn't know how. And given all the uncertainties and doubts raised by the new developmental world work has created, it is understandable why the working mother and her child would be vulnerable to an insecure attachment.

In the pages that follow, I have several goals, the most specific of which is to show you how to apply Dr. Ainsworth's concept of sensitivity to your world. You will learn how to identify your child's needs in almost every situation and, even when you can't identify them or when there doesn't seem to be an appropriately comforting response, you will learn to respond in a way that will make your child feel uniquely understood and loved. You will also learn how role strain, time pressures, knowledge gaps, and guilt can alter a woman's sensitivity, and you will learn how you can prevent these work-related distractions from altering yours — how, in other words, you can develop what we call *situational sensitivity* to your child.

In the three chapters that follow, this situational sensitivity will be explored as it specifically, and differently, relates to the key points of your and your child's day. We will examine how at breakfast, at morning leave-taking during the shared time at the day-care center, during drop-off, or upon your caregiver's arrival, upon your arrival home after work, at dinner, at bedtime — you can respond in a manner that will make your child feel that "Mommy knows."

If situational sensitivity is about your response to your child's needs during the day, *developmental sensitivity* is about your awareness of and response to those needs over the years. Occasionally, a working mother has to step back and examine larger developmental trends and issues in light of her work. The chapters on developmental sensitivity — chapters 6 and 7 — will show you how to do this.

Beyond these specific aims, however, the pages that follow have another, broader, and more ambitious goal. They are designed to show you how to build a strong, rich attachment bond between you and your child so that no matter whom he is with or where he is or what he is feeling, *you,* in the form of an evoked companion, will be there beside him to soothe, to comfort, to reassure, and to love him as only a mother can.

3

The Work-Shaped Family

LYNN RAAB'S CALL surprised me.

I hadn't spoken to her since the finish of a parent-infant interaction study we had conducted at the center sixteen months earlier. Lynn and her baby daughter, Melissa, had been among our participants, and I remembered her as a vivacious woman with a bright smile, dark curly hair, and a mischievous twinkle in her eye. I also remembered Lynn telling me during our last conversation that at one point she wanted to return to work. And when my secretary, Jane, told me about the call, I wondered whether it had anything to do with that.

The young woman who walked into my office a week later was a sleeker, slimmer version of the Lynn I remembered. Gone were the slightly battered baby-bag-cum-backpack and floppy University of California sweatshirt Lynn used to describe as "my battle dress"; in their place were a leather briefcase and a smart tan suit. As Lynn began to talk, however, I noticed that something else was gone: the exuberance that had made her one of our study group's most popular mothers. And as the conversation turned to Melissa, I understood why.

She was three now, Lynn said, holding up a picture of a dark-haired, intense-looking toddler taken from her wallet, and up until four months ago Melissa had been doing wonderfully. That was when Lynn had returned to work; and while she had expected the transition to produce some temporary adjustment problems, she told me she had been surprised by the intensity of Melissa's reaction, particularly since she had gone to such great care to prepare her daughter for the change. For the first few months, Lynn had spent three instead of five days in the office of the accounting firm she had joined. She also had kept her promise to herself to return home twice a week for lunch with Melissa. But neither these measures, nor the fact that Alana, Melissa's new caregiver, had worked out so well, did anything to mollify her daughter's distress. In the weeks immediately following Lynn's return to work, Melissa was cranky and whiny and began sucking her thumb again. When Lynn's three days at the office became five, Melissa's behavior became outright alarming.

"One minute she is hugging me, the next she is pointing to me and saying, 'You are a bad mommy.' It just breaks my heart to hear that. What's wrong, Dr. Sanger?"

Melissa's alternations between displays of affection and anger are a common symptom of an attachment disruption, I told her. And while they're by no means inevitable, I explained that recent studies do show that such disruptions occur more frequently in working families because of the ways that work can subtly alter the quality known as *maternal sensitivity*.

I told Lynn that this key building block of attachment usually is defined as the ability to see clearly and respond promptly to a child's needs and concerns. One reason why work affects it is that a woman's *daily absences,* the *time pressures* on her, and the way she feels about her *role* as a working mother often can spill over onto the dinner table in the evening in the form of preoccupations, distractions, and the knowledge gaps that subtly alter her ability to respond sensitively to her child.

"Take time pressure," I said. "Children like a relaxed, open-ended, spontaneous maternal style; it fits their way of doing things. Intuitively, you know this. If you watch yourself and Melissa at the park on a Saturday morning, you will find that is the style you use. But often during the week, the pressures of time can

conspire to make you—and other working mothers—forget
your weekend knowledge and lead you to adopt the kind of fast-
paced, directive maternal style that young children find confusing." I pointed out that the knowledge gaps that arise from being
away from a child all day also challenge a woman's sensitivity.
"Responding to an excited, preoccupied, or upset child at the
other end of the dinner table can be difficult if you don't know
why he is excited, preoccupied, or upset. Is it the fight he had with
Julie today at the center that is upsetting him, or is it because the
center was unusually noisy today? Is he excited because of the new
toy you brought him or because, unbeknownst to you, today he
did what he has been dreaming about doing for weeks, jumping
from one bed to the other? Being away for eight or nine hours
makes it hard for a woman to answer such questions."

One of the things I had noticed about Lynn from our earlier
talks during the interactive study is that whenever she is upset she
begins fidgeting with the buttons on her blouse, and as I finished
speaking I noticed that she had started fidgeting with them.

"If you had told me five months ago that things were going to
turn out the way they have, I wouldn't have believed it," she said.
"Who would have dreamed Leonard [Lynn's husband] would
react the way he has? Or that I was going to find it so hard to get
back into a nine-to-five rhythm? Or that Melissa would have been
made so unhappy? When you've got a lot on your mind, giving
anything your undivided attention is hard. Though with Melissa, I
have really tried. I try to make every moment we are together
count for something." She paused. "Do you really think she is
angry with me?"

"No," I said, "I don't. At the moment she isn't feeling as special
as she usually does, and she misses that feeling. That's why she is
upset."

I told Lynn that one important way the program could help her
is by showing her how to overcome work-related preoccupations,
which from our conversation I suspected might be interfering
with her ability to respond sensitively to Melissa. "You will find
that as these strategies enhance your responsiveness, the rift that
has grown up between you and her will heal, and as that happens
Melissa's behavior will change in two important ways.

"First, the tension in her greetings will be relieved once she feels securely attached. Your appearance will produce only the thrill and excitement that it should. Second, you will find a change in Melissa's behavior when she is away from you. She will be much better at comforting and soothing herself when you are not there."

Seeing that Lynn was puzzled by this statement, I described Dr. Stern's work on the evoked companion. I also explained why it indicates that when a child feels understood and loved, his mental image of mother shines with a brightness that enhances his ability to soothe himself when she is not there to do it for him.

Next, as I do with all my new arrivals to the program, I asked Lynn to imagine herself and Melissa together in the evening—at the dinner table and during shared time. Then, step by step, I described how gaps in knowledge, time pressures, and her degree of satisfaction in being a working mother might alter her ability to respond to Melissa in such a way that Melissa would feel "Mommy understands me." What follows is an adaptation of that technique, although in translating it from a clinical setting to the printed page I have put an emphasis on the way these work-created spillovers can be shaped to promote attachment.

TIME PRESSURES

From experience, I've learned that the aspects of work that most trouble women are the time pressures it creates. So when I talk to a new program mother, such as Lynn, I usually take those pressures and the two strategies we have devised to offset them as my starting point. The strategies are *limiting* and *pacing,* and the fact that neither involves what is commonly called "quality time" often — and understandably—surprises new program mothers.

For the past fifteen years, quality time has been held out as the answer to the working mother's time problem. The idea expressed in the words "quality time" is admirable. What troubles us at the center, though, is the way this idea has come to be defined and practiced. Advised that when it comes to creating quality time with a child, more action is always better, an unwitting working mother often will try to squeeze five, six — a whole day's worth of activities into two hours of shared time with her child in the evening.

Lynn is an example. Encouraged by what she had read in magazines and manuals, Lynn had become a skilled practitioner of the more-is-better philosophy. The best way I know of demonstrating the effect this philosophy has had on her sensitivity is to describe how two imaginary audiences might react to an interaction I witnessed one evening between her and Melissa. My first imaginary audience would be made up of other working mothers, and I believe that knowing the special time pressures Lynn faced, they would find much to praise in her behavior.

Indeed, in many ways, Lynn's performance in the exchange is a model of quality time. Over the course of the thirty minutes they spent in our videotape studio, Lynn managed to move herself and Melissa through six separate activities. They sang songs, read two books, rearranged the furniture in a dollhouse we keep in the studio, dressed two dolls we also keep there, inspected the entire contents of Lynn's purse, and played ring-around-the-rosy. It was clear from the brisk, purposeful way she moved Melissa from activity to activity that Lynn had come to the exchange with a set agenda of activities in mind. And I think that, meeting later to discuss their impressions, the mothers in my first audience would agree that Lynn should be congratulated for carrying out her agenda with great efficiency and dispatch.

I think they would also agree on another point: because Melissa had never been permitted a moment of boredom and had been exposed to a wide variety of activities in a relatively short period of time, Lynn's behavior was a model not only of quality time but of maternal sensitivity as well.

Being composed of one-, two-, three-, and four-year-olds, my second audience would have difficulty articulating a dissenting opinion. But if it were possible to magically endow the members of this audience with adult powers of speech and reasoning, I think they would quickly point out to their elders that the exchange had ignored two important needs of Melissa's — and of every young child. The first is the need for spontaneity. One of the ways infants and toddlers judge the sensitivity of a maternal environment is by their ability to pursue their interests and whims. And as my two-, three-, and four-year-old viewers would undoubtedly note, in the interaction they had just witnessed Melissa was never given an opportunity to pursue her interests. The agenda of activities was set by Lynn, geared to her pace and enforced by her. At one point, for example, when Melissa's eye went to a wall-mounted video camera we were using to tape the exchange, instead of letting Melissa explore the camera (which was secure and safe) as she obviously wanted to do, Lynn quickly directed her attention back to the dolls they were dressing.

I also expect my younger viewers would be greatly dismayed by how little opportunity Melissa was given to initiate activities on her own. To a one-, two-, or three-year-old, another important measure of the maternal environment's sensitivity is the mother's willingness to confine her role to that of responder or reactor. If the child smiles, she should smile back; if his eyes go to a block or Busy Box, she might reach over in that direction or name them. But she should not lead him to that Busy Box or ignore his attempts to seize the initiative, as Lynn did, when midway through the book she was reading Melissa suddenly burst into a refrain from "Fifteen Miles on the Erie Canal."

If challenged by their elders to substantiate their claim that Melissa had not enjoyed herself during the shared time, I'm sure the infants and toddlers would cite as exhibit A the crestfallen look on her face when Lynn interrupted her song to say, "Not now, honey. We will sing when I'm finished reading." And if challenged still further, I'm sure the youngsters would cite as exhibit B the relatively few times Melissa smiled or cooed with pleasure during the shared time.

At the center, we call the make-every-moment-count approach Lynn used in the exchange with Melissa a *directive maternal style*. Recent studies show that because of the way that quality time is currently interpreted, this style has become common among time-pressured working mothers. Dr. Sarale Cohen of the University of Michigan, for example, reports that all of the working mothers she studied recently employed one variant or another of the directive style. She also found that their real-life children didn't respond to it any more enthusiastically than my imaginary audience of infants and toddlers.

One of the best barometers of how much pleasure a youngster takes in shared time is the amount of cooing and smiling he does during it. This is an infant's or toddler's way of saying, "I feel myself in the presence of an environment that is sensitive to *my* interests, *my* rhythms, and *my* pace." Melissa's relatively infrequent use of both behaviors also constitutes a message of sorts. It is a young child's way of saying, "This shared time is geared to your rhythms, your pace, and your agenda, Mommy."

Dr. Cohen heard this message from a great many of the children of the working mothers in her study. As a group, she reports, they smiled and cooed markedly less than did the youngsters of at-home mothers — not because there was anything superior about the at-home mothers' mothering but simply because, being used to having a great deal of open-ended time with their children, these women more often displayed a relaxed, natural, spontaneous style.

What Dr. Cohen's study didn't document, but our work at the center has, are the developmental effects of a directive style. It has three, and all are worrisome. They are:

1. *A directive style inhibits the growth of a sense of mastery and personal competence.* A two- or three-year-old's sense that "I can make things happen" originates from his discovery that "I can make Mommy respond to my cues and bids." The problem with a directive style is that it is so preoccupying that a woman misses many of these important cues and bids. In an informal study we did here at the center, for example, we found that nearly 50 percent of a child's attempts to make his mother respond to him went unacknowledged when a woman used a directive style. And a youngster who, at two, feels he can't make his mother respond to him isn't, at twenty-two or thirty-two, going to feel that he can make others respond to him.

2. *A directive style makes it hard to move a child through his day.* Aside from being too fast-paced, this style is also too instructional; directive behavior like Lynn's says to an infant or toddler not "How can we get this done and have fun together?" but rather "Here is how we should do this." And one

effect of this message is that it tends to emphasize the chorelike qualities of bathing, dressing, and other routine events. I have seen this directive style contribute to battling over clothing and food in working families. Nothing is so likely to enhance a child's resistance to getting dressed or bathing than making these events seem like work to him.

3. *Evidence suggests that a directive style may be why boys with working mothers are at a higher risk of incurring learning problems.* One of the ways a mother helps her child learn is by attuning her stimulation level to his capacity to absorb sights and sounds during their exchanges. This is why maternal sensitivity is more than a way of pleasing a child — it is a way of helping him grow. Properly attuned and paced, a mother's words and gestures help keep a youngster focused and interested, and the longer he is able to remain alertly engaged in an exchange, the more he is able to learn from it. The reason a directive style can make such focusing harder is that it is intensely stimulating. And the reason boys are markedly more vulnerable to stimulation overload than are girls is that physiologically, girls are more mature, so they are able to adjust with relative ease to higher levels of maternal sight and sound. Not having this advantage, and faced with the threat of overstimulation, a boy will often tune out his mother and withdraw into himself.

How does a woman like Lynn maintain a relaxed, spontaneous, sensitive style in the face of the time pressures work creates? One strategy is a technique we call *limiting*. It is designed to structure shared time in a way that allows a child to follow his interests and inclinations. When a game or toy catches his fancy, he wants to be given time to explore it fully and freely. And he is much more likely to be permitted that time if the night's agenda for shared time has been restricted to two, or at most three, activities. The impulse to want to fit as many different activities as possible into a given night is understandable. Like Lynn, many working mothers see this as a way of compensating for their absence during the day. But aside from leaving an infant or toddler no room to express his interests and initiate activities, a crowded nightly agenda gives shared time a rushed, foreshortened quality that leaves a youngster longing for more of mother rather than feeling contented.

Limiting has the opposite effect. Because it provides the child with an opportunity to explore every aspect of a game, toy, or project, it has the effect of elongating time and giving it a shapeliness that makes the hours spent with mother seem satisfyingly complete.

As our program mothers learn, a key element in making limiting work is a second strategy we call *pacing*. Letting a child establish the rhythm of nighttime activities not only may ensure that those activities will naturally end up limiting themselves (think how long it takes to read a story to a toddler when all his questions and comments on the text are patiently heard and answered), it also ensures that whatever activity takes place is done at a pace the youngster finds satisfying and — equally important — shaped to his desires and rhythms.

ROLE SATISFACTION

Role satisfaction means the degree of happiness or unhappiness a woman feels about being a working mother. I don't think you will be surprised to learn that like too intense time pressures, too little satisfaction in being a working mother also can alter maternal sensitivity. What you might be surprised to learn, however, is that, contrary to popular belief, role dissatisfaction rarely is rooted in deep-seated ambivalence or conflict about work or about motherhood. In our experiences at the center, we find that usually our role-dissatisfied women, individually, are very happy with their careers and very happy with their children. The reason for their role dissatisfaction is that they haven't yet learned how to organize the three life areas that allow a woman to combine her maternal and working sides happily and successfully into the single larger role of working mother. You can guess what those three life areas are from the strategies we use to enhance role satisfaction: (1) getting your support system firmly behind you, (2) reexamining your goals, and (3) learning how to structure time more effectively.

By a wide margin, it is the breakdown of a woman's support system that is responsible for most cases of role strain. And most often the breakdown arises because the system's key member, the husband, fails to make the contribution he should. In practical day-to-day terms, knowing that he is in the basement doing the laundry or that he will take charge Saturday enhances a working mother's sensitivity because it gives her two fewer things to worry about when she sits down with her child. Even more important is the sense of emotional validation his activities confer. A husband who accepts his fair share of household chores is telling his wife, "I support and applaud your decision to work"; a woman who gets this message night after night is going to have the kind of peace of mind that fosters a deeply attuned maternal sensitivity.

Indeed, an important reason why Marta Hafferkamp and her son, Adam, have escaped attachment problems, while Lynn Raab and her daughter, Melissa, have not, is that Marta's husband, Keith, has provided a great deal of help and support, while Lynn's husband, Leonard, has not. When Lynn announced she wanted to go back to work, Leonard was very vocal in his support of her decision. But once Lynn returned to work, Leonard's attitude changed. The prospect of having a working wife had pleased him, but the reality—or rather, one aspect of the reality—didn't.

Leonard complained that the house wasn't as neat as it had been when Lynn was home, and he complained that his and Melissa's meals weren't as nutritious as before. Lynn's work was taking something away from him—and from Melissa, Leonard claimed. To signal his displeasure, Leonard retreated from his promise to "do more around the house."

The result was predictable: Within weeks of returning to work, Lynn began to develop a serious case of role strain. Having to do all the household chores herself was difficult enough, but Lynn would have adjusted to that if she hadn't also had to bear the weight of Leonard's not-always-silent displeasure. Melissa's "I love you / I am angry at you" behavior was her way of telling Lynn: "Mommy, you have become so preoccupied by Dad's displeasure that you are not paying attention to me anymore."

The best way to deal with a husband-caused support system breakdown is to bring the problem out onto the table. You and your husband should sit down and talk his attitudes through. When you do, you might remind him of several facts I reminded Leonard of the Saturday afternoon he, Lynn, and I sat down for a talk. The first is about the contribution your work makes to the family's standard of living. A recent study on male attitudes toward a wife's work shows that the vast majority of men welcome a second income in the family. Leonard was no exception. Lynn's return to work had taken a great deal of economic pressure off him, and he was immensely (if quietly) pleased by that fact. The reason for his reproachful attitude is that, like some men, he wanted to have it both ways.

Leonard wanted the second income Lynn's work provided, but he didn't want any of the personal inconvenience it caused him. One of the goals of the talk we had that Saturday afternoon was to make Leonard do what he clearly wasn't going to do on his own —confront the contradictions in his attitude and think them through. Given the choice between having the extra income a wife's work provides and doing the extra household chores it entails, or forgoing both, a man will opt for the first choice. Women's studies make the more general point that work is integrated into your overall dignity as an adult. With the modern longevity of women the old division between man-the-provider and woman-the-homemaker has become obsolete.

During your talk with your husband, you might also tell him about a study done by Dr. Candice Feiring of the Educational Testing Service in Princeton. It shows that the sense of support and validation a woman feels when her husband helps with the chores transfers directly into her mothering. Dr. Feiring found that the more support a man provides, the more sensitive his wife's behavior is with their child.

Setting unrealistic career goals for yourself also can produce role dissatisfaction. Do you expect to be vice president of marketing or make senior partner in your law firm by thirty-five? Is it essential that you serve as the team leader on every new project? Although there is nothing wrong with aiming high, what *is* wrong is pinning one's entire life and being on achieving them. The woman who does this sets herself up and, in a way, also sets up her child, because holding onto a dream too tightly makes losing it seem like a tragedy. The woman feels embittered and defeated, and because the need to deal with these feelings will inevitably absorb most of her energy, in time she will come to seem preoccupied and inattentive to her child. Looking at her across the dinner table, he will wonder, "Why doesn't Mommy pay attention to me anymore?" Hopes and dreams are something we all need, but a working mother has to know how to shape her hopes and dreams in a way that is flexible enough to accommodate an occasional career setback.

Setting unrealistic maternal goals for yourself is, if anything, even more likely to make you unhappy about being a working mother. There is *no* contradiction between being a good mother and leaving a child in the care of another adult for a part of each day. Millions of good mothers do it every day. Unrealistic goals, however, can make this look like a contradiction; a woman who sees being with her child every moment of the day as an essential prerequisite of good mothering will view not being with him as an act of betrayal. And the guilt that this false sense of betrayal engenders can interfere with her ability to see her child's needs clearly and to respond to them appropriately.

You can see the cause-and-effect relationship clearly in the results of a recent study by Dr. Ellen Hock of Ohio State University. The working mothers in her study group had equally happy children and equally stable and trustworthy caregivers, but Dr. Hock noticed something odd as she examined their lives. Her subjects' ability to see and be reassured by these happy facts was contingent on how they defined the role of a "good mother." Dr. Hock concluded that if a woman's definition of a good mother was broad and realistic enough to encompass the fact that a good mother also can work, the woman worried very little about her child and her caregiver.

But the women whose definition of such a mother left no room for daily separations or for the presence of other adults in their children's lives *did* tend to worry because those beliefs blinded them to what was apparent to everyone else: they had nothing to worry about. Dr. Hock called such women "conflicted mothers," and she found that in time their conflicts began to affect their sensitivity. As a group, she says, these mothers were much more likely to see problems where none existed and to respond inappropriately in moments of distress.

A case in point is the way conflicted mothers often unwittingly intensify their children's departure-time protests. Giving in to their guilt, they frequently tend to become either overtly distressed or excessively apologetic in the face of such protests. And because both responses tend to fuel a child's own departure-time anxieties, leave-taking protests frequently degenerate into tears and screaming. What investigators often call role-satisfied mothers also become upset by departure protests, but because they believe what they are doing is right, the research shows that this confidence has a reassuring effect on their infants and toddlers. Seeing that mother believes her leave-taking is no reason for alarm, the child comes to think, "Well, if Mommy believes her going is right then it must be right."

Studies like Dr. Hock's — and there are a great many of them — are why once every six months every working mother should ask herself the following three questions:

1. Even when my child is in a good mood, do I become anxious when I leave in the morning?
2. Am I continually switching caregivers because I am unable to find someone I can trust?
3. Do momentary upsets always make me feel guilty or inadequate?

If you find yourself answering "yes" to one or more of these questions, it would be advisable to reevaluate the goals you have set for yourself. Are they realistic? Even if you were able to achieve them, whose needs would they serve? Riding home on a hot, crowded subway at six in the evening, who wouldn't want to be an earth mother leading her brood of four freshly scrubbed children across a beach in Sausalito at sunset? But if you were to look at this embodiment of nurturing perfection through the eyes of a three- or four-year-old, you would see her differently. Young children like mothers who make mistakes and forget things and give them some emotional room to grow and learn on their own — in other words, mothers who are fallible and human. Mother already looks powerful enough to them; if she were as perfect as the imaginary earth mother, they would find her oppressive.

As part of your goal evaluation, you might also remind yourself of all the things you would be doing if you were home all day. Studies show that laundry, shopping, preparing dinner — all the routine chores that fill up the at-home mother's day — so occupy her hours that she spends no more time in direct one-to-one exchanges with her child than you spend with yours. It would also be a good idea to look at your own childhood memories of your mother. Given the way the years alter our perceptions, it is easy to idealize people and situations. The point of this part of the reevaluation isn't to dredge up unhappy recollections but simply to help you realize that your standard of mothering may be one created by illusion. Judged against that impossible standard, your own mother would very likely be found as lacking as you now find yourself.

Finally, it would be a good idea to talk to other working mothers you know. No one is better at putting a working mother's concerns into perspective than another working mother.

Along with unrealistic expectations and support system breakdown, inability to structure your time, and especially your energy, can lower your role satisfaction. Routine work and office pressures magnify a hundredfold when you feel tired. And, as you know, on the days when those pressures seem overwhelming, it is hard to focus your full attention on the child at the other side of your dinner table. The principal reason why a working mother lacks that energy is because she uses what we call a flat-out style. Typically, the practitioners of this style go at the day in one concentrated burst of energy, and a not uncommon result is that, in time, they begin to develop a sense of oppression. Because no discrimination is exercised, because the hard and the easy get the same level of effort, everything seems more difficult than it really is.

One sign that a woman has fallen victim to the flat-out style is trouble getting out of bed in the morning. The burdens of the day have become so onerous that she wants to pull the covers back over her head. Another is exhaustion; often practitioners of the style find that precisely at the point in the day when they most need energy and liveliness — during evening shared time — they have none left.

The best antidote to the flat-out syndrome is time structuring. Give tasks the energy they require, but don't be a spendthrift. Save your major efforts for the projects that really need your energy and concentration. A second antidote is to build rest stops into the day. Every hour or so, give yourself a few minutes. Tiredness always makes a problem look bigger than it is.

Designing your week so that it affords you at least one mini-vacation from responsibilities also helps. As you slip away for a drink with a friend or an aerobics class, remind yourself that you are doing this as much for your child's sake as your own.

KNOWLEDGE GAPS

If you were to poll one hundred working mothers on the aspect of work they find most frustrating, I think at — or near — the top of the list would be the knowledge gaps that arise from being away from a child all day. It is frustrating not to know what is on the mind of the two- or three-year-old who greets you at the door or who sits down at the table. Even more worrisome, these knowledge gaps can interfere with a returning mother's ability to respond sensitively to her child. A technique we call *creative uncertainty* helps a woman close these gaps by giving her the clarity of mind and the time she needs to find that one special word or gesture that will make her infant or toddler think, "No one knows me better than Mommy."

The ability to find this right word or gesture is a key component that flows from maternal sensitivity, and being able to track a child's fluctuations of interest and mood on an hour-by-hour — sometimes minute-by-minute — basis does give the stay-at-home mother something of an advantage.

The knowledge gaps that arise out of her daily absences put the working mother in a different position. The element of time and the fact that he has had his "own" day will make the feelings and interests of the child she greets tonight different from those of the one she said goodbye to this morning. So before she can offer the just-right word or gesture that produces the magical "How did you know, Mommy?" she has to gather up the threads of her boy's or girl's day, examine each thread, and weigh how it has altered the preoccupations of the child who greets her at the door.

One way creative uncertainty assists a returning mother in doing this is by helping her to deal with her own tiredness and tension. Slipping into your child's world requires clarity of mind, and few things can so distract or preoccupy a mother — and hence rob her of sensitivity — than exhaustion or anxiety about a meeting that didn't go well. The procedure's first step, then, involves relaxing yourself during the bus, car, or train ride home.

One good way to do this is by using a technique called *leveling*. Adopted from stress management programs, leveling is a form of autosuggestion; it involves summoning up especially tranquil images or memories. You might, for example, imagine you and your child walking together on a deserted beach or sitting together in the park. Or you might recall the especially sweet expression on your child's face last night when you bent over to kiss him goodnight.

Creative uncertainty's second step involves emptying yourself of all preconceptions about what your child will be thinking or feeling when you walk through the door. Although issues and activities that dominated the morning hours may resurface, don't try to pick up morning-time themes unless your child indicates a desire to do so. Upon walking through the door, you should have a clear mind and an open, receptive attitude. This will give a one-, two-, three-, or four-year-old the time and emotional space he needs to tell you how his day was and what he is feeling now. Just as important, it also ensures that a homecoming won't be disturbed by the kind of disharmony that results when a returning mother says or does something that makes her child wonder, "Why don't you know, Mommy?" Most often, this question arises out of the running dialogue your toddler conducts in his

mind with you all day. Each time something significant happens
to him, he immediately tells you about it and imagines the way you
will respond to his news. The fact that you are not there to hear it is
a distinction he can be counted on to ignore. This is why he will
expect you to be thoroughly cognizant of and eager to discuss the
fact that Tommy hit him today when you return tonight, and why
he will be upset and baffled if, instead, you begin talking about the
game the two of you played this morning.

One way of dealing with such expectations is through the skillful use of questions. The three-year-old who is bursting to tell you
about Tommy, for instance, very likely will begin his story in the
middle. And this gives you an opportunity to find out what really
happened, but in a way that already makes you seem "in the know"
about Tommy. Specific statement-queries such as "Yes, but I'll bet
the two of you had an argument first," or "Was the fight about
that paint box you both like so much?" convey an informed maternal air while allowing you to collect information before you
commit yourself to a final opinion about Tommy or your child's
behavior.

Another important toddler expectation that creative uncertainty enables a returning mother to fulfill is the expectation that
"I will be able to follow my own interests and wishes." When
returning home to find a two-year-old sprawled on the floor absorbed in a coloring book, every woman's first impulse is to think,
"Oh, God, he is ignoring me; he must be angry." Understandably,
she misses the big bear hug that usually is the endpoint of this
thought chain, but her concern is unjustified for two reasons.
First, it is based on a misinterpretation of the child's behavior (he
isn't mad; he's just absorbed in his coloring). And, second, sweep-
ing him up into your arms defies his expectation that you will
respect his wish to finish what he is doing. Creative uncertainty,
which in this case means limiting your initial greeting to a soft
smile and an unintrusive "hello," is a way of telling him you do
understand and respect that wish.

If you think a three-year-old is too young to notice when mother
is responding sensitively to his desires, let me repeat a story Gloria
O'Connor, one of our REAP mothers, told me. One night not

long ago Gloria walked in the door expecting an especially fervent reunion with lots of hugs and kisses and squeals of joy. That had been the pattern on days when morning leave-takings had been full of tears and baleful looks. And today had been one of those mornings for her twenty-month-old, Jesse. The Jesse who greeted her from the living room floor, however, was clearly interested in finishing the book he was reading with his caregiver, Eileen. Gloria's first impulse was to snatch him up into her arms, but remembering a talk on creative uncertainty she had heard at the center, she resisted the impulse and instead went into the kitchen and began preparing dinner. Hearing the patter of footsteps a few minutes later, Gloria looked up from the kitchen table where she was sitting to see a beaming Jesse standing in the doorway. "He didn't walk, Dr. Sanger," Gloria said later, "he ran all the way across the kitchen and flung himself into my arms. For the rest of the night my husband, Henry, kept asking me, 'Gloria, why are you smiling like that?'"

One other way REAP has helped Gloria to meet Jesse's expectation to be understood is by showing her how to read his behavioral clues. From a child's point of view, a mother who gives him room to state his thoughts and feelings is just as terrific as a mother who can tell from what he says or does what is on his mind, what kind of day he had, why he had that kind of day, and what he wants from her now. If you know what to look for, a child's behavior will tell you a great deal about his current thoughts and interests and mood — not just when you arrive home, but when you leave for work, during shared time, and on weekends. Knowledge of these behavioral cues — or themes, as we call them — also will help you to tell what kind of day he had at the day-care center or at home with his caregiver.

Learning how to read these themes is the subject of our next chapter.

4

Themes
How to Read Your Child

On the Friday before Halloween, Mona Rubenstein arrived in my office bearing twelve pumpkin cupcakes and a paradox that had been troubling her all week. The cupcakes were for the center's annual Halloween party; the paradox involved one of our guests, Mona's three-year-old son, Jeffrey.

Last Sunday, Mona explained, Jeffrey had thrilled the entire Rubenstein family by solving on his own a fit-in puzzle that had stumped him since he had received it three months earlier. Even five-year-old Ben, Jeffrey's brother — and not always his most un-critical fan — had been sufficiently impressed by the triumph to offer his little brother a few grudging words of congratulations.

What Mona found paradoxical was Jeffrey's response when she laid out the puzzle for him on Monday night. Instead of repeating his triumph, as Mona had expected, Jeffrey refused to focus on it. He got up and, tucking his good friend Brainy Smurf under his arm, stalked into his bedroom, slamming the door behind him!

Having experienced all the imaginative ways a preschooler can say "no," I found Jeffrey's behavior easy enough to interpret. And knowing that Monday was one of the three days a week he spent in day care (the other two were spent with Allison, his part-time caregiver), I thought I knew what had inspired his rebellion. Such "no's" are an assertion of self, and parents such as Mona tend to hear them a great deal on the evenings of days when a child's projects (which represent an assertion of that self) at the center have been interrupted too frequently. Sometimes the culprit will be a peer who took away the blocks he was using for his house to build a bridge; sometimes it will be a schedule-conscious day-care worker who kept saying, "You're not going to have time to finish that game now." Whatever the source, the interruptions make the child feel frustrated and rebellious.

"The next time Jeffrey behaves the way he did Monday night," I told Mona, "check with his day-care worker. He probably didn't get to finish all the projects he wanted to finish."

Mona gave me a rueful smile and said, "You know what I need, Dr. Sanger. I need my Sunday night knowledge of Jeffrey all through the week." In one form or another, we hear that wish expressed a great deal at the center. It isn't just daily absences that challenge a woman's ability to respond to her child; not being able to track him on a continuous basis over an extended period of time can make even leave-taking, shared time, or Saturday morning behavior very puzzling. That's why Sunday night has come to occupy such a special place in the hearts of working mothers like Mona. After two uninterrupted days together with her infant or toddler, a woman usually finds herself able to answer easily a question that often seems difficult to answer during the week: "What does my child mean by that?"

This capacity to track a child's innermost thoughts and feelings represents an important form of sensitivity, and working mothers know it. It is why women such as Mona feel so vulnerable when their special Sunday night knowledge vanishes during the week. Simply put, the goal of this chapter is to show you how to transfer that special knowledge to Monday, Tuesday, Wednesday, Thursday, and Friday nights.

A young child's body language, the questions he asks, the requests he makes — often these clues will give a parent who knows how to read them a concrete and specific idea of what her boy or girl is thinking and feeling. For example, the toddler who insists on showing you the bed he has made for his teddy bear the moment you walk in the door has one thing on his mind; the toddler who asks you to swing him around has another. We call these interests and preoccupations themes. In the pages that follow, you will be introduced to the most common themes young boys and girls use during homecomings, departures, shared times, and weekends, and when they want to signal a concern about a significant other (caregiver and/or day-care worker).

One word of caution: don't expect perfection from yourself. Even with a knowledge of these themes, there still will be nights or mornings when your child's behavior will be a source of bafflement. It is all right to wait, to be quiet, to inquire. What you should not feel at these times is guilt; what you should feel is creative uncertainty. Children are very tolerant. As long as mother leaves enough emotional room for them to tell her what they are thinking, they won't mind if sometimes she is uncertain about or puzzled by their behavior.

HOMECOMINGS

Creative uncertainty is the one essential precondition for understanding the most common homecoming themes. As I pointed out in chapter 3, it means divesting yourself of any preconceptions about your child's current mood or attitude so that when you walk in the door at night he will have the space to tell you what is on his mind. Very likely you will find yourself greeted by one of four themes.

"Hey, Look at Me!"   is the theme of pride and achievement. The "me" refers to me-and-what-I-can-do: some accomplishment the child is especially proud of and can't wait to share with you. Sometimes it will represent a real breakthrough; for example, this morning in nursery school he finally mastered the difficult art of zippering a zipper and can't wait to demonstrate it to you. Other times it will take the form of a new game or a new form of play he has invented. A common example is the two-and-a-half-year-old who leads his returning mother directly into the living room to show her what a great tent can be constructed out of sofa pillows and sheets.

One defining characteristic of this theme is urgency. Whatever the particular nature of the "me" being shown off, its demonstration can't be delayed by the need to take off a coat or put away a briefcase. Mother has to come *right now,* and if she shows the slightest hesitation, her hand is taken and pulled. A second defining characteristic is subtlety. Often what the child wants to show off or have praised isn't as obvious as it seems, so don't comment on the accomplishment until you are sure what it is. Otherwise you may find yourself in the position Sharon Pacin, one of our program mothers, found herself in one night. Walking through the door, Sharon was immediately taken in tow by her three-year-old, Timmy. He led her to his bedroom, where four stuffed animals were carefully seated around a table, a plastic cup and saucer in front of each animal, and in the middle of the table, a small pitcher of apple juice.

The placement of the objects suggested a party to Sharon, so she said, "Oh Timmy, how wonderful — you are giving your animals a tea party." Instead of the pleased look she had expected, however, this response seemed to disappoint Timmy. "It wasn't until the next morning on the way to the center that I understood why," Sharon said when she told me about the incident. "Timmy mentioned that the day before, for the first time, Irene, his day-care worker, had allowed him to pour juice for the other children. That was why he had arranged the party; he wanted to show me he could pour juice without spilling it."

I told Sharon one way to avoid such missteps in the future is to use direct questions. If Timmy grasps your hand the moment you walk in the door, ask, "What is it you want to show me?" An even better way, I explained, is to use affirmative but neutral statements, such as "Wow, you certainly are excited" or "I just know something terrific happened today." These allow you to join in the excitement, but also leave room to find out exactly what is causing it. Usually, the child will tell you what it is on his second or third "Look, look" or "See what I can do." I told Sharon if she had waited an extra moment before commenting, for example, Timmy would have made it clear that the "me" he wanted praise for was his skill in pouring apple juice.

If you are not sure, don't react. Better to let the child wait a moment while you figure out the source of his excitement than to respond in a way that is going to leave him wondering, "Why doesn't Mommy know?"

"Hey, Look at Us"   is a theme of interaction. The child doesn't want to show you something; *he wants to be with you.* Sometimes he will state this wish directly; but more frequently, he will ask you to play dolls or superheroes or read a book to him the moment you walk in the door. He may even ask you to swing him around or play a game of hide-and-seek. Trudi Fields, one of our REAP mothers, for example, has found that when her three-year-old, Steven, wants one-on-one time with her, often he will greet her at the door with a dare: "I'll bet you can't find me, Mommy."

One way to distinguish "Hey, Look at Us" from "Hey, Look at Me" is that the child's requests require your direct involvement. The youngster who wants to show off a new triumph will be content to let you play spectator; a child who wants your presence won't. Whether it be reading or playing a game, if "Hey, Look at Us" is the theme he has in mind, he will want to do something that requires your active participation. Another way of distinguishing this theme from "Hey, Look at Me" is that the activities the child requests are ongoing. After offering the appropriate round of applause, the two-and-half-year-old who wants to display a new triumph will usually let mother go; the child who wants mother won't. After she has read one book, he will go and get another one.

It should be read, too. When your child wants half an hour of quiet with you, reading is a good way to provide it. Requests for a swing-around or hide-and-seek are more problematic, as they can be tiresome for you and divert your child from his deeper purpose. The way to deal with them is to do what Trudi Fields does: grant them initially, and then channel. Trudi always finds Steven once or twice when he is hiding, but then she will say, "I was thinking today about that book we got from the library Saturday. Why don't we read it?" Or she will invite Steven into the kitchen to "help" her prepare dinner. In other words, she will gradually channel him toward what he really wants: direct one-on-one time with her.

"Leave Me Alone" most often indicates anger, and usually it announces itself in a way that is easy to mistake for legitimate preoccupation. The reason I didn't get a warm "hello" tonight, the returning mother thinks, is that Robert was absorbed in "Sesame Street" when I came home, or he was involved in his Lego set again. The surest way for a woman to tell if she is right is to see what happens once "Sesame Street" is over or the Lego set put away. The preoccupied child will come over and offer a big hug on his own. The angry child won't. Your hug or kiss will have to be coaxed out of him; his behavior will be evasive and remote.

What should you do until the child reveals his true feelings? Any form of preoccupation should be respected. Walk over and offer a warm "hello"; but if that doesn't inspire an interaction, don't ask, "What's wrong?" or hover. Go about your chores. If it turns out the toddler is angry — in other words, if he doesn't offer that hug you want — don't probe; it will only deepen his sulk. If you wait, one of two things will happen. Either the child will volunteer the reasons for his anger, in which case you should discuss them with him then and there; or, deciding that after all Mommy is terrific, he will without explaining why come out of the sulk on his own. This is the time to ask him about tonight's nongreeting. It is important to know the source of his withdrawal or anger, but you shouldn't try to explore it with him until there has been a restoration of positive feeling between the two of you. Get together in a game or some continuing project, then ask, "What was the matter earlier?"

"Let's Make This Quick, Mom" could be called the "one-minute greeting." It consists of an initial exchange of hugs and hellos, followed by a period of fidgetiness during which the toddler points with increasing eagerness toward the game or television program he was watching before you arrived.

The reason a working mother often finds the one-minute greeting upsetting, of course, is its brevity and the youngster's obvious desire to return to what he was doing. "Could he really miss me that little?" you wonder. This concern is misplaced, however, because the child's eagerness to slide off of your lap isn't the sign of uninterest it is usually taken to be. Instead it is a two- or three-year-old's way of telling you that he has comfortably settled an important security issue. He now is absolutely certain that even though you leave each morning you will *always* return at night, smoothly fitting in to his ongoing events. This confidence is why he is willing to release you after such a brief exchange of hugs and hellos. Experience has taught him that when it matters and he needs you, you will be there for him.

DEPARTURES

Leavetakings typically are characterized by one of three themes.

"You Can Go Now" is a theme that causes a great deal of unnecessary ambivalence among working mothers. The ambivalence arises from the fact that although it is always important to be out the door on time, and a woman can't help but feel relieved when she is allowed to make an exit without a struggle, a part of her also can't help but wonder, "If he lets me go this easily, does he really miss me?" In that respect, this theme is like the one-minute greeting. The reason the ambivalence is unnecessary is that "You Can Go Now" — again, like the one-minute greeting — actually indicates something quite different and much more reassuring.

What makes the separation smooth isn't that the child finds it easy to distance himself emotionally, but that his mental representation of mother — the evoked companion he carries in his mind's eye — is so strong and vivid that it is able to step in and begin its work as her surrogate without special prompting. This is why the "You Can Go Now" theme characteristically announces itself through self-absorption. Having mother's spiritual presence with him in a sense, the child no longer needs her physical presence and so moves on to become involved in something else. In the case of a child at home, this something else could be engagement with a toy or television program or an interaction with a caregiver. In the case of a youngster at day care or nursery school, the self-absorption usually takes the form of immediately coupling up with another child or heading for a favorite object.

One stricture: in both cases, don't go over and give your boy or girl a last kiss. This says, "I feel uncertain and guilty about leaving you"; and as I've pointed out, a woman whose behavior says, "I am upset about leaving you," is going to upset her child, even if he has his own normal departure-time anxieties well under control.

Timmy Pacin, the little boy I mentioned earlier, is a case in point. One thing that brought his mother, Sharon, into the program was concern about what Sharon called "Timmy's transition problem" when she dropped him off at his day-care center. Timmy would whine and cling. It emerged later that his departure-time anxieties coincided, for the most part, with the days that Sharon had *her* departure-time anxieties. The morning I was observing at the day-care center Timmy linked up with a friend the moment he got inside the center's door. He didn't become upset until Sharon, having said goodbye once, returned for a last hug and kiss after going halfway out the door. While the impulse that brought her back was understandable, her return told Timmy something he didn't need to hear at this delicate point in his day. A leave-taking should *always* be geared to your child's inner mood. "See you later," said casually, was all that Timmy required.

"Go Quickly" is a theme that is played out on mornings when, for whatever reason, the child is finding it difficult to make the separation. Not wanting to let go, but not wanting to break into tears either, he summons up all his emotional reserves to hold himself together through the departure. Every youngster has mornings like these, which is why the "Go Quickly" theme is both common and normal. The best way for a mother to signal her sensitivity to it is by acknowledging his struggle for self-control, yet continuing to leave. Although well intentioned, lingering will only deplete further those already strained emotional reserves, producing the tears and embarrassment the child is struggling so hard to restrain.

Typically, one of the stratagems he uses to keep himself together is to focus on something other than mother. "Go Quickly," though, produces a special kind of focusing; it is distracted and disjointed, as if the child were saying, "I want to lose myself in this, but I can't quite yet." "Go Quickly" is also on the mind of the boy or girl who spends the breakfast hour clutching a favorite toy animal or other soft, cuddly object as if it were a life preserver. Holding on especially tightly to a caregiver's or day-care worker's hand is another way a child signals his desire to bring leave-taking to an end as quickly as possible. That evening you might mention to him how brave and strong he was that morning.

"Don't Go Yet"   in its most straightforward form, means exactly what it says: "You can't go yet, Mommy," and usually it is presented in a way that does require an extra minute or two of comforting. *No matter how pressed for time you are, the child's tears and clinging should be soothed before departing.* The same is true for the second and more subtle form of the theme. The behavior it prompts should be dealt with before going. That can be more difficult, however, since in this variation of "Don't Go Yet," although the child doesn't want mother to go, he isn't consciously aware of it. So he does what all of us do in such circumstances: he acts out his wishes.

Often the acting out will take the form of dawdling in getting dressed, making a mess at breakfast by, say, spilling cereal or misplacing an essential toy. These are stalling tactics. And while as stalling tactics go, they may seem relatively benign — particularly in comparison with tears and clinging — each behavior requires a sensitive response, because each touches on an important psychological issue. Mess making, for example, is related to the potent question "Why does Mommy go?" Seeing her clean up his spilled cereal reassures a youngster that one reason she does *not* go is because he is a bad boy who makes messes. The danger of becoming exasperated by the child's attempts to stretch out breakfast, thus causing you to leave before he finishes, is that it can set up an association in his mind between strong emotions — in this instance, sadness about mother's departure — and food, which can lead to eating disorders later. One simple way to solve this problem is to serve a small breakfast. The caregiver can serve the main morning meal later, or if the child is going to day-care, pack an especially fortifying snack for juice break. During the evening following a particularly stressful leave-taking, you should also talk a great deal about how much you look forward to coming home after work. Using hand puppets, stuffed animals, stories and pretend play, together you and your child will arrive at a better understanding of this process.

WEEKENDS
Saturday Mornings

By the time a child is twenty months old, the qualities that mark a Saturday morning as special and different not only are recognizable, but have become cues in the child's mind. Seeing mother and father still in their bathrobes and hearing none of the sounds that usually ring through the house at this hour, he realizes that the rules that normally govern the family's morning behavior are in a state of happy suspension. And often he will respond to the opportunity this represents by introducing one of the following themes.

"Let's Go Forward" signals a desire to move into the weekend. Eager to begin making use of the free, open-ended time it offers, the toddler will ask to do something that is both uncharacteristic and involved — in other words, something there is no time for during the week. It could be baking cookies or bread or finger painting; it could be splashing around the tub in last summer's flippers. The sometimes antic nature of the requests shouldn't obscure the primary message of "Let's Go Forward." While it represents a desire to have fun, the theme's underlying message is more serious.

The need to feel oneself linked with mother in an unlimited expanse of time — what we call "just being" — assumes a special intensity in the child of a working woman.. Unstructured, free-floating activities provide a means of satisfying this need, which is why the cooking utensils or flippers the two- or three-year-old asks for on a Saturday morning are really his way of saying, "Mommy, let's just be with one another."

Leaving Saturday morning — and as much of Saturday afternoon as possible — open is a parent's way of replying, "What a wonderful idea." A way of making this "together time" seem even more abundant is to structure shared activities in a manner that highlights their beginning, middle, and end.

For example, you decide to make cookies together. Such statements as "Now we are going to get started by taking the butter out of the refrigerator" (beginning); "Now we are putting the cookies in the oven to bake, and this is the time we need to wait" (middle); and "Wasn't that fun?" (end) do more than just demonstrate the different phases of cookie making. They give a child an opportunity to think through and savor the process as it happens, as well as to watch the sequence draw to a logical (and hence, satisfying) conclusion. And all of us — not just toddlers — perceive time as being more generous than it is when we have been helped to feel that we are a part of the structure and flow of an event.

"Let's Be Together"   is a family theme. The child wants to feel himself united with his mother and father in that single integrated whole, the family unit. Weekday mealtimes provide some opportunity to satisfy this need. It is only on Saturdays and Sundays, however, with their abundance of open-ended time, that a youngster has the space and relaxed atmosphere he needs to fully express the wish to be more than "me," to be a part of "us." Crawling into bed and rolling back and forth between mother and father is one way a child announces this desire. Another is by trying to draw one parent into an activity he is already doing with the other. An example of this is the two-and-a-half-year-old who insists that mother put down the paper and watch him and father play with the fire truck. A third way is by mimicking an activity one parent does for the other. Helping father make mother's coffee or mother put away father's shirts is a three- or four-year-old's way of saying, "I want to join in and feel a part of things."

Two-and-a-half-year old Emily Weinstein has devised a particularly imaginative way of stating this message. Recently Emily appointed herself to the position of "passer" in the Weinstein household. According to her mother, Ann, at one point during Saturday breakfast Emily usually will stand up in her chair and start passing the salt and pepper back and forth between Ann and her husband,

Sam. Ann concedes that neither her desire nor Sam's for salt and pepper is nearly as great as their daughter seems to imagine, but she says that she and Sam support and encourage Emily in her position as passer because they know it is her way of saying, "We all love one another very much in this family."

The Weinsteins also do something else that is important. Whenever Emily announces that she is about to begin passing, Sam and Ann begin talking about a recent adventure the family shared or a trip they have planned. And as they do, they drop the pronouns "you" and "I" from their speech and add the more communal-sounding "we" and "us." "Let's Be Together" is a theme that needs to be more than acknowledged — it needs to be celebrated. So when it appears, do what the Weinsteins do: begin talking about subjects that focus on your family as a unit.

"Let's Go Backward" is a theme of distress. Something upsetting happened during the week, and the child is still trying to come to terms with it. Behaviorally, the distinguishing characteristic of this theme is its lack of sociability. A youngster with "Let's Go Forward" or "Let's Be Together" on his mind will, immediately on rising, involve you, or you and your husband, in some form of zesty interaction. A child with "Let's Go Backward" on his mind usually won't. You may find him following you from room to room; you may even find him rubbing up against you. But he rubs up against you the way he would rub an amulet he believes has healing powers. What he wants is the magic of your presence to heal his upset. You won't hear him suggest activities that will involve the family in spontaneous, free-flowing interactions.

What is at the root of his distress? Sometimes the child will tell you by acting out his upset. The Saturday morning Marge Brookner heard her three-year-old, Benjamin, scold his teddy bear for spilling his apple juice, Marge correctly deduced that earlier in the week Benjamin's day-care worker had criticized Ben for spilling *his* apple juice. Other times the nature of the child's clinging may indicate the cause of the upset. A two-year-old who tugs at your skirt every time you pick up the phone on a Saturday morning, for example, very likely didn't receive much attention from his caregiver or day-care worker during the week. At still other times the child may tell you why he is upset in direct words.

Usually, however, you won't be able to identify the exact source of his distress, at least not until you have talked to his caregiver. The following Monday morning ask her about the previous week. Did something happen out of the ordinary? Did he show signs of a special distress? In the meantime, don't probe or question your child, and if he wants to regress by becoming clingy, let him. Your responsiveness to his wishes will tell him that you know he is upset; and just knowing that Mommy is uncritical, calm, and present will help make him feel better.

Sunday Nights

By this point in the weekend, a woman doesn't need any help in identifying and tracking her child's preoccupations. After two uninterrupted days together she has acquired that special Sunday night knowledge that allows her to sense what her child is thinking and feeling. The one exception to this otherwise general rule are themes of organization. And what makes them able to defy even a working mother's Sunday night knowledge is that they are related not to any specific thought of the child's or thing that happened today, but to a larger and more complex developmental issue.

"Organization" is the technical term for what a parent would call her child's "nature" or self. And one of the best indexes of a young self's stability and security is how it rebounds after confronting stress or anxiety. Almost any significant upset will produce passing tears, clinging, and an inability to focus in a one-, two-, three-, or four-year-old. But what happens later after the stress has been removed? The reason Sunday night behavioral problems carry a special significance is that they are a way of answering this question.

By this point in the weekend, the effects of an upset that occurred Thursday morning and produced a normal spillover into Thursday night (in the form of a regression) should have dissipated. And in a child with a healthy sense of self, it will have dissipated. He will be easy to interest and keep interested. His play will be relaxed and focused. Even the things that sometimes cause problems during the week — like toothbrushing or the transition from bath to bed — will go well tonight. Everything about this child says, "I'm okay," and it is an okay whose implications extend beyond Sunday night. A child with this thought in mind is making a general statement. His smooth, integrated, focused Sunday night behavior is his way of telling you that his self-development is proceeding normally.

The child whose Sunday night behavior lacks these characteristics is making a developmental statement as well. His difficulty concentrating, his clinging, his reluctance to listen, are his way of declaring that his self is so weak that even after a three-day interval it remains too disorganized by Thursday's stress to produce coherent, integrated behavior. In most cases, if you followed this child's difficulty to its root, you would find that it was caused by a work-influenced alteration in maternal sensitivity. A child's sense of self is a by-product of the maternal environment. If preoccupations or conflicts about work or the knowledge gaps it creates change the sensitivity of that environment, often the self that emerges from it will be less vigorous and thus vulnerable to stress and anxieties.

"What should I do?" Gloria Velez asked when I explained this to her. Gloria had brought her two-and-a-half-year-old, Maria, to the center, not because she was concerned about Maria's Sunday night behavior, but because she was concerned about Maria's behavior generally. Her Sunday night difficulties with transitions, her frequent tears, and her distracted, out-of-focus airs were a repetition of what happened every other night of the week. This is typical of a youngster whose Sunday night theme is "I'm not okay." His behavioral problems usually are evident during the rest of the week as well. It is just that it is easier to see them on Sunday nights because the things that might cause transitory behavioral problems on a Monday or Tuesday night, like a difficult morning at the center, have been removed.

If "I'm not okay" is a theme you encounter a great deal on Sunday nights, I would recommend you do the following:

• *Give your child more of yourself.* Cut back on business trips and late nights and weekend work for a while. Your boy or girl needs significantly more time with you. The way to make the most of this time is to keep it free of agendas and to keep the focus firmly centered on your child. This will make your time together what we call "just-being" time (it involves pacing and limiting as well as several other techniques we will look into in the next chapter), and one of its advantages is that its slower pace allows a parent to notice things about her two- or three-year-old — a special like or dislike, or a way he signals when he is stressed — that she may have overlooked before.

• *Consult the caregiver and/or day-care worker.* Ask if they have noticed any special behavior problems, and if they have any ideas about how to deal with those problems. Both of these individuals know your child well, and they know children well; you shouldn't feel self-conscious about taking advantage of their knowledge and experience.

These measures usually help you to define what is happening in the inner world of your child. If after two months you continue to see the same problems, I would recommend a consultation with a child-care professional.

SHARED TIME / PLAYTIME
THEMES

"I Don't Want to Play Anymore"   is a theme of detachment or, more precisely, of attachment disruption. Although the disruption is usually minor and easily mended, often it is linked to some aspect of the child's work-shaped lifestyle. He may still feel upset about being rushed this morning at breakfast, or angry because when he fell and hurt himself at the center this morning mother wasn't there to comfort him, or anxious because she came home late tonight. (Lest these examples sound guilt-inducing, keep in mind that being an at-home mother also carries its own attachment risks.) Knowing the source of the disruption isn't as important as knowing how to identify its presence, and how to correct the minor frays it can produce in the attachment bond.

Typically, these frays will announce themselves in the form of lack of interest or engagement. The child will start to read a book or play a game or build a castle with mother, then suddenly and inexplicably begin tuning out what usually is for him a riveting activity. To a parent, it may appear that her child is having trouble focusing (as opposed to being in an angry or rejecting mood) tonight. And in a sense he is: since the tensions caused by the disruptions are inhibiting his ability to concentrate, he is too upset to focus.

Engaged, involved interaction is the most effective way to dissipate these tensions and heal the underlying upset. And there are two techniques that will almost always produce such exchanges. The first is to drop back to an activity you know your child likes but in the past month or two seems to have outgrown. Depending on his age, this could be anything from peek-a-boo, to water play, to a Busy Box. The reassurance of being involved in something familiar and enjoyable often will have a soothing effect on even the most scattered and disjointed of toddlers.

Another way to dissipate tensions is to suddenly produce a new toy. At the center, we advise our mothers to gather a secret supply of presents so that they will always have a surprise immediately available for such minor emergencies. The toys don't have to be elaborate; something as simple (and inexpensive) as a balloon, which the child can help mother blow up, frequently will be enough to lift him out of his distress and draw him closer to her.

"I Don't Want to Play with You Anymore" is easy to confuse with the last theme because the child introduces it the same way — by pulling away from mother. In this case, though, the pull doesn't take him off into himself but moves him toward father, who becomes designated playmate for that particular evening. Don't take this as a sign of rejection. "I Don't Want to Play with You Anymore" is *not* a negative theme. The child simply wants to add some freshness and variation to his nighttime play and switching partners is how he has decided to do it. His usual partner can then take the night off, or if that is going to make her feel guilty or left out, she can make a bid to turn their play into a three-way interaction. This latter option, however, carries two ground rules with it:

(1) Don't make an attempt to involve yourself immediately; give
father and child twenty or thirty minutes by themselves first. (2)
Insert yourself into the play unobtrusively. Quietly join them in
what they are doing rather than suggesting a new game or activity
to bring yourself into the action.

"I'm Bored."   No matter how imaginative or inventive her play
style, there are going to be nights when a working mother finds
herself sharing the floor with a bored one-, two-, or three-year-old.
He is easy enough to distinguish from his peers with other playtime themes in mind. Unlike the youngster whose attachment
bond has been stretched, he won't pull himself away from a shared
activity; and unlike the child who wants a new playmate, he won't
direct his attention to father. What characterizes him is a marked
lack of enthusiasm and zest; although he continues to play with
mother, his play is listless and uninspired.
    The "I'm Bored" theme offers a working mother a special op-
portunity. Her helping to alter a familiar form of play in a way that
makes it new and exciting again shows a child just how unique her
ability to please him is. In the case of a four-year-old, for example,
suggesting a new adventure for his Batman and Robin action
figures might be a way to reinvigorate play. In the case of a two-
year-old, it might be transforming a juice tray into a bridge (by
turning it upside down) so that the toddler has a new way of
playing with his toy car. An example of what *not* to do is suggest an
entirely new toy or activity. Limit your recommendations to ways
of juicing up what the child is already doing. You do not want to
do his thinking for him. If the only thing that will lift him out
of his boredom is an entirely new activity, let him discover that on
his own.

"Don't Tell Me You Are Going Out Again!"   Parental nights out
are like Saturday mornings: the house feels different in a way that
makes even a two-year-old take notice. That's why, often even
before the baby-sitter arrives, the child is acting cranky and whiny.
The baby-sitter's appearance only confirms what the unusual bus-
tle in the house and mother's and father's dress have already made

him begin to suspect: tonight is a night out for them. The "Don't Tell Me" theme is, in part, an expression of his disappointment at losing his nighttime play partners; but even more, it is an expression of the fact that for any child under five, two parental leave-takings in the same day represent a significant psychological stress.

This isn't to say mothers and fathers don't deserve an occasional weeknight out. They have earned it, and the time alone together is important for their relationship. Still, even when sensitively handled, you should expect nights out to produce upset in a toddler who has already heard one "goodbye" that day. The upsets won't be lasting, but don't be surprised if you encounter an unusually difficult child at breakfast the next morning. Testing, clinging, and sullenness are all typical "morning after" behaviors.

Handle them with a special gentleness; this morning your boy or girl deserves to be indulged a little.

THEMES RELATING TO SIGNIFICANT OTHERS (DAY-CARE WORKERS, CAREGIVERS)

Day-Care Workers

"I Need a Bottle." The voice at the other end of the line was nasal, high-pitched, full of urgency, and very familiar. It belonged to Sarah Kline, M.D., former student of mine and the mother of two-and-a-half-year-old Leslie Kline. On returning to medicine full time six months ago, after two years' hiatus at home, Sarah announced that she intended to do two things immediately.

"I'm going to go out and buy a dozen new white smocks and a pair of stiletto heels to go with them — and I'm going to enroll in your program, Sirgay."

The impish humor was typical of Sarah. But in the six months since rejoining the obstetrical staff of the hospital where she had practiced before Leslie's birth, Sarah had found little to laugh about. Leslie's new day-care center had added a complex, puzzling element to their relationship. It was evident to Sarah that many of her daughter's nighttime behaviors were now rooted in things that had happened to her at the center during the day. But what things? Sarah's increasingly frequent calls to me were pleas for answers.

This particular call was inspired by Leslie's request for a bottle. "It's been almost nine months since Leslie's been weaned. Why would she want a bottle now?" Sarah asked in the high-pitched voice she uses when she is nervous. I told her that regressions such as asking for a bottle, wanting to spend the night on Mommy's lap, or whininess are typically how a young child announces that she is having a difficult day at the center. And, I explained, usually the difficulty is rooted in one of two things: either the center was very noisy that day, or there was a major change in the schedule.

"Talk with Irma [Leslie's day-care worker] tomorrow," I told Sarah. "And in the meantime, I would recommend that you let Leslie have a bottle."

When Sarah protested, I said, "I know you had a hard time getting Leslie off the bottle, but a difficult day at the center represents a special case. It isn't that Leslie *wants* to be babied; it's just that she *needs* to be now."

"I'm in a Running, Jumping, Hitting Mood."   Also a sign of a difficult day at the center, this theme usually expresses itself in the form of disorganized, unfocused, and sometimes violent physical behavior. Often it indicates that the day-care worker has been inattentive; the child has been allowed to run wild at the center and now he expects to be able to do the same at home.

You should talk to his day-care worker the following morning; in the meantime, the best way to soothe the child is through quiet time. Quiet time is a good idea for every boy and girl who attends day care, but it's an especially good idea on days when the child seems out of control. If this is apparent when you arrive at the center — in other words, if you notice that your child's behavior seems unfocused and excessively energetic — devote the first half hour or so of your at-home time to soothing. Songs and repetitive games are helpful.

If the child seems as tired as he is overstimulated, then try a short nap, or — if the nap will throw off bedtime — shut off the lights in the living room, put on some soft music, and have him lie on the couch. If he is too restless to sit still, try a television program, such as "Mr. Rogers' Neighborhood." In most localities, this program is on in the early evening, and I can think of few things better suited to soothing an overwrought child than Fred Rogers's engaging, low-key manner.

"Why Don't You Know, Mommy?" is a theme of puzzlement arising from a child's expectations that what his day-care worker (or caregiver) already knows, his mother also will know. And it is a reflection of a belief about adults all preschoolers share. The notion that there exists a single adult consciousness that automatically gives every grown-up access to information about every child is why, for example, a three-year-old will expect the waitress in the restaurant he is visiting to know that he likes grilled cheese sandwiches, or why the four-year-old will expect the police officer who escorts him across the street to know that the woman on the curb in blue, not the one in red, is his mother.

The "Why Don't You Know" theme deserves the special attention of a working mother because inevitably there are going to be times when she finds herself in the same position as that waitress or police officer. The confusion and distress this can lead to is illustrated by an incident that occurred to Sandra Obst, one of our REAP mothers. One night Sandra was surprised to see her four-year-old daughter, Robin, walk across the living room with a pair of scissors. What surprised Sandra even more than the scissors was the look on Robin's face when she took them away. "I couldn't understand why she looked so crestfallen," Sandra said. "After all my talks about safety I would have expected her to know better than to try and play with something so dangerous."

A talk with Robin's day-care worker the following morning, however, threw new light on the incident. It turned out that the previous afternoon, Robin had spent several hours making paper cutouts with some of the other children at the center. Analyzing this fact on her way to work, Sandra realized Robin had assumed she would know this and wouldn't object if Robin continued the project at home. "I guess I disappointed her," Sandra said. "Taking away the scissors made Robin realize I hadn't known about the project.

I told Sandra that in the future, whenever Robin does something uncharacteristic, before reacting see if it is part of a larger pattern. "The fact that, in this case, she had laid out some paper on the couch before getting the scissors was an indication that she wasn't trying to test you or had suddenly become intrigued with a dangerous new plaything." I also told her that, in every case, she should give Robin the benefit of the doubt. "Unless she does something to indicate otherwise, assume her behavior arises out of innocence," I said. "Not only will this attitude give you time to discover if what Robin's doing is part of a larger project, it tells her in a way she can understand, 'Mother trusts you.'"

"Give Me Space"   is also a common theme among youngsters who spend a portion of their day in day care, and it takes the form of pleasure in doing things on one's own. The child shows a real enjoyment in involving himself in independent activities and, as at the center, he expects this capacity to be praised at home as well.

One way his working mother can attune herself to this expectation is to realize that when her youngster goes off to play on his own, he is not withdrawing from or rejecting her but simply doing what he is encouraged and praised for doing at the center. Another way is by realizing that even when his independent activity produces a mess — such as pulling all the jewelry out of your jewelry box — he will expect to be praised for his initiative. And while that doesn't mean you should announce yourself "delighted" at finding your jewelry all over the floor, it does mean that in such situations your response should contain an element of praise, such as "I think it's very nice, but let's see if we can't find something besides my earrings to decorate your castle."

Caregivers

"I've Had a Terrific Day."   One way a child expresses this theme is by making a smooth transition from his caregiver to you. Another way is by being alert and focused when you walk in the door.

A three-year-old who is focused and concentrated when he greets his returning mother, or an eight-month-old who is able to remain alert in one-to-one interactions with her, is the product of a skillful and nurturing caregiver who knows how to promote the cause of attachment.

"Please Don't Make That Call." The two-year-old who, instead of amusing himself as he usually does when his mother picks up the phone, suddenly protests by either crying or throwing a temper tantrum is telling her that the caregiver has spent a sizable portion of the day on the phone. In other words, he is responding not to her but to the caregiver and the feeling of neglect her calls have engendered.

The best way to deal with such situations is to give the child what he wants: undivided maternal attention. Calls can always be made after he is asleep. Also, the next day it should be made clear to the caregiver that while phoning is permitted, it should be limited, and whenever possible calls should be placed during nap time or before the nursery school pickup.

"Stimulate Me, Mommy." This theme usually expresses itself in the form of a desire for some type of exciting play. The child wants his returning mother to swing him around again and again and again, or to engage in some other form of overly rambunctious physical activity. Most often the theme is encountered in children who have spent the day in front of the television set with a bottle. Having been deprived of exciting play all day, by evening the child, understandably, is craving it. Within reason, give the child the stimulation he wants; also make it a point to talk to the caregiver the next morning. A steady diet of television does nothing for a child's cognitive or emotional growth, and this should be made clear to the caregiver. One subtle way to deal with this problem is to draw up a list of things you would like the caregiver to do with the child each day (varying it as needed); then go over the list with her on your return home.

"Whom Do You Believe?" One of the most complex and troubling themes a young child can raise, "Whom Do You Believe?"

takes the form of a complaint against another significant adult. The toddler may claim that the caregiver is ignoring him ("She was on the phone all afternoon"), or that she is being unfair ("She wouldn't let me play with the new blocks"), or, in extreme cases, that she hit him. More often than not these complaints are a child's way of asking his working mother for her understanding and sympathy, which is to say that, while strictly speaking often they aren't factually true, they do contain a kernel of emotional truth.

Frequently, for example, it will turn out that although the caregiver isn't on the phone all day, she does have a habit of interrupting shared activities to take or make calls. Or perhaps her corrections and warnings are so intimidating that sometimes it almost seems to the toddler as if he *were* hit. As nicely as possible, make it clear to her that you expect her to be as gentle and considerate with your child as you are.

One thing not to do is accuse the toddler of fabricating or embellishing in order to win your sympathy. Not long ago, a magazine aimed at businesswomen cited, with some approval, the response of a mother who, on being told by her five-year-old that his caregiver had hit him, replied, "You are just making that up because you don't want me to go to work today." The woman happened to be right, but her curt dismissal could only enhance her child's feeling of isolation. Statements such as "I wish I could have been there to see what was going on," "You are such a good boy that I don't understand why anyone would want to hurt you," or "You are such fun to be with, why would Nanny be on the phone all day?" are a more appropriate way to respond. These tell a toddler that mother recognizes the emotional truth behind the factual fabrication and that she sympathizes with it. Often this will make the child feel so good that, without any prompting, he will tell you what really did happen. "Well, Nanny didn't really hit me, but she did. . . ."

Let me conclude by telling you about another visit Mona Rubenstein made to my office. This one occurred on the Tuesday before Valentine's Day, and this time Mona came bearing a box of twelve chocolates and a big smile. "You know," she said, "since we last talked, we've spent three group sessions on themes and it's really made a difference. For the first time since I went back to work I find I'm able to understand Jeffrey's weekday behavior nearly as well as I do his Sunday night behavior."

Then a suddenly solemn Mona asked, "Now what can you do to help me improve my relationship with Brainy Smurf?"

5

The Most Important Points in a Working Mother's Day

ON MY DESK is a photograph with the same bittersweet quality that made so many of Norman Rockwell's *Saturday Evening Post* covers memorable. It is of a mother and little boy saying goodbye at a day-care center, and in its own way it says as much about the way we live now as Rockwell's paintings did about the way Americans of his time lived. Having an eye for the very young's first confrontations with implacable reality, Rockwell, I imagine, would find the child in the picture irresistible and, despite the contemporary setting, familiar. He is about three and a half and is being as brave as a little boy can be when saying goodbye to a mother he doesn't want to go. His head is slumped on his chest, and with a partially clenched fist he is rubbing away what looks like a tear. Nearly hidden by a pair of oversized jeans, a sneakered foot can be seen curling upward at the toe.

What I think Rockwell would find unfamiliar, however, and what I expect would give him trouble if he tried to depict it on canvas, is the attitude of the mother in the photograph. He was as expert and as experienced at painting mothers as little boys, of course. In the crook of a smile or the bend of a laugh line, he could distill what seemed to be the entire body of maternal knowledge into a single gesture. But the woman in this picture is neither smiling nor laughing. The look on her face is serious and complex, and to someone of Rockwell's generation I suspect it would seem altogether novel.

It is impossible to say what was on the woman's mind the instant the photograph was taken, but her expression, with its combination of uncertainty, guilt, and a touch of rue, is one working mothers often wear in situations where they don't know what to do. How do I say goodbye to a tearful child at the day-care center, for example, or help him make a smooth transition to his caregiver? And what do I do if my toddler won't eat breakfast? Should I make him, even if it produces the kind of food battle that will sour my leave-taking? Like the woman in the photograph, there are many times in the day when a working mother feels that she has suddenly stepped into a world where the rules of sensitive maternal behavior have yet to be defined.

The purpose of this chapter is to help define those rules for her. Knowing what kind of goodbye to give at a day-care center, or what to do about morning (or evening) food fights, not only can have important developmental consequences for a child, it also has an important influence on the mother-child relationship. So step by step, we will go through a woman's average working day, paying particular attention to the ten most significant points in it and what maternal responses are most appropriate to them. Because these times set the mood and tone of the day, we call them touch-points and they are described below.

WAKE UP
6:00 A.M. to 7:00 A.M.

Mother

The early morning hours are a time of renewal and reunion in working families. In a very real sense, they form a kind of sunlit space between the separation imposed by sleep and that imposed by work. The point of rising first is that enjoyment of this space's special magic will be dependent on whether you have had time beforehand to remove the obstacles that can clutter it. These take the form of pants, shirts, blouses, and dresses that need to be ironed; papers that need to be read; briefcases that require checking; breakfasts that have to be started; and all the other chores that, although necessary, can distract a woman's attention from a child in the morning.

WAKE UP
6:30 A.M. to 7:30 A.M.
Child

Because morning time pressures have a way of assuming a life of their own, while you are going about your chores waiting for your child to wake up think about the next hour and a half to two hours and the qualities and values you want to emphasize in them. Begin by reminding yourself that dressing, bathing, and eating are more than just way stations on an assembly line that, at eight-thirty or nine o'clock, deposits a fed, dressed, and scrubbed child into the arms of a waiting caregiver or day-care worker. Each is also, and most important, a potential social interaction. Remind yourself, too, that by taking the time to stress the social and interactive aspects of these events, you can give the hours a continuity that will serve you both.

For the child it will transform the morning into one long, seamless interaction, the unifying thread of which is the playfulness and sociability that link together the disparate activities of dressing, bathing, and feeding. For you the continuity will provide a way of avoiding that greatest of all threats to a working mother's morning schedule — a resisting child. Having his focus firmly set on you and the fun you are having together, a youngster will be much less likely to protest the move from bed or crib to changing table or bathroom. Indeed, in many cases he will be so absorbed by the fun he is having that he won't even notice the change in venue.

In terms of the morning's minute-by-minute logistics, this approach has several important implications, the first one of which awaits you as you enter the now awake child's room. On greeting him, expect a request — by word or deed — for a few minutes of just being together. The way to reconcile his expectation with your need to get him up and into the morning is to offer him what we call a start-up activity. In the case of an infant, this could be a game like peek-a-boo or thumbkin. For a toddler, it could be reading a book or playing with a stuffed animal. These activities' playful aspects will engage a child while giving you a discrete bridge into the day. The baby whose attention is focused on peek-a-boo won't mind being moved from the crib to the changing table if the game comes along with the move. The same is true for the toddler. He won't walk to the bath as if he is walking his last mile when, on arriving at the tub, he knows he will hear you finish the story you began on the bed.

Ideally, one more playtime should be scheduled in between dressing and breakfast. For a two- or three-year-old, this should include at least one activity that will remain unfinished until your return at night. Throughout the day the partially built castle or half-colored drawing you begin now will not only serve as a symbol of your return but will also give the child a way of linking himself more directly to the healing and comforting powers of that evoked companion in his mind's eye.

Ginny Fisher, one of our REAP mothers, came up with an imaginative way of enhancing this linkage: she put up a chalk-and-tape board in the room of her three-year-old, Jason, so that every morning the two of them could begin a picture/collage. "I make sure we do enough drawing so that the images are satisfyingly clear to Jason," Ginny says. "I'll draw a mommy and child holding hands; we'll tape a cut-out bird overhead; and Jason will do a few zigzags for a fence. But we always keep the right-hand side of the board empty. During the day Jason and his caregiver, Ruth, flip through my old magazines for pictures that catch Jason's eye. Then when I get home, I cut those pieces out for our collage, and we finish the drawing and tape on the pieces together. Jason's very proud of this work. Ruth says he makes references to what he and I are going to do to finish the picture all day. Sometimes she says he even goes over to the board and pats it."

At breakfast, the playfulness and sociability that have lit up the morning generally should continue. In other words, your focus

should remain fixed on the child's spiritual and emotional nourishment. If he resists eating, don't make an issue of it. One way or
another a skipped meal will be made up in the course of a day. But
what can't be made up so easily is time together that has been
marred by an upsetting food fight. The afterimage of you that the
child carries into his day should not be disfigured by the memory
of an angry scolding. One other point: if the next stop of the
morning is the day-care center, then raise the interactive energy
level between the two of you at breakfast and on the way to the
center. Get the child to join you in an exciting game like patty cake
or hide-and-seek during the breakfast hour, or in a song as you put
on your coats. Swapping silly jokes, which children love to do, on
the bus or car ride to the center also will raise the energy level
between the two of you.

And raising this level is important because a recent study by Dr.
Susan Loomis of the University of Waterloo in Alberta, Canada,
indicates that energetic interactive behavior serves as a kind of
warm-up, facilitating a toddler's adjustment to the faster pace of
the center. In her study group, Dr. Loomis found that the fifteen-
to twenty-month-olds who were provided with a high-energy interaction just prior to separating from mother scored differently
on two important indexes of adjustment. After their mothers'
leave-taking, they were much quicker to link up and play construc-
tively with a peer and slower to become upset by the high energy
level around them. As a result, says Dr. Loomis, these children
spent very little time at the center walking around in that out-of-
focus state a child falls into when the sights and sounds around
him become overwhelming.

June DiSalvo, REAP mother of two-and-a-half-year-old Luther,
found a way of building the warm-up into the tail end of breakfast,
which Luther usually eats slowly. Picking up on Luther's fascination with the speedy pace and agility of the waiters and waitresses
he sees at coffee shops, June gets out two aprons just as Luther is
taking his last slow nibble of toast. "When we put the aprons on
the whole energy level changes. We play waiter-and-waitress,
clearing the table (of course I do ninety-five percent) with that
whiz-whiz pace Luther loves to watch. At the sink, I let him splash

a little water over the dishes and squeeze the sponge." June says the higher energy level this game creates has made a difference in the rest of Luther's morning. His day-care worker reports that usually Luther adjusts very easily to the center's faster pace.

LEAVE-TAKING
8:00 A.M. to 9:00 A.M.

Maternal departures are really a composite of two different situations: one involves mother and child; the other involves mother, child, caregiver, and/or day-care worker or nursery school teacher. And since each situation has its own individual dynamic and requires its own set of behavioral responses, it will be more useful to analyze them separately.

Mother and Child

Situational factors have an important influence on how well we deal with stress. One of the most important of these is context. The more reassured and secure we feel in a setting where stress is introduced, the less threatening it will seem. A second factor is time. While an abrupt presentation can be emotionally destabilizing, gradually introducing a stress in a way that affords time to think about and absorb its impact makes it much less upsetting. Children — even infants — are no different from adults in this regard. And that has important implications for how the stresses of leave-taking should be presented.

Rather than bring up the subject of your impending departure all at once at the end of breakfast, sometime during the meal mention that soon it will be time to leave, or place your briefcase or the coat you will be wearing that day on a kitchen chair where the child can see it. By eleven or twelve months, a child already will have begun to associate certain articles of clothing and objects with your departure, so the message behind your action will be clear enough. But having introduced the message (and in context, the breakfast table, where the child feels secure) and having provided some lead time to think about its meaning, by the time you actually reach for the coat or briefcase, most of the stress associated with that message will have been processed and absorbed. Seeing you reach for one or the other, the boy or girl will think, "I know, Mommy, it's time for you to go."

Inevitably, of course, there are going to be mornings when nothing this simple works. You should expect these; they are normal. They will occur most often on Mondays after the child has had two uninterrupted days of you, or when he is overtired, ill, or under the weight of some other extra stress. One way to respond sensitively on these mornings is to make common cause with the child.

Telling him that you also are saddened at the prospect of leaving lets him know that you join in his upset and, even more, understand it. And knowing that mother understands just how hard her going is for him this morning is a source of solace and comfort to a two- or three-year-old. One word of caution: if you do use this strategy, make it clear to the child that what saddens you is parting, *not* going to work. Work always should be presented positively as something mother enjoys and has a right to. A statement such as "I don't want to leave you either, honey; but look, we're both going off to do things we like, me to work and you to play with your friends at the center" makes both points in a way a toddler understands.

Focusing on the nighttime reunion also can help ease distress on difficult mornings—directly, because this connects the youngster with a happy thought, "Mommy and I are going to play with my new Lego set tonight," and indirectly, because such statements are a subtle way of reminding a twenty-month-old that while your life may be marked by temporary separations, you share an endless future together.

Above all, you should avoid surrendering to the child's distress on difficult mornings. If nothing else works, gently but firmly insist that you have to go to work; it is a responsibility, something mother has to do. Telling this to a tearful child or one who is clinging to your coat or dress is wrenching, I know. But apologizing or otherwise indicating guilt will only make an already trying situation more trying still for both of you.

Mother, Child, and Caregiver

The morning's final activity is the "handover." Although where it occurs makes a significant difference in a child's response, even a one-, two-, or three-year-old who welcomes a caregiver within the familiar context of his home often needs an added measure of reassurance during the actual moment of transition. This is why the following two rules apply, not only to day-care and nursery-based handovers, but also to those an infant or toddler is able to observe from the relative comfort of his own bed or high chair.

1. *Reassure the child in language he understands.* The appearance of another adult — even one such as the caregiver who is known and trusted — can produce momentary twinges of anxiety. Most mothers know this, which is why they make it a point to give the arriving nanny a very high-profile greeting. In letting their two- or three-year-old see how much they appreciate Carol or Andrea or Leyola, they are in effect saying, "I value your caregiver highly, *and* I know you will be safe with her." The intended reassurance in this message can help alleviate leave-taking anxieties, but it sometimes does not because it is delivered in the wrong behavioral language.

The reason is that up until the age of about two and a half, a child doesn't yet have the social sophistication to understand how his mother is responding to another person. You can see this very clearly in the results of a study by Dr. Michael Lewis of Rutgers University. The study is worth examining for a moment because its findings are especially pertinent to the issue of leave-taking transitions.

Essentially, Dr. Lewis found that a young child is most at ease when another adult appears if mother smiles *first at him,* then at the new person. The investigator says the reason for this is the toddler's still incomplete knowledge of human social signals. He doesn't yet know enough about adult behavior to know that in smiling first at the caregiver, mother is trying to tell him how much she values, and how safe she thinks he will be with, Carol or Andrea or Leyola. Her smile and its meaning quite literally go over his head. A toddler — or even a three-month-old — can understand maternal friendliness directed toward him, however.

Mother's smile tells him he is loved and understood. This is why if, on the caregiver's appearance, the first thing mother does is tell him via a bright smile how much she loves him, any anxieties he may harbor about the caregiver will quickly vanish.

2. *Keep the focus on the child.* Making the child feel part of, rather than the object of, the handover also can do much to allay transition-time anxieties. One way of doing this is by asking the caregiver to get down on one knee and greet the child at eye level. Another way is by not letting your own anxieties about running late disturb your normally calm demeanor. A third is by making sure that the handover conversation is brief and that it involves the child.

An example of how to combine all three elements into a transition is the handover strategy we devised for Margo Kemmerling and Yvette Brown, the young woman who looks after Margo's three-year-old daughter, Lacy. I suggested to Margo that she and Yvette move the transition to the table and chair set she had bought for Lacy when Lacy "entertained" friends. This may make things a bit tight, I conceded, but it will put you and Yvette at Lacy's eye level, and because the transition is taking place at "her" table, Lacy also will feel as if she is hosting it. A week and a half later Margo called to report that much of Lacy's transition-time whining and clinging had disappeared. "I'm going to have to be careful, though," Margo added. "I think Lacy is beginning to think of herself as a replacement for Johnny Carson."

Mother, Child, and Day-care Worker and/or Nursery School Teacher

While someone who has to greet fifteen or twenty charges can't be expected to get down at eye level to welcome each one, the other rules that govern at-home transitions also govern those outside the home. During the drop-off you should look and smile first at your child, then at his teacher or daycare worker. You should also make an effort to keep the conversation between you and them relatively brief.

Most important of all, don't allow guilt to intrude now. Not only is that unfair to you, it will produce the kind of insensitivity that will make the drop-off significantly more stressful for your child. The reason can be seen in the results of a recent University of Miami study on day-care-based leave-takings, which found that the four parental behaviors most likely to produce protest and tears in a two-, three-, or four-year-old are all (in one way or another) linked to maternal guilt. The four are: *hovering* or dallying at the center instead of leaving immediately after the drop-off; *distraction* or trying to take the child's mind off of the transition; *explanations* in the form of overlong and complicated discourses on why mother has to leave now; and *sneaking out* of the center when the child's attention is focused elsewhere.

The study's principal author, Dr. Tiffany Field, believes that what makes these tactics so upsetting is the message of maternal distress they convey. Toddlers and infants are the world's greatest experts on maternal behavior, and when it tells them "I am distraught and guilty about leaving you here," they respond by becoming distraught themselves and so begin to cry and protest. Conversely, when parental behavior says, "Day care is a normal and expected part of your day just as work is of mine," children understand this and respond accordingly. Dr. Field found that the infants and toddlers in her study who made the smoothest adjustment to leave-taking had parents who believed in the value of day care and thus acted straightforwardly during the handover. They didn't, for example, dally excessively at the center; after saying goodbye, they left. Nor did they feel the need to explain what they were doing. And they always drew their child aside before leaving, looked him in the eye, and said goodbye.

One other finding from Dr. Field's study is noteworthy because it illustrates how a schedule that takes advantage of each parent's individual strengths can help ease a child smoothly through his day. At the center that was the focal point of her study, Dr. Field found that a large proportion of the infants and toddlers who made the best adjustment to leave-taking were dropped off by their fathers. The men behaved sensitively during leave-taking. They didn't engage in distractions, or try to avoid a last goodbye by quietly slipping away, or otherwise apologize to their child for the fact that he was going to spend the rest of the day at the center. And the children were quick to pick up on this attitude. Because everything about father's attitude said, "I believe this is good for you," the children segued smoothly from him to their day-care worker.

Does this mean drop-offs should always be the man's responsibility? No, what matters is the attitude conveyed, not the parent's sex. But if you find it difficult to control your feelings during transitions, it might be a good idea to divide the responsibility: your husband makes the drop-off; you make the pickup.

MIDMORNING CHECK-IN CALL
11:30 A.M. to Noon

This is the day's most difficult touch-point to generalize about. Scheduling factors and caregiving arrangements vary so widely that what may be a good call-in time for one mother may be thoroughly impractical for another. The way I have resolved this dilemma is by describing the ideal. Although not every woman has the flexibility and easy access that an at-home caregiver provides for check-in calls, seeing how they are used in this context should give you some idea of how they can be used to maximum advantage within the confines of your own schedule.

The check-in call's primary purpose is to establish a sense of interconnectedness, to let the child know that even in the midst of his mother's busy day, he remains uppermost in her mind. One way of doing this is to make a joint activity the focus of your phone conversation. Remind him how much fun the two of you had this morning at breakfast, or tell him about the plans you have made for your night together. Another way of enhancing the child's feeling of connectedness is by creating the right setting for the call. Language — even simple language — is still a complicated medium for a two-, three-, or even four-year-old. In this period, sensory phenomena — the look and feel and smell of things and people — speak most directly to a child. This is one reason an at-home caregiver is such a valuable ally in optimizing the midday touch-point. She has the time and resources to create the kind of setting that gives a mother's call the added dimension of tactility. Talking to Mommy while looking at a photograph of her on the table, holding a picture she helped draw this morning, or even smelling her perfume may not be the same thing as actually having her there. But because each of these things speaks directly to the child's senses — and through the senses to his memory — they give mother an immediacy and vividness that her words alone, however warm, cannot.

Another reason that an at-home caregiver can maximize the impact of a midday call is that she can choose just the right moment to place it. Is the child absorbed in a television program or game? Is he hungry or tired? Being there at around noon, a caregiver is in a good position to judge precisely when he will be most receptive to a phone talk with you. She can also monitor what happens when the phone is hung up.

Is the child sad, angry, or otherwise upset by the call? These are important questions, because how he reacts in the moments immediately after the call reflects on quality of attachment. Occasional reports of distress should not be a cause for alarm. On some days your absence weighs more heavily. You should expect that, and you should make it clear to the caregiver that you would like the child's sadness or upset to be respected. Tell the caregiver that while cheering up is appropriate, you would like the child first to be given a few moments to ventilate his anger or upset. These are legitimate emotions, and a toddler has a right to them.

What *is* a cause for concern is an ongoing pattern of postphone distress. A child whose emotional equilibrium is so fragile that even a five-minute call from mother is upsetting probably does not feel secure at other times and in other situations. In these cases, the phoning should stop for a month or two and shared time increased, with happy, playful interactions. Put night and weekend work in abeyance for the time being. The distress is a child's way of saying, "Mommy, I need more of you."

COMING HOME
5:30 P.M. to 6:30 P.M.

Reunion

Many of the rules that govern morning transitions apply in the evening as well. Eye contact and smiles should be directed first at the child — because you want to put your hello into his language, and (just as important at this moment) you want to let him know who stands first in mother's affection. Also, as in the morning, keep the conversation between you and the caregiver or day-care worker brief. Although you will need to know about your infant's or toddler's day because it will influence your night with the child, you don't want to frustrate or confuse him with a great deal of adult language. If you have business to conduct about parents' committees, book fairs, shopping, or cleaning, do it by note or over the phone later in the night.

Most important of all, again, do not let guilt intrude. Conducting the evening pickup as if the day-care center is the Beirut Airport, or Desert One and you are Rambo on a rescue mission, is going to make the two-, three-, or four-year-old wonder, "If Mommy is so anxious to whisk me away, maybe I shouldn't be at the center in the first place." The child's comfort quotient — with his caregiver, the center, or a nighttime baby-sitter — is a mirror image of your own. The best way to let him know how happy you are, and how much you believe in the institutions and figures that care for him, is to linger a moment. If you find the child and the caregiver in the middle of an activity when you get home, encourage them to finish. Or — in the case of the center — as you are about to leave, ask, "Are you ready or would you like to finish coloring that picture first?" Relaxed, casual, approving, these behaviors tell a child how highly mother values the center or Amanda, the caregiver; and knowing that makes him feel better about them.

In the moments immediately following the evening transition, the joy of being together again is so great that this touch-point may not seem to require any special attention. But sometimes scheduling pressures can undercut the mutual happiness mother and child share at having one another again to look at, talk to, hug, and kiss. One way this often happens is when the need to pick up a package, catch a bus, or get to the cleaners or supermarket is allowed to dictate the pace of the posttransition period.

Actions speak louder than words to a young child. At the end of the day when he asks himself, "How happy is Mommy to see me?"

(and in one form or another all boys and girls do), he looks not so much at what she says — although, of course, verbal expressions of happiness matter — as at what she does that indicates her attunement to his inner self, to his changing moods. And important as they are to you, adult chores are not among the ways a toddler defines his needs. Do them before the pickup so that on the journey home you will be free to help him satisfy his need for adventure by stopping when he wants to explore something, and his need for variation, occasionally altering the route home even if it adds extra time.

Carrie Goldstein was especially creative about devising alternate routes home for her four-year-old, Ari. Four is the age when a child wants to know how things work — how buildings get built, for example, and why fire trucks have sirens. So on nights when she and Ari had some time to spare, Carrie would use one of the two alternate routes she had created to help Ari satisfy this desire. One route brought them past a construction site. Ari had an enormous collection of steam shovels, dump trucks, and derricks at home, and seeing their real-life equivalents operating at the site gave him a big thrill. The second route took them past a fire station. Like most stations, this one left its garage doors open, so as they walked past Ari could peer in and examine the fire engines parked inside. A visit to the station added an extra forty-five minutes to their homeward journey, but, said Carrie, it was worth it to see the way Ari's eyes lit up as they approached the station.

To describe a visit to a fire station as an example of maternal sensitivity may sound surprising. But that is what it is. Carrie was telling Ari, in a way that means the most to a young child, that "Mommy is so happy to see you, she shares your interests and enthusiasm, and enjoys making *you* happy." And it is through such messages that a child comes to feel uniquely loved and understood.

The same reassuring message of maternal happiness is conveyed by the woman who, after saying goodbye to the caregiver, doesn't immediately disappear into the kitchen to begin preparing dinner, or pick up the phone, or start cleaning, or turn on the television news. Instead she quiets the house and herself, then gently takes the child up onto her lap and asks, "How was your day, darling?" Or in spring and summer, when the days are long and the evenings inviting, she moves the transitions outdoors to the park so that after the caregiver has left she can join her toddler's construction crew in the sandbox, or be dazzled by his prowess on the monkey bars, or just sit quietly on a bench with him and savor the wonder of their being together on a night like this.

These are the kinds of things caregivers — whether baby nurses or day-care workers — don't do, partly because they don't have time, but mostly because even the most loving and devoted of them don't think about a child the way a mother does. This isn't to say the infant or toddler who spends a substantial portion of his day in the care of another adult is "losing out"; he isn't. While the sensitivity of a caregiver or day-care worker is usually nonspecific in the sense that it is designed to please *a* child, it is more than sufficient for most of the situations a youngster encounters during the day. Putting on "Sesame Street," or buying him an ice cream, or engaging him in an exciting sing-along — all these things not only please a child immensely but make him feel that the adult or adults around him care deeply about his well-being. What they don't make him feel, however, because they are too general, is that he is uniquely loved and understood.

What distinguishes Mother's sensitivity and makes it so special and important to him is that it does make him feel uniquely loved and understood. It isn't designed to please any child, but *him*. And that by the sixth or seventh month an infant already has distinguished who is mother and who is caregiver shows how quickly a child picks up on the special intimacy and specificity of maternal sensitivity. The caregiver may point out a fire engine as it passes by on the street, but the youngster knows that only mother will go ten blocks out of her way to show him a fire truck parked in a real fire station. On a more general level, he also knows that although the caregiver may be able to soothe him, she isn't able to soothe him as deeply or quickly as mother, or able to read his thoughts and feelings as accurately. And it is through his awareness of these differences that a child comes to realize that mother, in her understanding and love for him, stands apart from and above all others.

The reason the tail end of the evening transition is a particularly good time for displaying your unique knowledge of your child is that, for both of you, it is one of the day's free points. From the moment of waking until the minute you left the center together or said goodbye to the caregiver, the mechanics of the schedule have governed your movements. And it will take over again in fifteen or twenty minutes when it becomes time to start dinner. In the meantime, the two of you have a rare chance just to be with one another. And it is in the act of "just being" that your special knowledge of his interior life and the secret dreams and fantasies that drive it is most likely to be noticed by a young child.

It is usually at this point in the talks on scheduling I give to parents' groups that I am asked, "But what about those nights when I come home exhausted?" Every working mother has them — evenings when she feels there isn't another ounce of energy left in her and she would give anything for twenty or twenty-five minutes to close her eyes. One way of handling these times is to ask your husband to make the day-care pickup so that you can go home for a quick nap. Another way is to switch one-on-one times so the child spends the first portion of the predinner hour with his father. A third is by learning how to unwind with the child present. You can do this by bathing or by lying down with your child nearby, looking through his books or making a Lego structure.

What should be avoided is asking the caregiver to cover for you while you take a quick nap. A one-, two-, or three-year-old doesn't yet have enough understanding of tiredness — at least as it applies to mothers — to realize why on her return home his mother heads not for him but for the bedroom. If you play for fifteen minutes, then nap, the child will be much more content.

EVENING

The three evening touch-points — dinner, shared time, and bedtime — also should be characterized by a mixture of playfulness and sociability. Also, with more open-ended time available, the extra element of rhythmicity should be inserted into the schedule. Events flow more smoothly and more is derived from them — in terms of both learning and enjoyment — when they are shaped to a child's natural pace. And thanks to the work of investigators such as Dr. T. Berry Brazelton of Harvard and Dr. Kenneth Kaye of the University of Chicago, over the last decade the nature of that pace has been identified. It is cyclical, revolving around bursts of energy and periods of quiet.

Careful frame-by-frame analysis by Dr. Kaye, in fact, reveals that this on-off rhythm is already apparent by the second day of life. In feeding patterns, typically, newborns alternate between bursts of energy at the maternal breast and pauses of rest in maternal arms. By the second or third year of life, it has become so pronounced that it spills over into every aspect of a toddler's behavior. One moment he is full of conversation, play, or physical activity; the next he is sitting quietly contemplating a block.

What Drs. Brazelton and Kaye's research shows is that each phase of this cycle is important to a child. In the bursts, he interacts with and collects information from the environment; in the pauses he rests, but it is a special kind of rest. He uses it to reflect on the information he has collected, and even more important, to process the stress that even the most satisfying interaction builds up in a one-, two-, or three-year-old.

Translated into the practical realities of nighttime behavior, what makes an awareness of this on-off pattern important is that a schedule that is sensitive to the needs it creates won't overstress, overstimulate, or otherwise emotionally destabilize a young child. Your boy or girl will get the most out of his nights with you and his father if his evening schedule flows something like this:

It will start with a burst of energy in the form of the nighttime transition, which involves the child in a great deal of interaction with his caregiver and/or day-care worker (saying goodbye) and with you and his father (saying hello). Following the handover should come a pause, in the form of a relatively low-key time with one or the other parent. In working families, dinner is usually an intensely social time, so it would serve as the next burst, and the cleanup afterward as the next pause. During it, the child might be left to play quietly by himself for a few moments, or he might read a book with his father.

This will put him in the right frame of mind for his shared time with you. One reason the energy women bring to this touch-point is sometimes destabilizing is that the youngster hasn't been given enough time to process the excitement built up over dinner. Inserting a pause period in between gives him a chance to regain his emotional equilibrium before you begin raising his energy level again.

Because bath time is usually the last intensely active point in the day, the final few minutes of your shared time should be quiet ones. This is when you might read a book or sing songs or play quietly with one another — in other words, start soothing the child with an activity he enjoys and finds easy. The same is true for the postbath period. After the excitement of water play and stimulation of being toweled, the child is usually feeling lively. This is why getting him into his pajamas or brushing his teeth sometimes degenerates into a wrestling match.

Stimulated by the bath, the last thing he wants to do now is relax. One way to gently bring him down is by creating an established bedtime routine. Repeated in sequence every night, such activities as putting on pajamas, brushing teeth, getting Big Bird or Tender Heart bear, become cues over time. As the child's pajama bottoms are slipped on, he knows bedtime is drawing near, and as he sees you approach, toothbrush in hand, that it is nearer still. The way to make these cues not just messengers of the night, but natural tranquilizers that relax and soothe an overexcited child, is to describe each event in the bedtime routine during toweling. Hearing you explain in a soft quiet voice, "Next, we are going to put on our PJs, and then get a glass of water, and then . . ." allows a two- or three-year-old to begin mentally preparing himself for the day's final transition from burst (his bath) to pause ("Goodnight, Mommy").

Having looked at its overall pattern, now let's look at the evening's three most important events.

DINNER
6:00 P.M. to 7:00 P.M.

This is an important touch-point for the same reason breakfast is: it is an opportunity to nourish the child's spirit. Why this opportunity isn't used to advantage as often as it might be is that work tends to increase a woman's concern with what might be called maternal forms. The emphasis is placed, not on how a child gets dressed but when, or — in the case of dinner — not on dining as a social experience, but on the amount of food consumed. This is understandable. Every working mother wants to believe that, whatever her other responsibilities and interests, her child is not suffering because of them. And being easily measurable, things like time or calories offer a handy yardstick. If her child seems to be on track in these areas a woman can say to herself, "See, I can do both."

Being less tangible, qualities such as empathy, cooperation, and humor usually don't get factored into such equations, and so the important role dinner (and breakfast) can play in nourishing them also doesn't get the attention it deserves. What a child sees and hears around him at the table, and the way he is treated at the table, are as important to the nourishment of his spirit as the food on his plate to the nourishment of his body. And if on certain nights one has to be given precedence over the other, it should be his spiritual nourishment. One way or another — as I said earlier — the youngster's daily caloric intake is going to be met, if not at dinner with your help, then at lunch or snack time with his caregiver's or day-care worker's help. That they may even be better than you at getting him to eat his carrots or lettuce is no reason to feel guilty or ashamed. Feeding a child is something any responsible adult can do, but only *you* can feed his spirit.

One other point about dinner: don't avoid talk of work. Some mothers do, out of fear that it will be resented as an intrusion. But mentioning work is no more likely to make a youngster think, "Even when Mommy's with me, all she talks about is work," than the mention of a supermarket at dinner is likely to make him think, "All she thinks about is groceries." Work is, after all, a central part of your identity, and it is important for your child to recognize this fact as early as possible. Furthermore, what they usually find most threatening about it is that it represents the unknown and mysterious. A two- or three-year-old's vivid imagination is capable of conjuring up all kinds of scenarios, but the most improbable scenario of all is that you do anything as humdrum as sit behind a desk all day.

SHARED TIME
6:30 P.M. to 8:30 P.M.

A number of qualities give the mother-child relationship its special texture, but two in particular stand out. One is the unusual depth of its intimacy. A measure of this is that on average, mother and child have been found to hold their mutual gazes almost twice as long as romantic lovers. The other is their sense of sharing a common history and destiny. Out of these two elements emerge that almost telepathic maternal understanding that makes a child think, "Mommy knows." And out of that thought evolves a sense of security that shines through in everything a child says or does.

During shared evening time, more than at any other touchpoint in the day, the one-on-one interaction without distractions helps establish the qualities of intimacy and the sense of sharing a common sensibility. Other intense periods of the day also offer special moments, but there is always the distraction of having to get something done soon. The child must be dressed or bathed or fed, and if not fed, cleaned off. Shared time is the only point where the two of you can just be with one another. And it is in the act of "just being" that the best things happen.

One of Pat Bias's sweetest memories of her daughter Rebecca's first year, for example, is the night she first discovered Rebecca's wicked sense of humor. Pat was sitting with Rebecca, then eight months old, when she noticed that one of her magazines had fallen onto the floor. Picking it up, she reached over to put it on her work desk, but as she did the magazine slipped out of her hand. Startled by this unprecedented display of maternal fallibility, Rebecca paused, looked down thoughtfully at the fallen magazine, looked back up at her mother, and then broke into an enormous grin. "As I looked at her smiling at me," says Pat, "I thought, 'Oh, what a little devil you are going to be, my dear.'"

That exquisite moment with Rebecca never would have happened if Pat's mind had been focused on an evening agenda. She would have been too preoccupied to have noticed the magazine. Even if she had noticed it, and it had fallen again, Pat would have been too concerned with moving the evening along to have given Rebecca the moment she needed to absorb what had just happened. This is why relaxed, unstructured, just-being time is so important. It lets things happen spontaneously, and because it does, it is the time when the mother-child relationship is most likely to accumulate the details of memory and feeling that give it its own unique shape and its special ability to nurture, comfort, and enlighten.

The reason that just-being, shared time — as opposed to what is known as quality time — has special power is that it puts the emphasis where it belongs: on mother and child. It involves games, songs, and other forms of play, but these are not ends in themselves. They are only a medium whose purpose is to give a woman and her infant or toddler a way of relating to and enjoying one another. What matters in such time isn't goals, in the sense of getting to the last page of a storybook or through every event on the evening's agenda, but *process,* the act of doing. Is that story or song you are sharing providing the pleasure you both should feel when together? More important still, is the story or song one that can be interrupted, or even discarded, so that if some moment of magic suddenly erupts you feel free to follow it?

This sense of open-endedness is one distinguishing characteristic of just-being, shared time. Another is what I earlier called *limiting.* Instead of trying to get through six or seven activities, concentrate on two or, at most, three. This gives a child time to explore them, comment on them, and think about them — in other words, time to do all the things he likes to do when involved and interested in an activity.

A third distinguishing characteristic of just being there is that it also stresses the importance of background quiet. Stereos, televisions, VCRs — all the intrusive noise-making machines that can produce annoying distractions — should be shut off when the two of you sit down together. Even more important, phone calls and conversations with other adults should be avoided. This is your special time together; nothing is more likely to make a two- or three-year-old realize the high value you place on him than hearing you tell a caller or visiting grandparent or interrupting husband, "Not now, we will discuss it after Andy and I have had our time together."

7:00 *P.M.* to 8:30 *P.M.*

Bath and Bed

Watching her child splash happily away in the bath, a working mother often feels a touch of sadness: another separation — in the form of sleep — is drawing near. This is why the bath and bedtime routines I mentioned earlier are, in some ways, as important for her as they are for him.

For a small child, a well-established routine constitutes both a road map to the end of the night and a form of autosuggestion. The last thing you should have to do in the delicate period leading up to bed is wrestle an overexcited two-year-old out of the bath, or chase him around the bedroom with his pajamas in one hand and a toothbrush in the other. A regular bedtime routine is a way of avoiding such struggles, because the child doesn't need anyone to show him what comes next or to soothe him; he will be able to do these things for himself.

Knowing that the schedule proceeds from bath to toweling, to toothbrushing, to goodnight kiss, gives him a recognizable map to the way stations along the road that leads to sleep. And since, through repetition, each of these stops will become a cue in his mind as he passes from one to another, unconsciously he will begin soothing himself.

For a working mother, bath and bedtime rituals also serve as a form of mental preparation. Because the evening always seems to go so quickly and because it is hard to say goodbye to someone you love, a woman needs time herself to adjust to the day's final separation. The routines give her a way of talking to herself. Watching her child move past the night's way stations, she is able to tell herself, "You are going to bed now, pussycat, but tomorrow we have a new day to share with one another." And reminding herself of that can help ease the pang of sadness brought by hearing that final "Goodnight, Mommy."

WAKE UP—MIDDLE OF THE NIGHT
1:00 A.M. to 4:00 A.M.

Stay in bed; you deserve the rest. One of the things working mothers often have to learn is how to be good to themselves. And one of the things their husbands often have to learn is how to help them be good to themselves. Getting up in the middle of the night to soothe a crying child is one way a man can help ease the enormous burden on his wife. Getting up also serves his relationship with his son or daughter. With you in bed, the house quiet, and all other distractions removed, father and child can enjoy their own just-being, shared time.

One last point: in this chapter and in the two preceding it we have been examining examples of what I earlier called *situational sensitivity*. At dinnertime, breakfast, and leave-taking, during shared time and on weekends—in each of these situations—we have explored how work changes a child's needs and desires in a way that will make him feel, "Mommy understands." Occasionally, however, a working mother also has to step back and look at the longer-term developmental trends in her child's life and how they are affected by work.

We call the capacity to do this *developmental sensitivity,* and in the next two chapters we are going to examine two important facets of it. One involves limit setting. What makes discipline a developmental rather than a situational issue is that its larger goal is self-discipline. The point of your admonitions and warnings is to instill a code of right and wrong that will allow your child to distinguish good from bad behavior without the help of your "no." But how does a working mother set limits and still remain responsive to her youngster's wish not to have precious shared time marred by fights and scoldings? In chapter 7, we will examine how you can meet both your needs and his by adopting a nonconfrontational approach to limit setting.

Another aspect of developmental sensitivity is a knowledge of the skills that can facilitate an infant's or toddler's adjustment to a work-shaped lifestyle. The capacity to self-comfort or to operate effectively in group situations arises first and foremost from a firm sense of security, but the emergence of certain developmental milestones will further enhance a boy's or girl's mastery of these and other important abilities. The developmentally sensitive mother is aware of these milestones and eager to put her child in touch with them at the earliest point in his developmental cycle.

The technique we have developed to help her do this is called *active guidance,* and it is the subject of our next chapter.

6

Active Guidance:
The Three Developmental Milestones Every Working Mother Needs to Know About

IF IT WERE POSSIBLE to compose a verbal snapshot of the "actively guided" child, I imagine it would look much like the evaluation report of three-year-old Alan Gillis that is lying in front of me. What makes it such an especially good illustration of the technique's effect on a young child is that, in a sense, the report catches Alan in freeze-frame. After eighteen months in the program, he is about to graduate, so in its pages you can see the cumulative effect of two years of active guidance on his development. This is why I have asked Alan's mother, Irene Gillis, for permission to quote from two places in it. The first quote is from Betty Mulligan, who is Alan's day-care worker and who, like all of our children's surrogate caregivers, was consulted in the process of preparing a final evaluation. Betty remarks:

> Alan has an unusual ability for a three-year-old. When another boy or girl does something he doesn't like, Alan protests appropriately. But he also is able to see past a moment of selfishness or anger in another child to all the things he likes about that child. This is why Alan never becomes involved in the bickering and petty jealousies that are so common among two- and three-year-olds. He doesn't get "stuck" on his anger the way other young children do when they feel themselves wronged. He knows how to forgive and forget.

The second quote is from our evaluator at the center. The developmental milestone he mentions may seem unrelated to Betty's comments about Alan's generosity of spirit, but that generosity reflcts the fact that, as the evaluator notes, "Alan displays an unusually advanced mastery of *object constancy*."

Of all the changes that occur in the first four years of life, this milestone and the two others we will examine in this chapter, *symbolic thinking* and *individuality,* have the most direct bearing on a young child's ability to adjust successfully to the stretches work imposes. Simply put, the goal of active guidance is to ensure that a child arrives at these milestones, and the special strengths and capacities that grow out of them, at the earliest point.

One of the most common fears I hear expressed by working mothers with infants and toddlers is: "Is my child too young to cope with the challenges and demands my work creates?" It is a fear with some justification. Every child does have the innate (biological) abilities needed to meet—and even thrive on—work-shaped challenges, but sometimes these abilities do not unfold as quickly as the youngster with a working mother requires them.

An example is the capacity to self-comfort. While its key building block is a firm sense of security, the distress produced by a late arrival home or a missed midmorning check-in call will be that much easier for a child to handle if he also knows how to use mementos of mother to soothe himself. Seeing one of her coats hanging in the closet or the storybook she read this morning lying open on his bedroom floor, the toddler feels linked to mother through that evoked companion—almost as if she were there comforting him at this stressful moment. The larger developmental milestone behind this ability to self-comfort through maternal mementos is symbolic thinking. And while by age two a toddler develops the ability to understand what mother's coat stands for, in the meantime how is he to cope with the stress produced by mother's late nights at the office?

What we call the "Mommy Here / Mommy There Syndrome" poses a similar dilemma. It isn't until nearly his third year that a child fully links up in his mind the mother who leaves in the morning with the mother who returns in the evening, for this is when object constancy, which makes this linkage possible, develops. How is the child — and how is the mother — to cope in the meantime with the confusion and distress that Mommy's comings and goings cause? The same troubling question hangs over other abilities that are of special importance to a child with a working mother, such as the capacity to operate comfortably in a day-care or nursery school environment, or to absorb the stress of a maternal leave-taking without dissolving into tears. Locked within him, every youngster has the ability he needs to adjust to these aspects of his work-shaped lifestyle. But they are the by-products of developmental milestones whose unfolding is governed by a biological timetable that, in the meantime, can leave the youngster prey to needless anxieties, uncertainties, and fears.

Active guidance is a way of hastening (but not hurrying) the emergence of these larger developmental milestones, and it does so in a *natural* way. What is not natural is isolating individual abilities like social adaptability or self-comforting and targeting them for growth. Guiding a child to the larger developmental milestone out of which capabilities like self-comforting and problem solving flow on their own *is* natural. And that is what active guidance does.

Alan's evaluation report also is noteworthy for another reason. It illustrates how attachment is affected when a woman knows how to exercise developmental sensitivity. This doesn't mean that an actively guided two-, three-, or four-year-old thinks anything as direct or specific as "Mommy is being very helpful; she is putting me in touch with the abilities I need to function effectively." Because of the way he is programmed, however, a young child does "know" on an instinctive level when he is being helped to learn and grow and function in a given environment. And such sensitivity to his needs does have an influence on his feelings toward the mother who displays it.

The special nature of the influence can be seen in the section of Alan's report that describes his behavior during the Strange Situation Test. Developed several years ago at Johns Hopkins University, the test grew out of the discovery that how a child greets his returning mother after she has momentarily left him in the care of a "stranger" (who is usually an evaluator) accurately reflects the quality of his attachment to her.

In such circumstances, a child responds in one of three possible ways. The first and rarest response is avoidance. The child who turns away from his returning mother is signaling a weak attachment, characteristic of children who feel themselves in the midst of environments that are insensitive or unresponsive. The second, somewhat more common response is ambivalence. The youngster who alternates between beaming smiles and turning away from his returning mother is saying he feels insecurely attached because, although sometimes mother seems to understand how to help him grow, other times she doesn't. The third possible test response is the one Alan gave to Irene. The hugs, kisses, and squeals of joy she met are signs of the secure attachment that develops when a child feels himself in a sensitive and supportive environment.

Here is how active guidance can help you shape such an environment for your child.

INDIVIDUALITY

One of the most remarkable things about the human infant is how quickly he begins asserting his special likes and dislikes. As early as the end of the first week, for example, a baby already will be using his coos and cries to signal the way he likes to be held when brought to the maternal breast for a feeding. By the end of the eighth week, he also will be using those coos to indicate how he prefers to be held — in his mother's arms or on her shoulder — when he is upset. And by the end of the twenty-sixth week, he will be using his gurgles, smiles, and other behavioral signals to tell her that he prefers this activity (say, rattle play) over that activity (say, peek-a-boo).

These likes and dislikes appear so early and sharply because they are a reflection of the child's innate temperament. What makes them so important developmentally is that they are the building blocks of individuality. Through a knowledge of his likes and dislikes a child is given a way of defining himself to himself. At seven months, a baby's special pleasure in being swung around may be experienced largely on a biological level, but by four the special pleasure derived from such activities will have given the preschooler a way of identifying himself. "I am a good runner," he will think. And by fifteen or sixteen his self-assessment will have become refined to the point where he will be able to say simply, "I am an athlete." An awareness of one's likes and dislikes also fosters individuality by helping a young child to define how he is different from his friends. The fact that Jimmy likes to draw and he likes to climb jungle gyms helps the child to distinguish himself from Jimmy in a way that makes him feel unique. Ordinarily a youngster's knowledge of his likes and dislikes doesn't reach the point of critical mass out of which a strong, clearly defined "I" emerges until sometime between the twenty-fourth and thirtieth month. Active guidance, however, often help bring a child to that point months earlier. There are a number of reasons why this earlier date better serves a working mother and her child, especially if that child is in day care.

The boy or girl who worries day-care workers most is usually the one who is unable to represent his needs effectively in group situations. Behind this inability lies an ill-defined sense of self. The child never speaks up simply because, not knowing what he likes and requires, he has little to say. Such a child is a special source of concern to a conscientious day-care worker not only because of the fear that his needs will be overshadowed by those children who do know what they like and are able to speak up for themselves, but also because in time even the day-care worker herself will, without realizing, begin to ignore him. One common result of this is what we call the "Little Child Lost Syndrome." The toddler ends up languishing in a corner, ignored, overlooked, and unhappy. One common result is that one day he begins to rebel against being sent to the center.

That is what happened to Rennie Paco. One morning ten months after her mother, Roberta, returned to work, three-year-old Rennie walked into the kitchen where Roberta and her husband, David, were having a final cup of coffee. In that voice toddlers reserve for their most irrevocable decisions, Rennie announced, "I'm not going there today, Mommy. I'm not going and don't try and make me."

"But I thought you liked your center. I know you like your day-care worker, Jane," Roberta replied brightly, hoping to contain an explosion. But Rennie refused to be brightened out of her resolve.

"No, no, no. I'm not going!" she screamed, and to underline the point collapsed to the floor in a lifeless heap.

The nightmare that followed still makes Roberta Paco shudder. First, there was the bus that had to be abandoned because Rennie was screaming so loudly Roberta was afraid the other passengers would think she had hit her daughter. Then there was the accusing look on the face of the taxi driver who drove them the rest of the way to the center. And finally there was the very unhappy look on her superior's face when she arrived an hour late for a meeting at which she had been scheduled to make a presentation.

Describing the incident later, however, Roberta confessed that Rennie's announcement hadn't been a total surprise. A worried Jane had called her to the center several times in the preceding months to discuss what Jane called Rennie's "noninvolvement" in the group. In most situations, Rennie was odd man out. The other children were always bursting with ideas about what to do and where to go if an outing was scheduled, but Rennie never seemed to have any opinions about these things. "She is such a passive child," Jane said. "I worry a lot that she is getting lost in the shuffle around here."

Alan enjoys his center so much because, unlike Rennie, he always does have plenty of input on his group's decisions about activities and plans. That doesn't mean he always gets his way, but his knowledge of who he is and what he likes has made him sufficiently assertive to ensure that he gets it enough times to make day care an always interesting and enjoyable experience.

One other way Alan's knowledge of himself has facilitated his adjustment to Betty's center is by making him easier to comfort in moments of distress. Upsets are less likely to end in tears if the day-care worker can distract a child by guiding him to some activity she knows he finds especially absorbing. On mornings when

Betty senses that Irene's "goodbye" has left Alan anxious, for example, she always takes him to the corner where she keeps a collection of old hats, coats, shirts, and ties because she has noticed that Alan's pleasure in dressing up has a soothing effect on him. As Betty noted to me once during a visit to the center, "you can't do that with a child who doesn't know what he likes."

The second important way individuality facilitates a child's adjustment to work is by making leave-takings less stressful. As Irene discovered, however, this is a truth that has to be qualified in one important respect. One morning about six months after she and Alan entered the program, Irene appeared in my office with a complaint. She was too diplomatic to put it so baldly, but the essence of her complaint was that instead of making Alan more tolerant of her departures as she had expected, the strategies we had shown her were actually increasing the intensity of his departure protests. I explained to her that this is one of the paradoxes a firm sense of individuality creates.

In the short run, it does intensify leave-taking protests because, as his awareness of his likes and dislikes grows and clarifies, a child begins to act on them. And since one thing he can be counted on *not* to like is his mother's leaving, for a period he does cry and cling more. I told Irene she could take comfort in the fact that this intensification in Alan's departure protests was a reflection of the effectiveness of the strategies she was using. I also reassured her that this period of increased intensity is mercifully brief because a knowledge of "Who I am and what I like" gives a child a means of dealing effectively with the deeper underlying stress mother's leaving produces.

One way is by enhancing the child's ability to comfort himself. Now that he knows what he likes, he can distract himself out of his upset in a favorite game or toy after mother leaves. Even more significant, a sense of individuality gives the youngster who has said goodbye something to hold onto — *himself*. Leave-taking anxieties are especially sharp in one- or two-year-olds because, not having separated entirely from mother, they feel that what leaves each day isn't another person but a part of them. And even worse, it is the competent part, the part that takes care of feeding, dressing, and bathing. In psychoanalytical terms, this can give rise to what are known as "disappearance fantasies." Because a part of him has vanished, the twelve- or thirteen-month-old fears that the rest of him will vanish, too. Once a child has a firm sense of self, this fear abates because, important as mother is, the child now realizes she is not he but is another person; knowing that makes it much easier for him to let her go.

If you were to plot the pattern of leave-taking protests I have just described on a graph, you would find yourself looking at a bell-shaped curve. For most children, the apex of this curve — the period when protest departures are most frequent and sharpest — would be the thirty-sixth month. That is the time when an awareness of likes and dislikes reaches critical mass. While climbing up the ascending side of the curve, the intensity of protests in the thirteenth, fourteenth, or fifteenth month would still be relatively low because often the anxiety produced by disappearance fantasies isn't expressed verbally.

If you were now to turn to a graph of Alan's departure protests, you would find the same pattern — a bell-shaped curve — but you would also notice three important differences in his curve. First, its apex wouldn't be nearly as steep as that on the first graph; second, it would be positioned in Alan's seventeenth month, not his twentieth; and third, instead of tapering off gradually on the descending side as the curve in the first chart does, his curve would drop sharply. This trajectory is a reflection of the dramatic behavioral change Alan underwent as he was helped to answer the questions "Who am I and what do I like?"

BUILDING BLOCKS OF INDIVIDUALITY
Menu Offering

The robust, vigorous, assertive "I" that three-year-old Alan displays in every area of his life is the outcome of a series of discoveries that every child begins making in his first months of life. Not that a three-month-old thinks, "Music really moves me," or a four-month-old, "Color excites me." Before that kind of self-knowledge can grow, a child first has to be helped to identify his special likes. And that is the goal of *menu offering*.

This is designed for use in the first year, and its name is a reflection of the fact that the wider the interactive menu of sights, sounds, movements, and objects he encounters, the more likely a child will be to find something among the selections that touches him in a special way. In designing your menu, the only limit you should put on your imagination is your child's age. What interests a three-month-old won't interest a seven-month-old. Here are some sample menus for three different age groups:

Three Months.   For infants in this age group, the menu theme should be *people* in the form of mother (and father). People are what interest a three-month-old most, especially when they present themselves in interesting, exciting, and varied ways. In exchanges, you should offer yourself in a wide range of guises: singing, talking, whispering with an animated and with a quiet face, smiling, mock frowning, playing finger games such as thumbkin and hide-and-seek games such as peek-a-boo.

Seven Months.   The appropriate theme for this age group is *objects*. Although mother remains of central interest, a seven-month-old's gaze has begun to shift outward to the wider environment of objects and things. Exchanges should reflect that change by including props in the form of blocks, shiny mirrors, teething rings, balls, and rattles. The more colorful and noisy (within reason, of course) the objects, the better.

Twelve to Fourteen Months.   For the toddler's menu *objects in motion* is the appropriate theme. Having familiarized himself with the things in his world, now he is eager to find out what those things can do. This eagerness makes his play more aggressive and inventive. Hand an eight-month-old a Slinky, a long coiled spring, and he will be intrigued. Each time he picks up the Slinky, however, he will do essentially the same thing: shake it and watch with fascination as it writhes snakelike before his eyes. Give that same Slinky to a thirteen-month-old, and he will bite it, swing it from side to side, throw it up and down, then finally bounce it against a wall. Surprising as it may seem, the thirteen-month-old's play constitutes a kind of scientific experiment. The toddler is being a little Einstein. He is exploring all the various things a Slinky can do.

In terms of menu offerings, this eagerness to explore the properties of things has two implications. First, the toys and playthings on a twelve-, thirteen-, or fourteen-month-old's menu should be durable. Second, in order to keep him interested, they should be multifaceted — have several different functions. Examples of multifaceted toys include Busy Box, dolls and stuffed animals that make sounds, and trucks, cars, and other movable objects that can be rolled across the floor as well as picked up and examined.

Throughout these months you should be closely observing your baby's responses. When a menu selection touches a special interest or preference, he will signal it by becoming unusually excited or attentive, or by quieting or babbling enthusiastically. These responses are a child's way of saying, "Hey Mommy, I really like that. Do it again, please." Take note of the things that produce this reaction; you will need them for the next building block.

Repeat Preferences

It is important for you to know what your baby likes, and it is, of course, also important for him to know. He can't begin to use his preferences to amuse, comfort, or define himself until he has identified them for himself. And because repetition is the way young children make connections between things, the more repeatedly an infant or toddler is exposed to a favorite menu selection, the sooner he is going to connect that selection with the special pleasure it gives him — and realize he likes it.

There are two ways you can provide such repetition. One is by shaping interactions so that a portion of each day always is set aside for activities or forms of stimulation you have noticed he likes.

The other, even more imaginative way is by incorporating your baby's preferences into the other things the two of you do. Estelle Chin, one of our REAP mothers, was particularly creative in this regard. Noticing that her two-month-old, Eric, became especially alert in the presence of bright colors — whether the colors took the form of a red dress she was wearing or the new chintz curtains the Chins had hung in their dayroom — Estelle decided to enliven their games of peek-a-boo by adding a touch of color. As she expected, hiding her face behind the swatches of pastel cloth she had bought rather than behind her hands gave the game a new excitement for Eric. But her variation also produced an effect Estelle hadn't anticipated. Because special likes have an almost magnetic effect on a young child's focus, Estelle found that her variation of peek-a-boo also became a way of distracting Eric when he was upset. Music will produce the same response in a child who is drawn to sounds. If your child alerts in a special way whenever singing fills the air, be sure that among his toys are a number of stuffed animals, jack-in-the-boxes, and Busy Boxes that ring out with music when opened, bent, or cranked. Alternatively, when he himself repeats an activity or sounds, he'll appreciate not being interrupted.

Encountering a favorite activity or object in every interaction not only hastens the day when the child begins to identify that thing as being a special favorite, it also does something even more important. It tells a four-, ten-, or twenty-two-month-old in a way he can understand, "Mother knows what you like." Through such messages, a youngster comes to realize that although there are many adults in his life and all of them understand something about him, no one understands him as deeply or completely as mother.

Inform Others about the Child's Preferences

The principal aim of this strategy is to widen the circle of repetition. The more people who know what the baby likes and the more often they repeat those likes in their interactions with him, the sooner still he is going to make the connection between a particular thing and the pleasure it gives him. One word of caution. Because fathers, caregivers, and day-care workers also have their own relationships with the child, and because each also considers him- or herself a child-care expert, be diplomatic in encouraging them to emphasize the youngster's special preferences. Further-more, your child's interests subtly vary depending on whom they are with. In noting that this game, that sound, these colors, or that toy seems to especially please the child, also point out that you have found this special preference to soothe him when upset and distract him when bored. You won't be exaggerating. As Eric's response shows, favorite things do absorb and calm a youngster. Emphasizing this fact will make your suggestion seem more like an effort to share your comforting skills with these other experts than like an attempt to control their behavior with him.

Encourage Decision Making

Having identified the child's special likes yourself and then helped him to identify them, the last step in the process of self-discovery that leads to the emergence of a strong, self-knowing "I" is the incorporation of these preferences into his day-to-day behavior. The best way to facilitate this incorporation is by encouraging him to make decisions based on them. In the case of a nineteen-, twenty-, or twenty-one-month-old (which is when this strategy becomes appropriate), the scope of decision making is necessarily limited. Nonetheless a toddler who is acquainted with his prefer-ences will be able to say, if asked to use his likes as guides in choosing, what he wants to do tonight. If he is drawn to sounds and color, he will probably select a favorite book for you to read; if his interests are mechanical, a set of blocks or a Busy Box. Al-though such choices do not encourage a toddler to think of him-self as a nascent intellectual or engineer, the selections do produce self-recognition. His choices say to him, in a way that nothing else in his life does, "This is who you are."

SYMBOLIC THINKING

One of Irene's sweetest memories of Alan is how he announced his arrival at this milestone. It was an unusually balmy Saturday in late March. Thinking "What a delicious day!" Irene decided to inau-gurate the year's park season by taking Alan to the neighborhood playground. Putting their lunch into the baby bag, Irene thought she saw Alan's facial expression suddenly change. But she told herself, "I'm imagining things." Alan, who was thirteen months old at the time, had never before evidenced any interest in a maternal behavior not aimed directly at him; why would he start now? Reaching for her tweed park coat, however, Irene saw that she had not been fantasizing. As she slipped on the coat, Alan began babbling excitedly and pointing toward his stroller. "Imagine that," Irene said when she told me this story. "Alan had figured out all by himself that we were going to go out."

Responses such as Alan's are how a young child indicates that he can now think symbolically. In the simplest sense this capacity means the ability to understand that this stands for that; and it is the by-product of two other capacities: memory and the ability to make associations. What had transformed Irene's coat and her baby bag from mere things into symbols of "going out," for example, was a pattern that over the months Alan had identified: whenever he and mother left the house together, Irene usually had these two articles with her. Remembering this pattern on that warm Saturday afternoon, Alan grew excited. Seeing Irene with the coat and baby bag, he suddenly realized, "Mommy and I are going out!"

Normally a toddler arrives at the ability to understand that this stands for that sometime between his fourteenth and eighteenth month. As Alan's response shows, however, a child can be brought to symbolic thinking as early as the thirteenth month.

This earlier date better serves the infant and his working mother. With the emergence of this milestone, a woman no longer has to be there physically for her child. Through her coats, hats, photographs, fragrances, and jewelry, even through the games she plays and the books she reads, she can leave a part of herself at home when she walks out the door in the morning. Most immediately, these maternal mementos link the child to her through the bridge of memory. Looking at a photograph of himself and Mommy splashing happily in the waves, the toddler is instantly brought back to the wonderful summer day at the beach when it was taken. Seeing his mother's blue parka draped over the back of a chair, he remembers how good it felt to nestle his head in its collar the day he fell and hurt his knee at the park.

Maternal mementos, however, also create another, even more intimate kind of connection. While everpresent, the sight of mother's red rain hat or tweed coat activates the child's mental image of mother — his evoked companion — in a direct and palpable way. Although he can't see or smell her, through such symbols he is linked to her in ways that allow him to feel her presence. And the more vivid a mother's presence, the less stress her absence produces.

As you might imagine, what most often attains symbolic status in a young child's mind are the clothes you wear and the objects you use. But once a toddler realizes how one thing can stand for another, shared activities also can be used as maternal symbols. An example is a technique we call *structuring*. It involves dividing an activity — the reading of a book, for example, or the building of a castle — into morning and evening segments. For the child who stays home all day, the partially built castle standing by his bed or the partially read book lying on his night table serves as a palpable symbol of mother and of the promise of her return that night. (Structuring is also appropriate for the child in day care.)

Diane Finkelstein, one of our REAP mothers, was skeptical when I first described the philosophy behind structuring. "I can understand how it might work for a three-year-old," Diane said, "but Aaron is only sixteen months old; he won't remember what we did this morning." I explained that a toddler of Aaron's age not only has a very good memory, because his mind isn't filled with worries about meetings that have to be prepared for and reports that have to be read, often he will be better at remembering your promises than you are.

Diane remained skeptical, but she was also sufficiently intrigued to try the technique one morning a few days after we had talked. Before breakfast she read Aaron the first half of *Dr. DeSoto,* a charming story about a mouse dentist who is almost devoured by one of his larger and less grateful patients. "I was really busy that day, and I had forgotten about my promise to finish reading *Dr. DeSoto* when I got home. But Aaron hadn't," Diane said when she told me about the experiment the following week. "He was sitting on the first floor landing with a big grin on his face and *Dr. DeSoto* wrapped in his arms." I told her that Aaron's greeting was more than just a reflection of his recall capacity; it indicated that he had been thinking about *Dr. DeSoto* — and about her — all day. That was why his smile was so radiant.

A second reason to hasten symbolic thinking's emergence is that it enhances a child's ability to self-comfort. Because symbols link him to you, in a general sense, everything that he invests with your presence serves to soothe him in times of special stress. There also is another, more specific way objects and things can be used to help a toddler cope with an upset or distress once he has attained the ability to think in symbols. An example is the way symbolic thinking facilitates his ability to use what are known as "transitional objects" as sources of succor. A transitional object is that blanket, bunny, teddy bear, or other special object the toddler carries everywhere and refuses to part with even for a moment.

What gives these objects their unique aura is the meaning a child attaches to them. They are, in other words, symbols, and they symbolize mother in a special way. A toddler's Paddington Bear or tattered blue blanket doesn't link him to mother through the agency of memory the way a photograph or piece of jewelry does; transitional objects rarely have specific maternal memories attached to them. Their unique powers arise from the association that grows in the child's mind. Over time that irreplaceable bear or blanket comes to symbolize not mother's face or smell or the special way she smiles when he does something especially pleasing, but her power to heal, to comfort, to be a companion, and to make him feel secure and loved. This is why a meeting with a new caregiver or a new day-care worker, a late night at the office, or an especially stressful morning at the day-care center will be incomparably easier for a child to handle if he is able to use a transitional object to soothe himself.

Even places can be transformed into symbols that enhance a child's ability to cope. On nights when Irene is working late, for example, Lilibeth, Alan's baby-sitter, gets a book and takes him into the corner of his room where Irene usually reads to him.

Sitting there, where he always sits with his mother, listening to the books she usually reads, invariably has a calming effect on Alan. Lilibeth may lack the psychological knowledge to explain why it does, but she is perceptive enough to know that the corner's soothing effect is linked to the fact that it is one of the special places Alan has come to associate with his mother.

Here are four ways you can actively guide your child to an early mastery of symbolic thinking.

BUILDING BLOCKS OF SYMBOLIC THINKING

First Year

Promote Memory Training.   Memory is central to symbolic thinking for the simple and fundamental reason that many of the objects that attain symbolic status in a young child's mind do so because of the rich trove of memories he associates with them. Think of that photograph of the mother and child splashing happily in the water. What makes it such a powerfully evocative symbol to the youngster looking at it on a cold January afternoon isn't the photograph itself, but the memories it stirs of the day it was taken. It brings him back to the beach, back to the special warmth of the sun that day, and — most of all — back to mother and the joy he felt being with her.

A child usually doesn't begin attaching such memories to objects or fragrances until the twentieth or twenty-first month not because he lacks sufficient recall capacity — at twelve months he already has a remarkably good memory — but because he lacks the opportunity to develop this capacity as early as he might. Memory develops the same way muscle tissue does: through repeated use. The more opportunities a youngster is given — especially in the first year — to exercise his memory, the sooner he begins to develop the kind of recall capacity that allows him to link himself to mother through the memories her coat, fragrance, photographs, and interactions evoke.

A memory exercise Irene found especially helpful is one we call *sequencing.* It involves taking a daily event, such as a feeding or bedtime, and developing a sequence of items that lead up to it. Since a key requirement of this strategy is consistency, in selecting an event around which to build your sequence you should take into account the nature of your child-care arrangement. Feeding sequences are appropriate if there is an at-home caregiver, since she will duplicate your sequences when she feeds the baby. Day-care workers won't; they don't have as much time. If your baby spends his day at a center, use bedtime as the focal point. Also keep the sequences simple; each sequence should contain no more than three or, at most, four items. Here are examples of feeding and bedtime sequences that can be used with four- to twelve-month-olds:

- *Feeding:* a song, a rocking, a stroking of the head, then your breast or a bottle.
- *Bedtime:* a finger game such as thumbkin, a soft song, a kiss on the cheek, and finally the word "goodnight" spoken softly.

You don't have to repeat the sequence exactly each time. To help the infant to lay down memory tracks of each item in it, however, you should repeat the items in approximately the same order and — just as important — at approximately the same pace. Over time, such consistency will transform the first item in the sequence into a symbol. Seeing your finger game or hearing your song, the baby will immediately think, "Feeding time" or "Bedtime." Which is to say, he will now have begun to understand that this can stand for that.

Since we remember not just what we see, but what we touch, taste, smell, and feel, *multimodal memory making* also can be used to help a seven-, eight-, or nine-month-old enhance his recall capacity. Modes are senses, and it is important to encourage a baby to explore an object with as many different senses as possible because such exploration gives him more ways of retrieving his memory of that object. Meeting the object next time, he may be able to identify it from visual memory alone. If that fails him, his memory of the object's taste, smell, feel, or sound can help him identify it.

Understandably, you may feel reluctant to subject a new hat or briefcase to the full brunt of multimodal memory making, but an infant's explorations can be shaped in a way that avoids tooth marks, stains, or wrinkles. If you notice, say, that a piece of jewelry has caught your child's eye, take it off and let him hold it in his hand for a moment; then jangle it in front of him so that he can form an auditory memory of it. We call this "supervised multimodal exploration," and it not only facilitates the memory — and hence symbolization process — in the infant, it also ensures that your coat, handbag, hat, or briefcase survives that exploration process intact.

Be Consistent.   Along with memory, the other foundation of symbolic thinking is the capacity to make associations. Your toddler is able to connect himself to you through a certain hat, coat, bracelet, or book because he has come to associate these articles with you and your love. And such associations develop more quickly in the mind of twelve- to fifteen-month-olds if there is a consistent pattern of maternal usage. Alan's quickness in associating Irene's coat and baby bag with "going out" is an example. Whenever he and Irene went out together, he always saw her with these two articles, and they became symbols of departure for him. Alan always thinks of his mother when he sits in the corner of his room next to the window for the same reason. This is the place where Irene always reads to him.

The things and places Irene targeted for consistent use are ones every working mother can duplicate. By creating a special "park" coat or bag, you will be quicker to establish the kinds of connections that lead your child to see these articles as symbols of you. Consistency in the use of a particular place produces a similar linkage. You needn't conduct your shared time in exactly the same spot each night, but reserving a special place for most shared times enables the child to use it to link himself to you when you are not there.

Use Objects that Lend Themselves to Symbolization.   Everything, even food, can attain symbolic value, but certain objects and articles do lend themselves more readily to the symbolization process

than others. In some cases this simply means that the article is
unusually visible. Your park coat is more likely to evoke you to
your child than your park shoes, for example, because he notices
the coat more. In other cases an object's potential as a symbol is
enhanced by its special *personal* quality. A storybook you read
together is more likely to become a memento of you than the toy
you play with together because the book has an intimate quality
and the toy doesn't. In still other cases, what facilitates the symbolization process is that the article — say, maternal jewelry — is
interesting to the child in ways that another, equally visible item
— say, your reading glasses — isn't. And finally, there are certain
other objects, principally photographs, that are just naturally *evocative*.

In order to facilitate the process of symbolization, the things
you surround the child with should contain at least two of the four
attributes highlighted above. Also important is easy access. In the
case of photographs, hats, coats, bags, or storybooks, this is no
problem. That favorite book can be left in a prominent place on
his night table or bookshelf. Also on the night table and hanging
on the walls of his room should be several photographs of you and
of you and him together. And one picture, preferably the one on
his nightstand, should be dabbed with a fragrance you wear. You
can provide easy access to things like park coats and baby bags by
leaving them hanging in the front hallway, where they can serve as
reminders of you during the week.

In times of unusual distress tell the caregiver to take the child
around the house and show him a photograph, bracelet, or pillow
that you have noticed he particularly likes, while the two of them
talk over the source of his upset. The sight of these mementos of
you will have its own soothing effect.

A word about transitional objects, because it is especially important to encourage the transference of your powers to comfort
and heal onto a transitional object: monitor the child's use of his
playthings closely. As soon as he begins to evidence a special liking
for one of his bears, bunnies, or blankets, make sure you and the
caregiver maximize his exposure to it. If he forgets to bring the
object to bed with him, put it in the crib yourself. On strolls, also

make sure the bunny or bear is in the stroller with him. Once the toddler has made a strong choice, immediately go out and buy a duplicate bunny, bear, or blanket. Imagine what he will be like on a morning when, just as you are about to walk out the door, he realizes he has lost that irreplaceable bear or bunny, and you won't have to ask why you need the duplicate.

OBJECT CONSTANCY

Talking with Alan is always an instructive experience. He is an unusually mature and thoughtful child, and these qualities shine through in his conversation. They are reflected in the way he talks about himself, his friends and playmates, and especially about Irene. Alan can't be said to "like" the fact that Irene's job as a purchasing agent takes her away from him for a part of each day. That would be too much to ask of any three-year-old. But what can be said is that the unhappiness these daily separations sometimes produces has not caused Alan to lose sight of the many more ways Irene knows how to make him feel happy.

He doesn't understand the meaning of words like *sensitivity* and *responsiveness,* of course, but in my conversations with him I am always struck by the ways in which Alan talks about Irene, ways that nearly always reflect on her mastery of these qualities. "Mommy," he will say, "knows what I like better than anyone else in the whole world." A statement like this indicates that Alan has developed the ability to form what we at the center call "all-and-all" judgments. His mental image of Irene is now sufficiently mature to accommodate the fact that some of the things she does displease him, but it also is sufficiently positive to allow him to see through these things to the larger truth underneath: that overall his mother loves and cares for him.

No child of four or under can be expected to actually like the work that takes his mother away from him each day. But whether his feelings about that work become an issue in the attachment process depends on whether he develops the ability to react as if he were thinking, "Although this is one thing I don't like, overall I do like most of the things Mommy does." If you think about it, a youngster's ability to make friends in day care or nursery school also is dependent on whether he is able to make similar judgments about the boys and girls he encounters in these settings — for example, on whether he is able to say about his friend Jessica, "Jessica wouldn't share her doll with me this morning, but usually she is a good friend so I will play with her now."

A three-year-old's ability to make such balanced and mature assessments is rooted in the mastery of a developmental milestone known as object constancy. During a child's first four years, parents encounter the milestone in two different and distinct forms. The first encounter usually takes place between the tenth and twelfth month as the baby begins to realize that mother does not, as he had thought, simply vanish on leaving him but leads an independent existence. In its simplest sense this is what object constancy means: the realization that mother continues to exist in time and space even when she can't be seen, touched, tasted, or felt. The reason why you should want to hasten the emergence of this first form of object constancy in your baby — and, actively guided, he can arrive at it in his sixth month — is that the appearance of another new awareness between the eighth and ninth month can intensify his leave-taking distress if he hasn't already discovered your permanence.

What makes the possibility of your sudden disappearance not unduly troubling to your six- or seven-month-old is that while he has begun to associate you with certain aspects of mothering, he hasn't yet put these aspects together into a single unified image that in his mind says "Mother." Once this happens — and usually by the eighth or ninth month the baby clearly identifies you as mother — distress about your leave-taking begins. Having identified you as the most important figure in his life, the infant naturally becomes upset by the prospect of your departure. But the degree of upset that maternal departures provoke will be lessened considerably if he has already come to an awareness of your constancy. Even an eight-month-old knows that objects that have permanence in time and space are much more likely to return than those which simply vanish into air. Conversely, if he identifies you as "Mother" before he becomes aware of your constancy, leave-taking will be fraught with added anxiety; each time you go, he will be left wondering, "Is she going to disappear forever?"

What links this first, elemental form of object constancy with the second, more advanced type, is that as soon as the baby becomes aware of your wholeness and permanence he immediately begins to divide you into two figures who might be called "Good Mommy" and "Bad Mommy." His angry wails are aimed at the Bad Mommy who failed to respond to his first cry to be picked up and fed; his smiles and contented coos, at the Good Mommy who rocks him back and forth as she feeds him. This division is normal. Every baby, regardless of his mother's occupational status, divides her into a Good Mommy and a Bad Mommy.

Usually, the way he eventually integrates these two figures back into a single "Mommy Mommy" is through the normal course of experience. Because mothers, on the whole, do a great many things that please their children and relatively few things that displease them, by about age four a youngster comes to have a three-dimensional image of mother that, while broad enough to encompass some of the things he doesn't like, is on the whole positive. This kind of shaped, balanced, but largely loving view of mother is what we call *positive object constancy*. Its nurturance deserves a working mother's special attention because while on the whole she does many more things that please than displease her child, often for the first four or five years of his life one aspect of her life will always cause some displeasure — the work that takes her away.

One consequence of this dislike is that the division between the Good Mommy and Bad Mommy may be sharpened to the point where attachment disorders erupt. An example is the "Mommy Here / Mommy There Syndrome." Natalie Washington, a mother I spoke to recently, described its effects on a toddler's behavior well when she likened it to the "Dr. Jekyll/Mr. Hyde Syndrome." Evenings and weekends her two-year-old, Althea, was sweet, loving, and reasonable; in the mornings she would suddenly and without apparent cause become angry, abusive, and unreasoning. During the discussion we had when Natalie came to the center for a consultation, I explained to her that

Althea's behavior was not atypical. Sometimes children in working families do divide their responses to a mother because they divide their attachment loyalties. They attach very securely to the Mommy Here figure because she is the Good Mommy who comes home at night and spends weekends with them. But like Althea, they rebel against and refuse to attach to the Mommy There, because she is the Bad Mommy who leaves each morning.

"Does that mean I am going to have to stop working?" Natalie asked in a suddenly low voice.

I replied, "No, you can help Althea heal the painful division she has created simply by emphasizing the constancy of the Good Mommy." This is the sensitive, responsive figure who has the ability to make Althea wonder, "How did you know that would please me?" I explained to Natalie that this understanding Good Mommy exerts an almost gravitational pull on a young child. If she is the figure Althea encounters in most situations, then the "Mommy Here / Mommy There Syndrome" will vanish of its own accord because Althea will be able to see: "There are things Mommy does that displease me — like leaving in the morning — but on the whole, she is a good and loving person."

The process that brings a toddler to this understanding, moreover, also will enhance his ability to get along with his playmates at the center or in nursery school. You won't, for instance, hear the child who has mastered positive object constancy utter such familiar toddler complaints as "Jimmy won't share his Big Wheel, I don't like Jimmy anymore." This is not because he won't be appropriately upset by Jimmy's lack of generosity; he'll just be able to understand that Jimmy's selfishness has not suddenly made him into another person. He will realize that Jimmy remains Jimmy however he behaves, and since Jimmy is ordinarily likeable and good about sharing his toys, he will say to himself, "Well, Jimmy was wrong this time, but I usually like him so I will give him another chance."

Here are strategies that will help you promote object constancy in your child.

BUILDING BLOCKS OF OBJECT CONSTANCY

First Form (Realization of Your Permanence)

Regularity

By the fourth or fifth month, a mother is easily recognizable by sight, sound, even smell, and her actions. But in a baby's mind these parts of her are like parts of a disassembled jigsaw puzzle. He knows there is a mommy who looks and smells and feels a certain way, but he doesn't yet know that these are simply three different aspects of the same person, someone who is the same smiling or frowning, wearing a blue or a brown dress, leaning over his crib in the morning or over her desk at work in the afternoon. Regularity in mood, in behavior, in routine, and in habits facilitates the development of object constancy because it highlights the similarities between various "you's" and makes it easier for the baby to put them together. Here are three contributions to regularity.

Regularity in Mood.   This doesn't mean flattening out your emotions, but confining your moods to moderate ranges, which creates a consistency of personal tone that makes it easier for your baby to link up the you who picks him up at the day-care center with the you who patiently soothes him back to sleep at three o'clock in the morning. Regularity in mood transforms your behavior into an easily identifiable identity card that tells the infant, "Here is Mommy, no matter what the color of her dress or the expression on her face."

Regularity in Habits.   Since habits are one of the most palpable expressions of personality, they can highlight maternal constancy in ways even a very young infant can understand. Drinking coffee in the same place each morning, for example, gives a three- or four-month-old a way of connecting Mommy yesterday with Mommy today. Seeing his mother in her usual spot and in a characteristic pose, the infant thinks, "Oh yes, Mommy." Established and well-defined morning and evening rituals send the same message. Knowing that Mommy always takes off her coat in the hall or sings a particular song as she walks through the door transforms these events into cues that make the baby think, "I know this is Mommy because these are the things she always does."

Regularity in Routine.   With older infants, household chores also can be employed to highlight maternal constancy. An example is how setting the table will help to reinforce the connection between Mommy in the morning and Mommy in the evening in the mind of an eight-month-old. By this age, a child's recall capacity is powerful enough to encompass an entire day's events. In the evening seeing mother place the silverware next to the plates she laid out this morning becomes its own subtle reminder of her sameness and continuity from one point in the day to the next.

Second Form (Positive Object Constancy)

One-, two-, and three-year-olds think not in grays but in stark blacks and whites. This is why they divide mother into such polar opposites, and also why the integration of these opposites is a complex and long process. When maternal acts that make the child feel understood outweigh those that make him feel misunderstood, the importance he attaches to these misunderstandings decreases and positive objective constancy occurs.

Translated into day-to-day behavior, this means that just as a child who on the whole feels understood can accommodate himself to mother's lack of step with his need to visit the toy store each day or eat jelly doughnuts for breakfast each morning, with maternal understanding he also can accommodate himself to the fact that mother can't grant his wish for her to be home every day. These are some important ways you can help make your child feel uniquely understood:

Display a knowledge of your child's world. Do you know who is Bert and who is Ernie? Did you know that Oscar the Grouch lives in a garbage can? Given all the things a working mother has to do, it may sound unreasonable to ask her also to sharpen her knowledge of the characters on "Sesame Street" or to notice when her two-year-old daughter begins transferring her affections from Raggedy Ann to Rainbow Brite. But a young child does expect a mother to know such things. Oscar, Bert and Ernie, and Rainbow Brite are very real to two- and three-year-olds. They think about these characters, follow their antics on television, and incorporate them into their fantasies. Asking at dinner "Did Oscar have anchovy ice cream today?" is a way of telling a two-year-old, "Mommy understands how important Oscar is to you." Even more important, it also is a subtle way of telling him, "Mommy understands you so well she is able to understand even the smallest details of your life." And it is through such displays of maternal sensitivity that a child comes to think, "On the whole, Mommy is a very Good Mommy."

Show your child you know how to read him. From a two-year-old's point of view, the Good Mommy is the Mommy who, even when he begins talking in midsentence, is able to tell what is on his mind. We call this capacity *reading.* Because of the eight- to ten-hour separations work imposes, tracking a child closely enough to read and join his moods is difficult, particularly since many of the clues he uses to signal those moods are obscure or cryptic. Even more than knowing who Bert and Ernie are, the toddler expects the Good Mommy to know what he really means when he asks her if he can help her put away Daddy's shirts or when he complains that the caregiver "hit" him today.

Show the child you know how to lift him out of his distress. Pulling a child out of his tears or upsets is like reaching into his mind and putting your hand over the Bad Mommy figure that sits in one corner of it. As his tears dry and his upsets subside, what he sees shining before him is the Good Mommy who can do what no one else in his life can do: turn his sadness into happiness. Irene is especially effective at this kind of soothing. An example is the night a very tired Alan proceeded in the space of ten minutes to spit out a half-eaten cookie onto the rug, knock a stack of magazines over, and — worst of all — turn on the stove, which he had been warned repeatedly never to touch. Ordinarily, Irene would have sent him to his room with a stern warning "to get yourself under control, Alan," but tonight, realizing he was too tired to soothe himself, she took him into her room instead.

Alan's careening around the house is typical of the out-of-focus energy very tired toddlers display. The first thing Irene did was to help him discharge the rest of his energy by encouraging him to jump up and down on her bed. As Alan began visibly wearying, Irene started singing and clapping her hands together—loudly at first, then more and more quietly. Slowly, this produced the desired effect. Alan's jumping gave way to singing, then to singing at the far end of the bed, to moving into Irene's lap, then to singing in her lap, to falling asleep in that lap.

Don't ignore the child's complaints about work. Just as you have a legitimate right to your work, your boy or girl has a legitimate right to his or her feelings about that work. There is no way of getting around the fact that, in the early years, daily maternal departures do sometimes distress a youngster. Acknowledging that distress won't make it go away, but it will lessen the child's disappointment because it says to him in a way he can grasp, "Mother understands and respects my feelings."

As Dr. Ainsworth noted in her definition, even when she has to say "no," "the sensitive mother is always tactful in acknowledging her child's communications. If your boy or girl complains about your work, tell him or her, 'I understand how you feel. I know my work is difficult for you sometimes. But there are also things mommy has to do for herself and work is one of them. I know you love me too much to want me to be unhappy.'"

It is also a good idea in these conversations to point out the benefits your work brings. There is nothing manipulative in reminding a three- or four-year-old that the toys he likes so much were bought with money you helped to earn.

What you never should do is dismiss or try to cut off complaints about work by changing the subject. Emotionally, such tactics are the equivalent of turning your back. They pull you away from the child and leave him wondering, "Does anyone care how I feel?"

This is a question Alan has never had occasion to ask himself— not because the active guidance Irene has used to help prepare him for his work-shaped lifestyle represents a form of fail-proof parenting for a working mother (there is no such thing), but because its techniques and strategies radiate so palpably her concern and love, Alan can't help but think, "Mommy cares about me very much."

7

Discipline Without the "No"
Setting Limits in a New Developmental Age

ONE OF THE FIRST THINGS new mothers notice when they return to work is how other mothers in their office, factory, or store talk about discipline. This reflects something we have observed at the center over the years. Working women with young children have developed their own special code for discussing discipline. The most remarkable feature of the code is the way it allows initiates to discuss all the facets of this complex issue in terms of just three words: *overcompensation* (as in, "I know I'm overcompensating for coming home late, but I don't think it will hurt if just this once, I let Alex . . ."); *overreaction* (as in, "I know I overreacted when Jenny began bouncing on the bed but . . ."); and *guilt* (as in, "I know I should have said no to Ryan, but I felt so guilty about . . .").

While the vocabulary's limitations say a great deal about the way working mothers feel about discipline, most of these thoughts can be compressed into two feelings — dissatisfaction and uncertainty. The dissatisfaction arises from the widespread — and correct — perception that traditional disciplining techniques are inappropriate in the new developmental world that work has created, the uncertainty from doubt about how to respond sensitively to the changes work has produced in the rules of discipline.

The first, and most mentioned, of these changes involves time; it has become too precious to squander in locking horns with a two-, three-, or four-year-old. But how does a working mother set limits without actually saying "no"? The second arises from the gaps work can create in a woman's knowledge of her child. How can she avoid the pitfalls — particularly the pitfalls of unfairly criticizing — that these gaps create? The third change stems from the multiple sources of discipline her child encounters. With three or four limit setters in his life, how can she ensure that he doesn't become confused or upset? The fourth change involves a need for flexibility. How can a working mother ease up on the rules on Saturdays and Sundays without undermining her authority the rest of the week?

REAP's answer to these questions takes the form of four strategies designed to reflect the new limit-setting imperatives maternal employment has created. They are *channeling, play acting, rolling through,* and *identification.* To illustrate how each works, in this chapter we have applied them to the most common disciplinary problems working mothers face.

CHANNELING

The strategy of channeling recognizes that while many of the feelings work produces in a young child may generate misbehavior, often the feelings themselves are legitimate ones. Behind the two- or three-year-old's refusal to go to bed, get dressed, or eat lie real needs, concerns, doubts, and fears that the child would express in nonoppositional and nondisruptive ways if he knew how. The goal of channeling is to help you show him how. Here are some cases in point.

Power Struggles

The reason for the often higher incidence of such struggles in working families is that maternal employment tends to accentuate the sense of powerlessness that is a common (and normal) part of the first years of life. To a very young child, the rest of the world not only looks bigger, stronger, and more competent but also seems to possess all the power he lacks. Work intensifies this perception because it becomes one more aspect of the environment the child finds himself powerless to control.

The happy, well-adjusted children we see every day at the center are evidence that youngsters do adjust to this state, and with time and growing maturity, come to feel an increasing sense of control over their environments. Nonetheless, it is important to realize that you live in an atmosphere that encourages the type of assertiveness that often leads to power struggles.

A case in point is the twenty-month-old who resists the gift his mother brought back from a business trip. Turning it away is his way of asserting that "I also have some power. If you don't have to come home at night, I don't have to play with the toy you bought me."

The most common outcome of this situation is a direct confrontation. The toy is urged on the child and just as continually rejected, and so an uneasy and unhappy truce descends on the family. A better way to resolve such struggles is to wait and channel. If the child at first spurns the gift, don't resist. He is not rejecting you, he is simply satisfying his need to assert himself. Respect it by putting the toy aside and going on to something else. In other words, for now, *let the child win.* Later in the evening when he is in a more receptive mood, you can channel the gift back into the play. A good way to help him to become more receptive is through the use of a related activity. Children are very quick to associate; if the toy they are playing with reminds them of the toy you have brought, often they will ask you to reintroduce it.

This technique worked well for one of our program mothers when the suit of armor, in the form of a plastic breastplate, shield, and sword she had brought back from a business trip to Nashville, was spurned by her three-year-old, Joseph. Instead of making an issue of the rejection, Blanche Bacarach, the mother, decided to enlist the aid of He-Man, Skeletor, and Hordak. These Masters of the Universe characters were among Joseph's most prized possessions, and introducing them into the play sparked the association Blanche suspected it would. Seeing his heroes dressed in their battle armor, Joseph looked up and said, "Mommy, where's my new sword and shield?"

Another common kind of power struggle channeling helps resolve by allowing both parties to win is getting dressed to go out on Saturday morning. Naturally you are in a hurry; this in the one free morning you have for grocery shopping, for picking up cleaning, for doing all the other errands you are too busy to do on the other days of the week. Just as understandably, your two-, three-, or four-year-old isn't in any hurry at all to get going. Having been rushed through the last five mornings, he would like to relax on this one. Besides, there are all those cartoons to watch. The upshot is a meeting of the irresistible force and the immovable object. No sooner have you wrestled him into his shirt than he has slipped out of his shoes.

Channeling in this instance involves the establishment of a looked-forward-to routine that dovetails with your chores. This could be having breakfast at McDonald's, picking up repair materials at the hardware store, visiting the local video store to pick up a new cartoon feature, or stopping at a friend's house. It should never be a weekly visit to a toy store, however, since the child is likely to misconstrue this as a reward for letting you work.

You are the best judge of what is most appropriate for your child; the only requirement is that the activity be a regular part of every Saturday morning. If your child starts resisting when you approach with clothes in hand, you can channel his attention from what he doesn't want to do (get dressed to go out shopping) to what he does want to do (get dressed to see what is happening at the playground).

Sleeping in Your Bed

Unanimity of opinion is fairly rare among child development experts, but on this issue there is agreement. A child should not be allowed to sleep in his parents' bed. It serves neither his interest, since it makes the separation process that much more difficult, nor his parents', whose need and right to intimacy is imperiled. There is also general agreement about why this problem is more com-

mon among working families. The boy or girl wants as much of
mother's presence as possible, and the mother, knowing this and
feeling guilty about it, tends to be more lenient about invasions of
her bedroom than she should be.

Channeling can be used in this instance not to satisfy an underlying need but to change your opposition to such invasions from a
negative to a nonnegative form. The best way of doing this is
through analogy. Stories with themes that center around viola-
tions of space, such as "Goldilocks and the Three Bears," tell a
toddler in a way he can understand how a person feels when her
rights to space and privacy are violated. The child's own well-de-
veloped sense of where things belong also can provide a basis for
your analogy. Few things upset children more than finding their
toys put away in the wrong place. Gently point out the next time
this happens that *you* feel the same way, on waking to find someone you know in the wrong place — your bed.

One word of warning: don't expect this technique to work every
time. Some nights you will have to say "no" directly, then get up
and physically put the child back in his bed. No matter how tired
you are, resist the temptation to give in just this once. You will
only make the problem that much harder to deal with the next
time. Besides, the child has to start learning sometime that certain
issues in life are nonnegotiable. And three o'clock in the morning
is as good a time as any to start teaching him.

Following You Around

"Disciplinary problem" is too harsh a term to apply to this common practice. Indeed, part of a woman is deeply flattered by the
little shadow she acquires the moment she steps through the door
in the evening. Such fidelity is a testimony to how much she has
been missed. At the same time, there is a part of her that would like
just a few minutes alone in the bathroom or in the bedroom to
change. One way channeling can be used to create this breathing
space is via parallel play.

Say, for example, you want to take a restorative bath. In order to
channel your child's need to be near you, place him in front of the

bathroom door with a favorite toy or book. This configuration will satisfy his need for closeness and also allow the two of you to exchange brief snatches of conversation. At the same time, because the toy will engage him, it also gives you the interval of calm and quiet you need to renew your energies for the night ahead.

PLAY ACTING

Play acting is a technique fathers often use, partly because its loose, slightly playful approach to discipline feels particularly comfortable to a man. But I think an even more important reason for its popularity among men is that their longer experience as working parents has taught them that play acting, in the form of dramatizing a concern in a half-serious, half-humorous manner, is ideal for disciplining in situations where time and especially lack of knowledge may be a problem. For example:

Forbidden Activities

Should you or shouldn't you criticize when one day your child suddenly jumps from the bureau onto your bed, or appears in the dining room carrying a plateful of food, or engages in some other activity that obviously gives him pride but that you have expressly forbidden?

Given the rapid pace of development in the first years of life, it is almost inevitable that at certain points a youngster's real abilities are going to outstrip his mother's or his father's knowledge of them. Because it takes a parent away for a large part of the day, work tends to increase these knowledge gaps and thus the risk of making the kind of unfair criticisms that leave a youngster wondering, "Why doesn't Mom know I have been doing this since last week?"

Play acting's value in such situations is that it allows a parent to state her concerns, but in a manner that also leaves some latitude for what she doesn't know. Not long ago, I found myself in just such a situation. I wanted to express my concern to the four-year-old I had brought to a playground near the center and who was now scurrying upward toward the top of a jungle gym. At the same time, I didn't want to criticize him for a climbing prowess he not only was very proud of but obviously wanted to impress me with. So, as he neared the top, I began making a sirenlike sound. Taken aback by the strange noise, my young companion stopped and said, "What's that, Dr, Sanger?"

"Oh, just the ambulance I am keeping around in case you fall and hurt yourself," I replied. Being very quick, four-year-olds have no trouble reading between the lines. The child knew I was telling him in a nice way that I didn't know if he could do safely what he was doing. He reassured me that the jungle gym he climbed at his park was even higher that this one, and so I let him finish scurrying to the top.

Since some mothers may feel uncomfortable about transform- ing themselves into an ambulance — especially in a public place — another way of drawing attention to your concerns, in a non- judgmental way, is through the use of questions: "Did you learn how to do that while I was at work today?" or "Are you trying to show me something new? I've never seen you climb so high. I'm going to have to get used to how brave you are." Such statements convey maternal concern but also compliment the child and leave him room to explain why he is doing what he is doing.

Getting Children to Pay Attention

It is one thing to tell a two-and-a-half-year-old, "Never cross the street alone" or "Never put your finger into an electric outlet." It is another to make these warnings stick in a child's mind. One means of doing this is through constant repetition; another, even better way, especially for a parent who isn't there all the time to repeat them, is to dramatize her concerns in a way that make them memorable.

Even if it is never repeated again, a three-year-old is always going to remember how dangerous it is to step into the street alone or to put his hand into an electric outlet if he has been provided with a vivid illustration of what can happen when you do these things. I'm sure if you pointed to an outlet in the presence of three-and-a-half-year-old Melinda Yallow, for example, her eyes would widen with alarm and in a voice full of urgency and concern for your safety, Melinda would say, "Don't touch; that's dangerous." This is because on the day after her third birthday, still upset by an incident that had almost brought the party to a dramatic and tragic halt, Melinda's mother, Helen, resolved to make the dangers of touching an electric outlet very clear to her daughter.

During the party, Danielle, one of Melinda's day-care chums, had picked up the cord from a lamp and with a hand dripping wet with Coke had begun trying to put the cord prong into a nearby outlet. Fortunately, Angela Arito, Danielle's caregiver, saw her and removed the lamp cord from Danielle's hand and Danielle from the vicinity of the outlet before any damage was done. But the incident had left a deep impression on Helen Yallow. The next day she found herself thinking about it a great deal, and riding home on the bus she decided to do something about her concern.

After dinner Helen told Melinda, "I want to show you something, honey." Then, while a very attentive Melinda watched, Helen got down on her knees and, pointing to the electric outlet, said, "Touching this is very, very dangerous." As Helen said when she told me the story: "At this point in my demonstration, Melinda was more curious than alarmed. But when she saw my whole body shake and heard me yell, 'Ouch!' as my finger touched the outlet, she became very upset. 'Mommy, Mommy!' she cried. I told Melinda that's why touching an electric outlet is dangerous; an outlet can give you something called a 'shock' and shocks not only hurt, they make you shake all over."

Helen knew her demonstration had been effective when, a few nights later, a very excited Melinda rushed up to her in the hall as she was taking off her coat and told her how in the new Donald Duck video she had gotten that day, Donald had also hurt himself when he put his hand in an outlet. "He shook just like you," Melinda said with the pleased voice of a scientist who has just seen a particularly intriguing hypothesis confirmed. "I'm never going to touch an electric outlet."

One word of advice: if you use play acting to dramatize the dangers of stepping into the street alone or of putting your hand too near an outlet or hot match, make the point in a way that engages as many of the child's senses as possible. Studies show that a child learns much quicker if a subject is presented in a way that involves not just his eyes and ears, or his touch and taste, but all of his sensory modes.

ROLLING THROUGH

Despite your best efforts, inevitably there will be times when gentler methods of discipline won't work. The child refuses to get out of bed, or won't get dressed, or begins running wildly through the house. And there doesn't seem to be any alternative left but physical force. Rolling through provides you (and the caregiver, since it also is appropriate for her use) with that alternative.

It is a three-step procedure designed gently but pointedly to escalate the stakes for an unruly child. The first step is called *presenting positive results*. It is meant to connect him with a thought he is well aware of but isn't focusing on at the moment: how happy the two of you usually are when you are together. Statements such as "We were having such a good time before you started misbehaving" or "How can we have any fun when you throw clothes around?" present his indiscipline as a breach of that happiness you normally share, and hold out the promise of its immediate restoration as soon as he starts to behave.

Consequences is the name of the second step. It is meant to remind the child who can't be enticed by "positive results" that his throwing, hitting, or resistance is going to result in disappointment ("no park this weekend if you keep this up") and lost opportunity ("I was going to invite Luke over for a play date, but I don't think I will now") for him, and sadness for you. Tell him how much it distresses you to see such a wonderful child behaving so badly.

If the child's unruliness continues, escalate to the third step, which might be called *we are both going to regret this*. Any kind of physical force, no matter how gentle and well meant, humiliates a child; he should be reminded of that and also of your great reluctance to be a party to such humiliation. Statements such as, "If you act like a baby you are going to force me to treat you like one" or "You are not going to like it if I have to physically remove you from that bed" tell him he has arrived at the danger zone. Unless his unruliness stops, you will have no alternative but to apply the force that will make him feel belittled and you disappointed.

Usually the prospect of meeting such a fate will bring even the most resistant child around. Tamar Rowe is a case in point. Like most four-year-olds, Tamar has mornings when she doesn't want to get dressed. This is a story of one of those mornings. Deborah, her mother, sensed trouble immediately. Tamar, being a chatterer, usually wakes up in midsentence, but not this morning. Outside of a groggy hello, she didn't say a word to her mother or her father, or her brother, or the family cat, for nearly ten minutes. As Deborah was getting Tamar out of her pajamas, Tamar suddenly went limp, and Deborah had to wrestle her out of them. The real trouble, however, didn't start until Deborah took Tamar's new red shirt from her clothes closet. Seeing it in her mother's hand, Tamar suddenly began rolling wildly in her bed.

First Deborah tried channeling. She described all the things Tamar was going to do today at nursery school. But seeing that her daughter was too upset to be distracted, Deborah decided a more dramatic measure — rolling through — was necessary. Remembering what she had learned at the center about the importance of careful escalation, Deborah began by presenting the little girl with a "positive result." She reminded Tamar of all the fun the two of them usually have in the morning, and told her, "If you stop this behavior, we can start having fun again." Failing to get any reaction, Deborah escalated to step two, "Consequences." "You know, Tamar," she said, "you are going to be very unhappy if we don't play dolls tonight; and we are not going to if you don't stop rolling around like a wild person."

Although this warning produced an appreciable reduction in Tamar's rolling, it didn't stop completely, so Deborah escalated to step three. "If you don't stop this," she said, "I'm going to have to get your father in here to hold you down so that I can dress you. I am not going to like that, he is not going to like that, and I don't

think you are going to like it either, young lady." Deborah was
right, Tamar wouldn't like it, and so the rolling stopped and the
red shirt went on.

Violent force in the form of hitting, slapping, or spanking
should *never* be used on a child. If all else fails, firmly roll the child
through his resistance by picking him up in your arms and carrying
him to his next step on the morning schedule, or by placing your
hands on his shoulders and leading him there. While rolling
through, as I've described it, will work in most situations, the
escalation process takes time. Sometimes when the child's behavior is an immediate physical danger to himself or to others, you
won't have that time. In those cases you should apply an abbre-
viated form of rolling through. Here are two examples.

Not Getting Out of the Bath

Most often, the two- or three-year-old who doesn't want to get out
of a bathtub will resist by turning your requests to "get going"
into a game. He will giggle and squiggle and otherwise engage in
tactics that help prolong what he is doing. A safe way to move to
the next stage is to say, "We'll play a bit more when you're in bed,"
while two hands reach into the tub, grab the toddler under the
arms, and firmly but gently whisk him out of it and onto the bath
mat.

Throwing Sand

Instead of shouting when you see your child toss a fistful of sand at
a playmate, give your voice and body a serious tone. Then if it is
necessary, climb into the sandbox and gently but unequivocally
seize his throwing hand. As you unclench his fist, releasing the
sand, remind him that you have come to the park today to play,
not to roughhouse. Then, to underline the point, sit down and
join the youngster in sand play. This will tell him that he is being
given one last chance, and it allows you to demonstrate what
civilized play is.

If this fails and the sand throwing resumes, remind the child
again that he needs to moderate his behavior, that he needs to

decide if he wishes to enjoy the sandbox. If he does not adapt, it may be necessary for you to announce that it is time to go home. If the child resists, pick him up and carry him out of the sandbox. This will leave him with a clear memory of your resolve, one that in the future will make him hesitate, not out of fear but simply because he now knows when you say something you mean it.

IDENTIFICATION

The parent who demonstrates through example what constitutes acceptable behavior produces two effects. Most immediately, seeing what she does or does not do in a specific situation gives her child a model of how to behave in similar situations; and in the long run, it facilitates the growth of an internal code of discipline. In time, through watching mother, the child comes to learn where the limits of acceptable behavior lie. The sooner this lesson is learned, the sooner he can be trusted to tell right from wrong on his own.

But isn't limit setting through identification something parents do naturally? In most cases, the answer is yes. The technique could be used more effectively, however, if a woman targeted specific situations, particularly work-related situations, that often lead to disciplinary infractions, and through example showed her girl or boy how to behave appropriately in them. Again, some cases in point:

Resistance to Day Care

One of the most valuable aspects of identification is that it can have an important influence on how a child behaves on those mornings when he would rather lie in bed or in front of the television than go to the center. Although tiredness and hunger contribute to the tears and baleful looks that make these mornings an ordeal for everyone, often the real source of the youngster's distress is that he is being confronted with a problem still beyond his grasp: the need to do something he doesn't want to do. And he requires some guidance on how to handle it.

A good (meaning both subtle and effective) way of providing it is by demonstrating how you behave in similar circumstances. Announcing a half dozen or so mornings a month, whether you happen to feel that way or not, "Gee, I'm so tired I'd love to stay in bed today, but I can't because I also want to go to work," shows a child how conflicting impulses can be confronted in a way that does not lead to emotional disintegration. You do what mother does; put aside your emotions and get on with the task.

Don't expect miracles from the technique. The child will still protest, but the incidence of the protests will be less. And now that the child has a model of how to behave, the protests themselves will no longer be of the kind that leave you and him limp with emotional exhaustion by the time the two of you arrive at the center's door.

Opposition to Being Corrected

This can be a problem for any parent, and it can become particularly pointed at half past eight in the morning when the three-year-old who has just buttoned his jacket the wrong way throws a major temper tantrum because you proceed to rebutton it the right way. No one, least of all a sensitive three-year-old, likes to be corrected. He will be much more amenable to such corrections if he has been allowed to witness you occasionally (and deliberately) put a shoe on the wrong foot or a jacket on inside out, and has seen how lightly and humorously you handle such errors. The parent who says, "Oh look, how silly of me. I've just put my jacket on inside out; could you help me fix it?" is teaching by example that mistakes are a normal, expected part of everyday life. And just as important, she is demonstrating that the best way to deal with errors is to do what she does: admit the error and ask for help in correcting it.

Marie Daimon, one of our REAP mothers, was especially good at this. She would turn her mistakes into little playlets. Casting herself in the role of "The Duchess of Dopedom," Marie would delight her four-year-old, Angela, by mistaking a lamp shade for a hat, a cereal box for her briefcase, and the salt for the sugar. The Duchess didn't know what she was doing, but Marie did. She was using the playlets to teach Angela that not only Duchesses can make mistakes without falling apart, but also mothers and even little girls.

Reluctance to Finish Tasks

This isn't of great consequence at age two or three, but at seven, eight, or nine it becomes very important. By then a working mother should find her own burden lightening measurably, but whether it does depends on the degree to which she can trust her child to complete tasks on his own. To ensure that four or five years hence you won't find yourself devoting nights to enforcing homework rules and days to wondering whether your nine-year-old has picked up his room, use modeling at age two or three to make a point about the importance you assign to finishing things. (Structuring — or the division of an activity into morning and evening segments — is the one exception to this rule. But when you structure, make clear to the child that the interruption is intended to have a specific goal: to give you and him something to look forward to during the day.) The best vehicle for doing this is a joint project such as cooking, coloring, or building, which allows a child to observe firsthand how conscientious mother is about completing what she starts.

Given the low boredom threshold of two- and three-year-olds, you can be sure that they will begin tiring of a task before you do. To help your child to remain focused when you sense that that threshold is being reached, add a degree of play acting to your modeling. Hearing mother say in an exaggerated and playful way, "Oh boy, do I wish we were finished. Why didn't you tell me this was going to take so long?" not only makes a project more interesting for a child by adding a bit of color and humor, it permits him to concentrate a bit longer.

MISCELLANEOUS DISCIPLINE PROBLEMS

The problems in this category share two characteristics. None lends itself to any single disciplining technique or approach, and each is unusually common.

Misbehavior Related to
Prolonged Maternal Absences

Most often these absences involve overnight business trips, but a succession of late nights or weekends at the office also can lead to disciplinary problems. Clinging, in all its various forms, and testing — in the form of demanding that mother repeat everything at least three times — are among the most common of these problems. Their appearance usually is an indication that a prolonged absence has prompted a child to ask himself, "Why isn't Mommy home more?" or, more troubling still, "Does she know how upset I become when she isn't here?"

Acknowledging these questions openly is important. The anxieties behind them are real, and letting the child know you understand that is its own source of reassurance. Statements such as "I realize it makes you unhappy and I feel bad about that" tell the older child in a way he can grasp that you are concerned about his unhappiness over your absences, but they do so without undercutting your right to work. For the younger child, you may want to use a pair of puppets to act out this scene.

What should *never* be done is to make light of anxieties aroused by a business trip or a late night at the office. Pointing out that "all the other mothers in the office make business trips, too," or saying, "You're a big boy now. You won't mind if Mommy is away for a few days," may be well intentioned. But it leaves the toddler's concerns buried under a pile of platitudes, making him wonder all the more, "Does anyone care how I feel?"

Sensitivity also should be displayed toward the disciplinary infractions that arise from the anxieties your trips produce. Often, your being away two or three nights running will make your child want to satisfy himself about his importance to you. One common way children do this is by requesting that the usual bedtime story be read three, four, or five times. The best way to handle this situation is to let the child win, at least initially. A second, third, or fourth rendering of a story may be tedious, but keeping in mind that what the youngster is hearing isn't so much the words you are reading as how much you love him will help you get through it.

At the fourth repetition — if it gets to that point — the line should be drawn. If more is requested, tell the child that as much as you would like to stay up and read to him all night, it is now time for bed. You will read the story to him again in the morning if he would like that.

Multiple Sources of Discipline

The reappearance of a previously overcome misbehavior is the most common indication that exposure to different and conflicting discipline philosophies is causing confusion. These regressions occur more frequently among youngsters in day care or nursery school because, on the whole, day-care workers and teachers are less likely than caregivers to attune themselves to a parent's thinking about discipline. Reverting to an old behavior is how a confused two- or three-year-old determines whose rules of discipline apply to his behavior.

From past experience the child knows how mother responds when he throws sand, and he may well use it as a test. How will she react to a very unruly Saturday morning in the sandbox — like the day-care worker or teacher or like her old self? The most appropriate way to deal with such regressions is through a conference. A busy day-care worker or teacher can't be expected to adopt any one parent's approach to discipline in toto, but a better understanding of it will help her shape her own responses in ways that will make them seem less discrepant to the child.

Unruliness at Day Care or Nursery School

If unruliness at day care or nursery school represents a manifestation of an already well-established home pattern, the root of the unruliness probably lies in a general personality disorder that is best dealt with in consultation with a child psychologist or psychiatrist. But if the problem is school- or center-specific — if outside of these environments the child is not boisterous or otherwise difficult to control — the unruliness usually signifies that the child is having difficulty adapting to the more structured day-care or nursery school environment.

One way to handle this unruliness is by asking the teacher or day-care worker to pace the child more slowly. Sharp transitions, in particular, often are troublesome to young children. See if he can be allowed to linger a bit longer over activities while he accustoms himself to the center's or classroom's more regimented atmosphere. Another way to facilitate adjustment is to have the youngster "twinned" with a child who already has the routines down. This is practical only for three- or four-year-olds, but it is especially effective because the twin becomes both an example and an inspiration whom the child actively seeks to emulate.

Having examined the two kinds of sensitivity — situational and developmental — REAP is designed to foster, we are now going to visit one of our discussion groups and see how the women in it used what they had learned about these two aspects of sensitivity to develop a more attuned maternal style.

8

The Optimist, the Worrier, the Achiever
Three Maternal Styles

THERE ARE PEOPLE you can set your watch by, and although Leah Rank isn't among them, in her own inimitable way she is a model of predictability. Coming through the foyer on Saturday mornings, when Leah's REAP discussion group meets at the center, Joan Hughes, another of the group's members, says she can always tell which coat on the rack is Leah's. It is the one hanging precariously by an armhole rather than by the loop at the back of the collar. And if it happens to be raining that morning, Barbara Molloy, also in the group, says she can tell which umbrella belongs to Leah. It is the one resting against the wall instead of in the cistern we use as an umbrella holder. And I know that if anyone is going to arrive at the absolute last moment, bursting with explanations about unset clocks, forgotten purses, and taxi drivers who lost their way, it will be Leah.

One of my graduate students, an observant young woman named Allison Blake who occasionally attends the group's meetings, calls Leah an *optimist*. And there is a good deal of truth in that remark. Leah does have an unshakable conviction that, in the end, things will turn out for the best. In her case, wishing seems to make it so, since things usually do for Leah. Precariously as it may be perched, her coat never does quite fall off the rack or her umbrella to the ground; and narrow as the margins are, she always does get to group just as I am about to give the opening lecture.

Leah's style with Jeffrey, her nineteen-month-old, shines with this same sunny optimism. If Leah has a worry at all about her style, it is that she doesn't worry enough about it and about the issues that seem to preoccupy Joan and Barbara, such as bed and feeding times and the knowledge gaps work sometimes creates. As a result, Jeffrey's habits have become as idiosyncratic as his mother's. "My little bohemian," Leah calls him, and this bohemianism makes Jeffrey a standout. In any given group of toddlers, you would not have trouble identifying Jeffrey. He would be the child whose play was most unregulated and mood changes most unpredictable. But if you spent some time analyzing that play, you would also realize how unusually imaginative and rich it was. And if you spent any time with Jeffrey, you would also notice something else — what a radiantly happy child he is.

Stylistically, Joan and Barbara, the two other women in Leah's group, couldn't be more different. Joan is the group's *worrier*. Despite all the demands of her work as a security analyst, she wants — and needs — to know everything about and maintain strict control over her twins' care. Barbara is the group's *achiever*. She comes closest to the conventional image of the supermom. Although I doubt that Leah would even notice it, Barbara would be deeply upset if a button were missing from the jacket of her twenty-two-month-old, Lisa, and the thought of going to bed with a sink full of unwashed dishes would put her in a state of acute distress.

For all their differences, however, Leah, Barbara, and Joan do share one link with each other and with you. The story of this chapter is the story of how these three women were helped to answer the two questions that work poses for every mother: "How do I remain sensitive to my child's needs?" and "How do I do that and still remain sensitive to my own needs?" What makes the way these very individual women were helped to answer the questions relevant to you is that each is also a representative type. Our experience has shown that most working mothers are optimists like Leah, achievers like Barbara, or worriers like Joan.

The most perfect answers in the world wouldn't have been of use to Leah if they had ignored her sunny optimism and predictable unpredictability, or to Barbara if they hadn't been shaped to her energy and drive. And they won't be of help to you unless they take into account who you are. This is why the most important lesson to be learned from Barbara's, Joan's, and Leah's stories is how to meet the two challenges work poses to maternal sensitivity and still be true to the optimist, achiever, or worrier in you.

LEAH RANK: THE OPTIMIST

People often tell Leah that she looks like Bette Midler, and there is a resemblance if you make allowances for the fact that Leah is a little heavier and much taller, and dresses with the no-nonsense practicality of a social worker rather than the flamboyance of a movie star. Leah has the same halo of frizzy red curls, the same expressive features, and the same twinkle in her eye. But on her they create a different impression. Instead of "saucy" or "mischievous," the words Leah most often brings to mind are "open" and "trusting." These qualities are also among her greatest strengths as a working mother, although it took the other women in the Saturday group a while to recognize that.

This is one of the odd things about optimists; often their best assets are underrated by others. Barbara, for example, was initially puzzled by Leah's willingness to confer so much authority on Darlene, Jeffrey's caregiver. "Aren't you annoyed that Darlene is always giving you advice?" she asked one Saturday.

"You're going to end up undermining your own authority with Jeffrey," Joan added, not bothering to disguise the reproach in her voice.

In time, however, both women came to realize that they had misjudged. Neither would want an egalitarian relationship with her caregiver, but they did come to see that for Leah, who didn't share their concern about detail or their worry about structure, it was important to have another source of independent decision making and authority available. They also came to realize that what allowed Darlene to fulfill this role so effectively was not only her own skill but that openness of Leah's they had initially found so puzzling.

Barbara acknowledged this one day in the form of what I thought a very gracious compliment. "One of the things I've learned to appreciate about Leah," she said, "is her ability to make use of advice. This is a sensitive point for me. I tend to get very defensive when someone else makes a suggestion about Lisa, and sometimes I think that we both lose out because of it. Leah doesn't get defensive; she listens, and if she finds the advice valuable she uses it."

Another strength Leah shares with many optimists is the ability to take one day at a time. Leah doesn't worry until something happens, and when it does she assumes that somehow the love she and Jeffrey share for one another will see things right in the end.

This has been important in helping her maintain a sense of balance and perspective — qualities some working mothers have trouble with. Leah doesn't immediately project or anticipate when something goes wrong, so she doesn't tend to make a problem worse than it is. An example is the way she handles Jeffrey's departure protests. Instead of turning his tears into an occasion for a general soul searching the way that many other working mothers do, Leah takes each morning and each protest on its own terms, which helps her maintain her peace of mind. Unclouded by guilt or self-reproach, she is able to see what these feelings often obscure — that the protest isn't a product of general anguish but of tiredness, hunger, or some unusual stress that has made today's departure particularly difficult for Jeffrey.

Like other optimists, Leah also places great value on spontaneity. Instinctively, she knows that what Jeffrey likes most is open-ended, free-flowing, spontaneous play, so she never has an extensive agenda of "things to do" when she sits down with him. She lets things happen naturally, and thus their interactions often are rich in those magical moments that will make mother and child smile when they look back on them later. The optimist's lack of inhibition might surprise, even shock, other women, but children love it.

That imaginary audience of infants and toddlers I described in chapter 3, for example, would have been delighted by Leah's improvisation at Jeffrey's first birthday party. Being particularly proud of the birthday cake she had bought, Leah planned to put it out on the table fifteen minutes early so that the other adults at the party would have an opportunity to admire it. Jeffrey, however, had other ideas. Intrigued by the gooey white mountain on the table, he toddled over and, while no one was looking, climbed up on a chair and stuck his fist into it. Instead of being upset, Leah was inspired. Walking over to the table, she took Jeffrey's hand in hers, licked the frosting from one finger, and, pronouncing it delicious, invited Darlene and her mother, Sarah, to "have a bite."

"Going with the moment" is how Leah describes her reaction to Jeffrey's assault on the cake. She believes that in the long run, the richness of such moments will contribute much more to his well-being than a precise bed or bath or eating time would. For Jeffrey's first eighteen months, the force that most often dictated his schedule was, as Leah put it, "whether we had something going." This made Leah an always imaginative and engaging companion, and these qualities lay at the root of many of the remarkable traits Jeffrey displayed during our preprogram evaluation. His unusually inventive play and mature social skills (always, except when he was tired) are both, in one way or another, a reflection of how sensitively his need for natural, spontaneous play had been met.

Our evaluation, however, also suggested that Leah's emphasis on going with the moment had reduced her sensitivity to another of Jeffrey's important needs — structure. A regular schedule of bed and feeding times is more than simply a parental convenience; such structure makes it easier for a child to organize his hunger and sleep urges into a coherent daily pattern so that they occur at predictable points in the day. It also gives him a sense of what we call "what's nextness." He can anticipate the day's scenario.

Imagine how frustrated you would feel if you never knew when you were going to find yourself suddenly too overwhelmed by hunger or sleep to continue focusing on a game or other activity you were enjoying. And imagine how much greater that frustration would be if, feeling hungry or tired, you didn't know when your next feeding or sleep time was. One of the ways such frustration often manifests itself in a young child is through hair pulling. And when he was very hungry or very tired, that is what Jeffrey did.

Darlene had created a regular lunch hour and afternoon nap time, but beyond that, Jeffrey's day was chaotic. Some nights he would be in bed at seven; other nights, if they were having fun, Leah wouldn't put him into the bath until almost ten. His evening meal hour was as erratic. It could be at five-thirty in the dining room with Leah, or at seven-thirty in front of the television with his father, Albert.

Our evaluation also indicated that the hair pulling was intensified by two other factors. One was that some of Jeffrey's key cues and signals were ignored. Jeffrey's frustration tolerance was lowest, and hence his tendency to grab another child's hair highest, when he was tired. But the cues he used to signal his tiredness — yawning, flattening of his cheeks, and rubbing his eyes — often were overlooked. So the soothing that might have calmed his frustration before it got out of hand was rarely provided.

This is apparent in a videotape we made during the evaluation. For the first half, the most remarkable thing about Jeffrey is how well he plays with the two other children on the tape. Toward the middle of it, however, he begins to yawn and then a moment later rubs his eyes. Absorbed in a conversation with another mother, Leah misses these cues, and the soothing that might have prevented the tumult that follows wasn't offered. Frustrated because the Big Bird doll he has been trying to stand up keeps falling down, a (by now) very tired Jeffrey suddenly turns and pulls the hair of one of the other children.

Our evaluation suggested that Jeffrey's communication skills were another contributing factor to the hair pulling. You don't have to grab to express frustration, annoyance, or tiredness if you have learned how to express these states through words, looks, or gestures. But like many working mothers, especially those with boys, Leah had automatically adopted a more physical play style with Jeffrey. This added to her excitement as a pal and playmate, but it deprived Jeffrey of a teacher and role model who could show him how to communicate complex feelings through a look, a tilt of the head, or some other gesture that didn't require physical contact.

In chart form, our assessment of Leah's optimistic style and its effects on Jeffrey would look something like this:

Characteristics of Optimist's Style

- Openness toward child and toward advice from others
- Ability to take one day at a time
- Spontaneity in play
- Unpredictability

Advantages

Allows a Child to Follow His Own Developmental Course. Few things are more harmful than trying to alter a child's course to fit a parent's preconceived notion of who that child should be. Leah's openness prevented her from falling into this common trap. She exulted in the fact that Jeffrey was always and uniquely Jeffrey.

Makes a Mother a More Exciting Companion. Jeffrey often over-rode his tiredness to stay up with Leah because being with her was such a delight. I can't think of a higher compliment a mother could be paid.

Promotes Sociability. Considering that a child's feelings about others are shaped by the quality of his interactive experience with his mother, it isn't hard to understand why, despite the hair pull-ing, Jeffrey took unusual enjoyment in being with others.

Fosters Independence. One other important consequence of Leah's openness is that it made Jeffrey an unusually self-sufficient child. And for a youngster who is out in the world earlier, this is an extremely valuable asset.

Potential Risks

Creates a Risk of Attachment Disruption. Jeffrey's attachment to Leah was secure, but the optimist's emphasis on spontaneity and casualness to structure can produce uncertainty in a child. The uncertainty arises from the fact that sometimes the environment seems very sensitive to his needs (particularly his need for companionship and relaxed, open-ended play); at other times it seems to ignore them (particularly his need for structure). And a child who is uncertain about how his environment will react next may become insecurely attached or regress.

Can Produce Bad Habits.   One such habit Jeffrey's chaotic environment produced was hair pulling. Another, which Leah was just beginning to encounter, was his resistance to toilet training.

Can Retard Skill Development.   One example of this was the level of Jeffrey's communication competency. Another was his resistance to toilet training. When most other areas of his life are unregulated, a child finds it hard to understand why his bowel and bladder habits must be.

Factors Needed to Make Optimist's Style Work

Here are the elements optimists need to prevent the inherent risks of their style from becoming realities.

A Competent Caregiver.   The optimistic style often puts much of the burden of decision making on the caregiver. So the caregiver needs the knowledge and experience to make decisions as wisely as Darlene does for Jeffrey.

A Flexible and Understanding Husband.   One of Leah's secret weapons is her husband, Albert. Not only has he been willing to assume an unusually large proportion of the child care and housekeeping chores, he is undemanding about such small but important things as meals. Albert will happily fix his own and Jeffrey's if Leah isn't there; and if she is, he will eat whatever is put in front of him, including a TV dinner.

Ability to Track a Child's Growth Through the Chaos.   This is the one essential element of the optimistic style Leah never mastered. In many respects, Jeffrey's behavior remained a mystery to her.

Often Leah had trouble tuning in to Jeffrey's moods and feelings.

When Leah asked how REAP would help her to acquire such knowledge, I told her we would show her:

• *How to read Jeffrey's cues and signals accurately.* Among the first things Leah learned were the often surprising cues and signals young children such as Jeffrey use to signal hunger and tiredness. For example, in addition to rubbing his eyes or growing wobbly, a tired one- or two-year-old will indicate sleepiness by clenching his fists, by dropping his head on his chest, by staring blankly into space, or by a sudden fit of coughing, sneezing, or hiccuping. Hunger, on the other hand, may be indicated by chewing on a teething ring, by crying for a bottle — even by crawling toward the high chair. Inexplicable irritability or whininess also can be a sign of hunger.

• *How to provide undistracted time.* One reason Leah had difficulty learning to read Jeffrey is that during their shared time together her attention often was not entirely focused on him. Either she would be half-watching television or half-reading a magazine, or she would be bantering with Darlene or Albert. This can be seen in the taped interaction I described earlier. Until the hair-pulling incident, Leah spends her time talking to the other mothers. This is why she misses it when, midway through the exchange, Jeffrey begins signaling his withdrawal by yawning and by irritably pushing aside one of the other children as he reaches for a block.

• *How to increase his knowledge of distal communication.* "Distal" means the ability to extract information from, and communicate thoughts and feelings to, others through the use of facial expressions, gestures, sounds, and other, nonphysical signals. Teaching Leah how to help Jeffrey to do this was less a matter of showing her a new skill than of reminding her of one she already possessed. New research shows that the reason women serve as the primary model for distal communication is that, just as children are genetically programmed to behave in certain ways, mothers are, too. One of those ways is to rely on the use of looking and listening in exchanges with their children. Sometimes, however, the pressures of trying to make every moment count or, as in Leah's case, the pressures of trying to provide a boy with a boy's kind of fun prompt a woman to forget her innate knowledge. The way to correct this is to do what we had Leah do.

Our first recommendation involved her use of physical gestures. Watching her and Jeffrey together, I had noticed that whenever Leah wanted to get his attention she would poke him gently in the tummy. It was a sweet gesture, and in a mother with a less physical style it would have been perfectly appropriate. But because Leah's style had become so physical, I suggested that instead of poking, "When you want to catch Jeffrey's eye, use an arresting facial expression, like an exaggerated smile or a mock frown." We also recommended that she reduce her reliance on physical props during playtime, again not because there is anything wrong with the Busy Boxes, balls, and blocks that are used to amuse children of Jeffrey's age, but because, in Leah's case, these props usually become a springboard for roughhousing. If Jeffrey picked up a block from a house Leah was building, she would pretend to wrestle it out of his hand, or if she saw him trying to turn a crank on his Busy Box, she would put her hand over his and begin turning the crank furiously. "For the next few months," I said, "make singing songs, word play, and reading books the focus of your shared time. Seeing you use your eyes, ears, and smiles and frowns conveys the book's or song's thoughts and will teach Jeffrey a good deal about how to communicate distally."

JOAN HUGHES: THE WORRIER

From a distance it is easy to mistake Joan for a graduate student. The Irish walking hat, the crewneck sweaters, and kilt skirts that are her trademarks give her a bright, tweedy air. But once you are near enough to notice the preoccupied look in her eyes and the deepness of the laugh lines around her mouth, that impression quickly fades. Close up, the word that best describes Joan is "overwhelmed." She looks as if she is carrying the burdens of the world on her fragile shoulders. And along with the special nature of her ambivalences and ambitions, this look defines her as a member of that perhaps most common category of working mothers — worriers.

In Joan's case, the sense of always being near the brink is partly a reflection of her unusual circumstances. She is the parent of twenty-month-old twins, Seth and Hillary. But mostly it derives from the expectations she has brought to her role as a working mother. These are a reflection of her long-cherished image of herself (as what she calls "a kind of earth mother"), her ambivalence about her work as a security analyst, and her determination that if, for economic reasons, she must keep that work then somehow she will "make it up" to the twins.

In one way or another, these attitudes are shared by most other worriers and account for the characteristic two-tiered shape of their maternal styles. Joan's is a case in point. On entering the program, she had a style that worked excellently on one level, but not at all on another.

In the months since the twins' birth, all of Joan's considerable energy and intelligence has been focused on their well-being. This attentiveness had produced an exquisite sensitivity to their thoughts and feelings. Joan was especially perceptive about the personality differences between Seth and Hillary. One morning she explained to the group — quite accurately — how those differences affected each twin's approach to language.

"Seth is a man of action," Joan said. "He wants to figure things out. Hillary is an experiencer. So in language, even though Seth knows more words, he doesn't pay much attention to their pronunciation; he just uses them as tools to get the job done. Hillary goes for quality; she only knows two words, 'daddy' and 'bubble,' but she can pronounce them almost as well as I can. Often she will repeat them over and over again just for the satisfaction of hearing their sound."

Joan's sensitivity has allowed her to enter into her children's lives in a special way. A nineteen-month-old excitedly yelling, "All, all," as he pointed out the window toward a night-darkened sky could at first glance, or second or even third, mean almost anything. But the evening Joan came upon Seth in this state, her knowledge of him allowed her very quickly to puzzle out the reason for his excitement, and even more important, to share it with him.

"He was standing halfway back in the room as he yelled," Joan said, "so I had to crouch down next to him to see what riveted him so. That's when I realized 'all' meant 'ball,' and 'ball,' the moon. As soon as I said, 'Yes, Seth that is the moon,' he stopped shouting. He was satisfied. All he wanted was for someone to acknowledge his discovery."

Joan's style works less effectively in creating a sensitivity to her own well-being. Every working mother needs to learn how to say "no" — to her work, to her friends, sometimes to her husband, and occasionally even to her children. She also needs to learn how to say "yes" to herself. No one can operate at full speed seventeen hours a day, seven days a week. Time and energy must be set aside for interests, for hobbies, for the luxury of being oneself.

Like most worriers, Joan had never learned how to do either. All the small but pleasurable things that had once given her life texture and variety — her running, Saturday nights out with friends, keeping up with new movies and books — had, one by one, been allowed to lapse after the twins' birth. Her marriage had also come under severe strain. Her husband, Robert, was alarmed by the emotional burdens Joan was placing on herself and resentful of their effect on him and on their relationship. They almost never spent time alone anymore, he told me one day, and when they did manage to put aside a few hours for themselves, Joan was usually tired to the point of exhaustion.

In the course of the interviews that preceded Joan's entry into the program, it also became clear that she possessed many of the other characteristics that define the worrier's style. One is a need to exercise detailed control over a child's care. In Joan's case, this need took the form of four check-in calls a day — two in the morning and two in the afternoon — plus a demand for a detailed nightly report on each twin's behavior. Not surprisingly, many caregivers find the requirement for such comprehensive intelligence onerous and intimidating. It says to them, "I don't trust you," and the caregiver who doesn't feel trusted will leave at the first opportunity. Josephine, Seth and Hillary's first caregiver, for example, left in their tenth month to take a job with one of the mothers she had met at the twins' park. And Joan's calls were now becoming a source of friction between her and Eva, the twins' current and much beloved nanny.

Loss of perspective is another defining characteristic of worriers that most often arises from their guilt. Wanting to "make it up" to her child for being away, the worrier will do things that, although well meant, are inappropriate. An example was Joan's announcement that she was thinking of enrolling Hillary and Seth in a French class. Joan's tongue was halfway in her cheek the morning she told the group about the plan, but only halfway. She was also probing. She had read in the previous day's *New York Times* that in the first years of life, a child's brain connections could be increased by increasing his exposure to learning. And a part of Joan wanted to run out immediately and enroll Hillary and Seth in every class she could find.

Leah's offer to get the twins admitted to her brother-in-law's physics class at New York University and the sight of Barbara's eyes rolling heavenward told Joan what a wiser side of her already knew: that French classes for two twenty-month-olds were inappropriate. Such perspective was critical to her, since without it she did tend to give way to that other, less wise side of herself. This was the side that had convinced her that she was favoring Seth over Hillary, even though it was evident to everyone who knew Joan that her behavior with each twin was equally loving. Even more inexplicable, it was the side that had convinced her she should continue the twins' breast-feeding into their eighteenth month.

As with Leah, our assessment of Joan's style revealed a mixture of positives and negatives. But in her case, the balance sheet took on the configuration characteristic of worriers: all the advantages were on the child's side of the ledger, all the disadvantages on the mother's.

Characteristics of Worrier's Style

- Exquisite sensitivity to child and his thoughts, feelings, cues, and signals
- Inability to say "no" to others and "yes" to oneself
- Tendency to lose perspective because of guilt

Advantages

Often Creates an Unusually Secure Attachment.   Joan's knowledge of Seth and Hillary, and the capacity this gives her to align herself almost instantly with their innermost thoughts and feelings, explain why one of the first things people notice about Joan and her children is how close they are.

Fosters a Sense of Individuality.   Another much-praised trait of Joan's is that she never confuses Seth with Hillary. She is always aware of how they differ in terms of personality needs and skills. In any given situation, she bases her responses on what she knows she can and can't expect from that particular twin.

Potential Risks

Can Create a Pattern of Guilt and Exaggeration.   Worriers tend to see trouble where none exists and often spend a great deal of time feeling guilty for no reason. Joan is typical. She worried about favoring Seth over Hillary, about the effects of her postpartum depression on the twins, and most of all, about whether her work was a harmful influence. One reason worriers are prone to this is that they try to track their children's growth too closely. Calling in four times a day and insisting on a highly detailed report each evening, a woman is bound to find something to worry about.

May Produce Tunnel Vision.   One of the things worriers almost never do is reality-test their fears. For all Joan's anguish about favoring Seth over Hillary, for example, she never stopped to ask herself, "Do I praise Hillary less? Do I spend fewer hours with her? Do I take less pride in her accomplishments? Am I slower to smile when she does something funny?" One of the most valuable things Joan learned from REAP was how to judge her thoughts and fears against her behavior.

Strains Marriage.   The intensity and self-absorption produced by the worrying style places a tremendous burden on a spouse. He feels excluded. Fortunately, Joan's husband, Robert, was unusually perceptive. Although Joan's focus on the twins often made him feel excluded, he was able to keep some perspective on that feeling.

Factors Needed to Make Worrier's Style Work

These elements are required to prevent potential risks from becoming realities.

Robust Good Health. This is important to every working mother, but it takes a special kind of endurance and stamina to maintain a style such as Joan's. Not only must she meet the demands of two young children, but her image of herself as "an earth mother" requires that she perform many of the chores other women assign to their support systems. What has allowed Joan to largely fulfill this ambition and withstand the succession of sixteen- and eighteen-hour days it involves is the conditioning she had acquired through years of running.

A Pliant Caregiver. A style like Joan's requires a special kind of caregiver, one who is willing to serve as Joan's eyes and ears when she is at work, without the corresponding satisfaction of having any real authority.

Requires the Ability to Maintain a Balanced Point of View. This is the aspect of her style that gave Joan the most trouble. "I'm not very good at deciding what I should and shouldn't worry about," Joan confessed the morning she was to attend her first meeting of the Saturday group. Robert, who was sitting next to her, nodded and added, "This has been a very hard time for Joan. What she has to learn to do, for her sake — for all of our sakes — is to step back and ask, 'Is this really worth the effort I'm giving it?'"

The staff evaluation lying on my desk that morning expressed the same thought in more clinical language. It also recommended a number of ways Joan could be helped to achieve a more balanced perspective on the twins and on her role as a working mother, and these became the basis for her experience in the program. The recommendations included:

• *Learning how to play results.* The most reliable way of determining whether something does or does not deserve worry is to look at its consequences. Has the source of worry changed either mother's or child's behavior in any demonstrable way? If the answer is "no," then the concern is unjustified; if it is "yes," then the next question is, "How long have you been aware of it?" Worrying about something that happened yesterday, or even last week, is often premature. Children's behavior is subject to many mysterious and self-correcting aberrations; only worrisome behaviors that have come to form a pattern — meaning ones that have been evident for three or more weeks — should be reason for concern.

This process of self-scrutiny is what we mean by playing results. An example of how it works in practice is the technique that helped ease Joan's fears about favoring Seth over Hillary. By learning to focus on her behavior — instead of on her worries — through a process of self-questioning, Joan could see that her fears about favoring one twin over the other were groundless.

• *Access to independent judgment.* It is a tribute to Joan's sensitivity that, if asked "How are Hillary and Seth?" she will reply, "You mean this morning?" But to be truly beneficial, such sensitivity must be complemented by, and balanced against, a view that sees growth in a broader perspective. One of the reasons Joan never became completely overwhelmed by detail is that Robert, having two children from a previous marriage, was able to provide her with a broader perspective on the twins' development. Friends also are able to provide the broader perspective worriers need to avoid becoming entirely enmeshed in the minutiae of their youngster's day-to-day life. For Joan, I think one of the most useful aspects of the program was that it provided her with regular access to two mothers who could help supply a sense of proportion when this began to happen.

• *Knowing how to recognize when it is time to pull back.* Joan also learned to do this for herself by learning the common, but often surprisingly subtle, signs that signal overinvolvement and a loss of perspective. A case in point is inattention to aspects of personal care, such as shopping for oneself or getting one's hair done. The same is true for the working mother who no longer seems to have room in her life for the little things that used to give her pleasure, such as aerobics classes, curling up with a new book, or a weekend minivacation with her husband.

As I said earlier, one of the most important skills a working mother can develop is the ability to say "no" to others and "yes" to herself. Without the kind of balance that allows time for one-self, a woman begins to lose the zest and imagination that makes her an exciting companion to her child. Being a good friend to yourself will make you a better mother to him.

BARBARA MOLLOY: THE ACHIEVER

Barbara is one of those people who seem to fill up a room with their presence. In her case, this isn't a matter of physical size. She is actually quite small — just barely over five feet. But what she lacks in inches Barbara more than makes up for in intensity, authority of manner, and controlled energy. If you have seen Bette Davis in *Dark Victory,* you have some idea of why, in every situation, Bar-bara stands out as emphatically as an exclamation mark.

People quickly notice Barbara's competence, organization, and perfectionism. She can't pass the Maurice Sendak drawing from *In the Night Kitchen* hanging near my office without stopping to straighten it, or, on rainy mornings, pass Leah's umbrella without stopping to shake it out and place it where it belongs. This desire to get all the details just right and in order has been as important to Barbara's success as an enterpreneur — she runs a successful net-working and computer dating service — as have her energy and talent.

We call the women who share Barbara's combination of drive, executive ability, and perfectionism "achievers." And one of their distinguishing characteristics is the way they use job-acquired skills and knowledge to enhance their role at home. An example is how Barbara selected a caregiver. The qualification most mothers seek is experience: how many families has the caregiver worked for and what kind of references will they provide for her? Barbara, however, found that in work situations this formula usually created friction for her. "I like things done my way," she said in response to a question from Joan, "and people who have been doing the same job for a long time usually like to do things their way. The people who work out best for me are the ones I hire directly from school, then train myself. So when Lisa was born, I decided to do the same with her caregiver."

Barbara's friends were surprised by her choice — a twenty-one-year-old whose only qualification for the position was an eight-month course in practical nursing. But as Barbara notes, over the last twenty-two months Miriam has grown into a highly competent and imaginative companion for Lisa. Secretly, I think Barbara is at least as pleased by the fact that over those months Miriam also has adopted her as a role model.

This is characteristic of achievers; they make excellent role models. In Miriam's case it isn't simply that, like most young people who come under the sway of an older mentor, she mimics the way Barbara walks and talks. Barbara's influence has been much more pervasive than that. Today Miriam has a self-confidence and, even more, a vision of herself that would have been unimaginable to the shy, insecure twenty-one-year-old who arrived at the Molloys' apartment for an interview nearly two years ago.

At twenty-two months Lisa is still some time away from noticing what a competent, effective, energizing force her mother is. But one day Barbara's modeling is going to have an important effect on the dreams she dreams. Having a mother who is able to ride the entrepreneurial fast track, Lisa will see no reason why she can't as well. And having a mother who is able to do this while still being a nurturing figure to her child and a companion to her husband, Lisa will avoid many of the conflicts that women have in trying to combine the roles of wife, mother, and worker. They will seem as natural to her as they do now to Barbara.

One morning during what had been a peaceful discussion, Leah touched — or perhaps more accurately pounced — on another aspect of the achiever's style. Annoyed by Barbara's criticism of Jeffrey's erratic eating habits, Leah suddenly turned to her and said, "Believe me, better that than to be obsessed with whether my child is in the right play group and takes the right classes."

"You've got me wrong," Barbara crisply replied. "I early on figured out that I wanted to protect Lisa from people rushing to pick her up or forcing her to join in. These things would upset her and I wanted her to have a positive attitude about socializing."

This drive for success and achievement in their children — as in themselves — represents one potential pitfall of the achiever's style. There isn't anything harmful about wanting to fortify a young child. But allowing a parental need for early competence and self-assurance to get in the way of a child's own developmental agenda *can* be harmful. In Lisa's case, this was already evident by the time she and her mother arrived at the center. Her Monday mornings were devoted to an educationally oriented play group, Tuesday and Thursday afternoon to "workouts" at Jamboree, Wednesday mornings to "early readers" class, and Fridays to the "twos" group at a local nursery school.

Barbara justified the schedule on the grounds of what she called "networking." Giving Lisa the advantage of early exposure to a wide range of social exchanges she felt would enable her child to discover one or two friends and the benefits of popularity. And up to a point this is true, but it must be balanced against an even larger truth: a child needs to follow his own developmental agenda.

This agenda takes the form of a series of biologically preprogrammed codes. We know that these not only prime an infant to expect that his environment will help him learn and grow in certain specific ways, but help him in his drive to express his true self. We also know that when a parent attempts to impose her own agenda, a common result is the creation of a compliant or a rebellious child. And this was the principal risk posed by Barbara's perfectionism and the energy with which she went about imposing it on Lisa.

Instead of seeking self-fulfillment by expressing herself, Lisa might grow up trying to fit herself into or be different from other people's visions of who she should be. At two, three, four, and five, that other person would be Barbara and her vision of what constitutes a perfect child; at twenty-five or thirty, it would be a spouse, a friend, or a boss. And the result would be that although Lisa would grow quite skilled at pleasing or frustrating those around her, she would never learn how to please the most important person of all — herself.

This vigilance for what was expected of her already was becoming apparent in Lisa's play style. In a quiet group situation, she was confident and productive. But if another child took her doll away, Lisa didn't protest; instead, she looked to Barbara, saying, "Mommy, get it." And if, in Barbara's absence, a teacher handed her a can of Silly Putty instead of the pegboard she wanted, Lisa pretended it hadn't happened. This wasn't because Lisa didn't know what she liked — she did — but, rather, because these priorities mattered more to her mother. She felt unable to cope on her own; Mommy wanted to and could do it better and more easily.

Cutting Lisa's schedule back from six to three activities per week was one of the first recommendations we made to Barbara. And it was motivated not only by our long-term concerns about Lisa but also by a more immediate worry — she was being defeated by her mother's competence.

One reason this sometimes happens is that being natural visionaries, achievers tend to see things as they could be and not as they are. This is what enabled Barbara to transform an empty room, two phones, and a rented personal computer into a successful dating service. Up to a point, her vision could also serve her as a mother. A woman should have an idea of who she would like her child to be two, three, or five years from now. What she should not do, however, is confuse that imagined child with the real youngster on her lap. And this is what Barbara sometimes did. She responded to the perfectly turned out, well-behaved seven-year-old in her mind's eye and not the often clinging, at times disorganized twenty-two-month-old that Lisa was.

As with the other mothers in the Saturday group, our assessment of Barbara's style and its effect on Lisa revealed a number of pluses and minuses.

Characteristics of Achiever's Style

• Inspiring (in that achievers make excellent role models)
• Instructive
• Controlling
• Perfectionistic

Advantages

Promotes Skill Development.   This is especially true for social skills. One thing Lisa is almost certain to be is socially adept. And as long as this doesn't become a substitute for pleasing herself, it can enhance her life in many important ways. Lisa will be a good friend, a good student, and one day an understanding mother and sympathetic wife.

Fosters a Healthy Sense of Ambition.   Through her example, Barbara is showing Lisa that there is no dream too big to come true.

Can Enhance Cognitive Development.   The importance achievers like Barbara attach to early education experiences is praiseworthy, but the experiences they provide should be appropriate. For a one- or two-year-old, "appropriate" means an environment that is rich in exciting colors, interesting pictures, and intriguing playthings, and that stresses learning through the kind of games and play that one- and two-year-olds are drawn to naturally. Inappropriate would be the use of flash cards or structured educational experiences in the form of early reading classes. For three- and four-year-olds, structured activity is not only appropriate, it's important. The social and playful side of learning, however, should receive primary emphasis in a child's first year of life.

Potential Risks

Can Create an Insecure Attachment.   Barbara's concern about Lisa's need for snacks between meals and her stubbornness about clothes was appropriate. When these form part of an ongoing behavioral pattern, they suggest an attachment disruption. In

Lisa's case, the reason for the disruption was that her developmental agenda was being ignored.

May Promote Rebellion Later.   Their energy and drive make achievers formidable maternal figures. There is a good deal of reassurance in having a mother who seems to know how to do everything right and who always has an answer for every question, but ultimately such omnipotence can become overwhelming to a child. Given the large shadow mother casts, there is no room left for me to be *me*. Such a child does what all youngsters do when other avenues of self-expression are denied them: rebel.

Factors Needed to Make Achiever's Style Work

A Husband with a Factual Style.   Criticism is not something Barbara takes well, but like other achievers she does have a healthy respect for facts. When they are presented to her in an objective manner she listens carefully. Her husband, Samuel, knows this. If an aspect of Lisa's care troubles him, he doesn't criticize or chide but instead presents the reasons for his concern in the quiet, factual, businesslike style he knows his wife listens to.

A Caregiver with an "Unshaped" Style.   Although Barbara's preference for a young woman she could shape and mold over an experienced caregiver may at first glance seem to have put Lisa at a disadvantage, it was the best possible decision for both of them. However competent, Lisa would have sensed Barbara's uneasiness with a more experienced woman, who then might have been the first of a multitude of caregivers.

Awareness of the Importance of the Child's Emotional Vulnerability.   This is the element essential to making the achiever's style work, and Barbara often missed it. Her view of Lisa was too much influenced by her own overachievement. Samuel provided some perspective, but it wasn't until she got to the program that Barbara learned how not to let her achiever's instincts blind her to Lisa's real need to find things out in her own way.

To help Barbara gain a new perspective, we showed her how to:
• *Think back on her own relationship with her mother.* For all her

imagination, often Barbara lacked the ability to see things through Lisa's eyes. This deprived her of a simple and effective way of reality-testing, since a child's needs often take on an entirely different shape when you look at them through a child's eyes. The purpose of having Barbara think back on her relationship with her own mother, Claire, was to provide this added perspective. In many ways the dynamic greatly resembled Barbara and Lisa's. There had been the same strong and domineering maternal figure and the same slightly overwhelmed and resentful child.

In recent years, however, Barbara had grown quite close to Claire. But as she started to think back on her childhood, her memories of always being what she called "the perfect little miss" resurfaced. "I really resented the way Mom would dress me up," she said one day. "I remember once in the third grade when our teacher took us on a field trip to a farm. The rest of the kids turned up in T-shirts and jeans, but I was dressed as if I were going to the senior prom. I felt so self-conscious in my frilly blouse and skirt I wanted to crawl into a hole and cry."

The round of piano and ballet lessons that had filled up Barbara's Saturdays was another painful childhood memory. "Everybody else was home watching cartoons or on play dates, and there I was going from class to class to class. No wonder I didn't have any close friends then." Putting herself in touch with these memories was often painful for Barbara. But the new perspective it provided was soon reflected in her more relaxed attitude about Lisa's missing buttons and whims for mismatched socks.

• *Learn to ask herself, "Who am I doing this for?"* This question is designed to help a mother like Barbara distinguish her needs from her child's. If you ask yourself, "Why am I buying a set of vocabulary flash cards for my twelve-month-old?" or "Why is my thirty-month-old attending five different classes a week?" or "Why am I spending a hundred dollars on a dress my twenty-four-month-old will outgrow in three months?" it quickly becomes apparent whose needs are being served.

One of the principal reasons a child like Lisa may not develop a strong self is that the inability to make such distinctions causes a parent to overlook or ignore the emergence of those special likes and talents that mark a youngster's true self. Until Joan pointed it out to her one day, for example, Barbara had not noticed what a flair for color Lisa displayed in her collages. Artistic talent hadn't been one of the items on her agenda for her daughter, so it had gone unnoticed and unnourished. As Barbara learned to distinguish her agenda from Lisa's, however, this changed, and it produced an important change in Lisa. Finding her displays of individuality responded to more sensitively, Lisa became noticeably more assertive. She still wanted to please others, but now she was becoming equally interested in pleasing herself.

• *Allow Lisa to become more involved in her own care.* No toddler can completely dress himself, of course. Even if he could, it would add a half hour to the dressing process, and he would emerge from it in a shambles of mismatched colors and clothing. Nonetheless, toddlers do love to "help" dress themselves, and allowing them to provide that help — by, say, picking a favorite T-shirt to wear or putting on a shoe — not only makes them feel that they exercise some control over their environment but also serves to check any perfectionist tendencies in the mother who is serving as valet.

Our Saturday group's final meeting took place on a cold, rainy October morning, much like the cold, rainy April morning that had marked the first meeting eighteen months before. Allison Blake, the graduate assistant who had been at that first session, came by the center for the group's last. She and I stood on the other side of the one-way mirror that fronts onto the playroom. Leah, Joan, and Barbara brought their children into the playroom to mark this special day.

As mothers and children cleaved into two separate groups, Allison also remarked on how changed everyone seemed. "Jeffrey isn't pulling hair anymore." And turning toward Leah, who had one eye on a drawing Barbara was holding up and the other on Jeffrey, Allison noted, "I see Leah monitors him much more attentively now.

"Is that Lisa Molloy in an old sweatshirt? I'd have thought Barbara would have walked over hot coals first," Allison said with a big grin. I told Allison if she watched Lisa play with Jeffrey and

Hillary and Seth for a while, she would also notice another change: how much more assertive Lisa had grown.

We both agreed we had never seen Joan look better. "You must be pleased by all the changes," Allison said, turning toward me.

I was, I told her, but I was also pleased by all the ways Leah, Barbara, and Joan had remained the same. "Look at Leah, she is as irrepressible as ever. And if you talk to Joan, you will find that while she worries much less and now has an antidote to her worry in the form of her runs, she still worries. Barbara," I said, "is forever and indomitably Barbara."

An hour later Joan, Barbara, and Leah exchanged a last tearful farewell. Then all three women gathered up their children, walked through the foyer and up the stairs, and stepped out our door into the rest of their lives.

9

The Single Working Mother

ANGELA BOYD is among the most discussed and analyzed women of our time.

Over the last decade, she has been the subject of dozens of journal articles, several studies, and at least three full-dress academic conferences. *Time, Newsweek,* and the television networks also have featured her often and prominently in their reports, while her advice has been solicited regularly by everyone from legislators to feminists.

The reason Angela's name may sound unfamiliar is that you know her by her generic identity: single working mother. And what has put that name on so many different lips and Angela's concerns at the center of so many different spotlights is that with Americans divorcing one another at unprecedented rates, it is now estimated that nearly *one-third* of the nation's children will spend some portion of their childhood in a home headed by a single working mother like Angela.

There is, of course, also a real-life Angela Boyd who has her own individual history. She is thirty-six; grew up in Mobile, Alabama; went to New York twelve years ago to study acting; and now lives in Hoboken, New Jersey, and works in telephone sales for a large magazine company. She also has two loving parents whom she sees three times a year, a four-year-old son named Adam, and a former husband named Peter who moved to Los Angeles two years ago and has provided his family with very little in the way of emotional or financial support since. But beyond these particulars, what makes Angela's story the story of America's millions of single working mothers is the special sense of isolation she feels.

As Dr. Michael Lamb of the University of Utah notes in a recent report, while single working mothers vary greatly in economic and social status and in educational and career attainments, a sense of isolation is the one constant in the life of virtually every woman who bears the responsibilities of parenting by herself. The feeling of being alone and cut off, which often arises when there isn't another adult there to offer help in emergencies and advice and support in the daily business of raising a young child, not only adds enormously to the weight of these responsibilities, as Dr. Lamb points out, but also creates three special hazards to a single working mother's maternal sensitivity.

The first of these hazards is *overintensity*. It is a developmental truism that no one adult can raise a child alone. Adults need other adults, not only to support them on issues like discipline and moral training and to provide a sense of perspective when they over- or underreact but to deflect a portion of the child's anger when he is mad or neediness when he is upset. Children need other adults to provide them with a sense of family, to serve as alternate sources of comfort and counsel, play, and identification. And both parent and child need other adults in their lives for the sake of their own relationship; otherwise the I-thou link, which every mother and child share, may become overstressed in ways that leave both individuals feeling misunderstood and alienated.

A second risk isolation poses for a single parent's sensitivity is *overinvestment*. While every mother dreams of a better life for her child, a single working mother's dreams have been shown to have a special intensity. The desire to be "all that I can be" is the most precious gift a parent can give a child. It is a key building block of mastery, competence, and self-esteem. But danger arises when a parent uses her child to realize her own hopes for herself. And studies show that this is more likely to occur in homes where there

isn't another parent to offer perspective — to warn when the maternal agenda is in danger of superseding the child's. A case in
point is a report by Drs. William Siegal and Ralph Ellison of Ohio
State University. Comparing single and married working
mothers, the investigators found that single mothers were markedly more likely to impose their own ambitions and goals on their
children.

This Ohio State study also highlighted the third risk isolation
poses to maternal sensitivity. It can make a single working mother
overly protective. Every mother is acutely conscious of her child's
vulnerability; it is a consequence of having carried him within her,
as a part of her own body, for nine months. In a single mother, this
sense of a youngster's vulnerability is intensified further by the fact
of her singleness. She knows all the hazards her child faces, especially if anything happens to her, and in time this knowledge can
begin to color her perceptions of her infant or toddler. She comes
to see him as much more vulnerable than he really is. One consequence of this, as the Ohio State study shows, is that a single
mother tends to be more restrictive about normal activities like
exploration; at all times and in all places her child is encouraged to
stay as close as possible to mother.

Translated into the language of development, the risk of overprotectiveness and the other hazards isolation creates is that it can
make a child feel that his viewpoint on issues that matter to him
— such as exploration, or freedom to follow his own developmental agenda — is neither understood nor respected. A common
result of such a misunderstanding is the growth of attachment and
emotional disorders. The markedly higher rates of both problems
among children, especially male children, in single-parent households testifies to the special challenge every single working mother
faces.

I have asked Angela to describe her story in this chapter not only
because it illustrates how, with help, one such mother overcame
the hazards of isolation, but also because her story demonstrates
the unique contribution a single working mother can make to her
child.

In his playful moods, Adam calls Angela "Wonder Woman."

While the nickname is a reflection of Adam's current fascination with superheroes, it is also a reflection of how he sees his mother. A great deal has been written about the working mother as role model, but usually the aspect that is emphasized is her professional competence, the example she sets as corporate vice president, doctor, or successful entrepreneur. There is another, more human kind of modeling working mothers do, however, and single working mothers such as Angela often excel at it.

Growing up in Mobile, Angela had taken it for granted that one day she would live the same kind of comfortable middle-class life she saw her parents living. "I knew I wanted to come to New York and act," she said one day, "but in most other respects I assumed that my life wouldn't be much different from my mom's and dad's. I'd have my own home, a family, and a happy marriage." Angela's expectations for herself, thus far, have gone largely unfulfilled. The house has turned out to be a four-room apartment in Hoboken; her acting career finally had to be abandoned for more regular paying, if less fulfilling, work; and instead of a supportive spouse, Angela finds herself alone with the enormous responsibilities of raising a young child. But like most other single working mothers, she hasn't allowed her circumstances to depress or embitter her. She takes one day at a time, coping as best she can, always with grace and dignity.

There are no simple one-to-one correlations in human psychology, but the memory of this grace and dignity will undoubtedly leave a lasting impression on her son. Reflecting on his childhood at twenty or thirty, what Adam is going to remember, cherish, and — most important — strive to emulate is the special example Angela is setting for him. Her humor in adversity, flexibility in crisis, and courage in the face of challenge are providing Adam with a model of behavior that, in its richness and universality, transcends narrow stereotypes. It is a model of woman not just as competent striver or achiever, but as competent, courageous, caring, and resilient human being.

This example is the special legacy all single working mothers have to bestow on their children. The reason Angela has been especially successful in bestowing it on her son is that she is an unusually thoughtful person. Long before she visited us at the center, for example, she had largely solved, on her own, one of the risks isolation poses for a single-parent family: an overstressing of the I-thou link between mother and child.

This sometimes happens because the need to be all things to her child — mother, father, confidante, disciplinarian, and task-master — ultimately becomes so taxing that, without realizing it, the single working mother begins to lose some of her sensitivity. Important needs go unfulfilled because she is too stressed to notice them. In the case of the child, the danger of stress in the I-thou link is that it can lead to feelings of resentment and ultimately to rebelliousness. The single mother's three-year-old protests when his play is interrupted for dinner not because he resents the interruption but because he resents the fact that the interruption is always being made by the same person.

Angela's way of escaping the dangers that arise when a parent has to be all things to her child was by bringing other adults into her and Adam's lives. An example is the way she transformed the women in Adam's day-care center into an extended family. In selecting a center, an important criterion for Angela, as for many single working mothers, was flexibility. She needed a program that would be able to accommodate her own one or two late nights a week at the office. She also wanted a center that was well equipped with toys and gymnastic equipment. But her most important criterion was the age and background of the staff, and this required her to make a trade-off.

Although usually well educated, caring, and competent, the young women employed by larger, chain-run day-care centers often lack the time (they have more charges to look after) and the personal experience of mothering needed to serve as an effective source of support and counsel to a single working mother or to her child. Since this was Angela's most important criterion, the center she selected for Adam was a small, home-based unit operated by two mothers in her neighborhood.

Unlike many larger centers, her choice offered a limited variety of gymnastic equipment and toys, but its smaller enrollment ensured that Adam would get a maximum of one-on-one time with the staff. Even more important, the two women who operated the center, Georgia and Diane, were not only mature and experienced but also eager to become involved helpmates. Georgia, who is herself a single mother, has become an especially important figure in the Boyds' lives over the past two years.

Angela has found her an invaluable source of advice and perspective, while for Adam she has come to serve as an emotional ombudsman. Nothing is so important to a young child as having a trusted figure there to wipe away his tears and enfold him in her arms when he feels upset or frightened. Like every mother, Angela would prefer to be there to offer that comfort herself, but when she can't be she has the reassurance of knowing that Georgia is there to do it for her. At least as important, Georgia also has become Adam's representative and ambassador. When he feels misunderstood, he relies on Georgia to present his case to his mother.

A small but significant example of this was how, through Georgia's intervention, Adam finally secured his long-dreamed-of Batman and Robin set. He had been fantasizing about owning these superheroes for months, but his requests for them had been refused by an unrelenting Angela, who felt her son should be exposed only to educational toys. "I think those action figures are junk," she noted pointedly one day.

To defend the Dynamic Duo on developmental grounds would be, to put it mildly, to stretch a point. Nonetheless, there is a reason for their perennial popularity among three-, four-, and five-year-olds. Superheroes give a young child a way of coping with his feelings of powerlessness and incompetence. To a four-year-old, everyone around him not only looks miles bigger, they are able to do everything he can't do, from cross a street alone to count to thirty. With their strapping physiques and amazing abilities, superheroes provide a way of vicariously enjoying those feelings of power and mastery that the child is so acutely aware he lacks. Having two sons of her own, Georgia knew this; she also knew how especially important those feelings are to a young boy. When she pointed this out to Angela, Angela finally relented, and Adam, now feeling more understood, began wondering when he was going to get the Batmobile.

Georgia's involvement has not stopped at the center's door. Her presence at Adam's birthday parties and her visits during the Christmas and Thanksgiving holidays have enriched these special times for both mother and son. "Georgia has become family to us," says Angela. "A birthday or holiday without her wouldn't be the same for Adam, and, I've realized, it wouldn't be the same for me either."

The other figure whom Angela has established as an important person in Adam's life is her own father, Sam Boyd. (After her divorce, Angela began using her maiden name again.) Distance has made this more difficult; living more than a thousand miles away, Sam can't be there on a day-to-day basis the way Georgia can. But he does see his grandson three times a year on family vacations, and being the only male in Adam's otherwise female world has given Sam a special status. It is always "Grandpa Boyd" to whom Adam refers when he boasts about his progress in those areas that mean so much to little boys, such as "How big I'm getting" and "How strong I am."

Angela's special insight has been to see that Adam's high regard for his grandfather could be used to transform Sam into an alternate authority figure. I say "special" insight because only recently has research documented what Angela largely intuited on her own: that one way a single parent can avoid the feelings of resentment that may arise when a woman has to fulfill every role herself is by creating alternate authority figures whose names can be invoked in situations of reward and punishment. After the third "I told you not to do that anymore, Adam," invoking Sam Boyd's name on her fourth warning still allows Angela to make her point but in a way that doesn't also make her seem overbearing to her son.

Also important is the fact that the name Angela most often invokes as an alternate authority figure is that of a man. The presence or absence of a male figure makes less difference in a girl's development, but it has been shown to make an enormous difference in a boy's. Sons of single working mothers have been found to have notably high rates of both learning and emotional disorders. Indeed, the weight of these data is such that a number of investigators have begun to describe boys in single-female-headed households as an "at-risk" group.

Exactly why the absence of a strong male figure has such a potentially worrisome effect on a son's but not on a daughter's growth is still not clearly understood. But we do know that most of the developmental risks associated with this situation can be eliminated if an uncle, a male cousin, a friend, or, as in Adam's case, a grandfather is available to serve as a role model. You can see clearly the effect their presence has on a boy in the results of a study by Dr. W. Biller of the University of Nebraska. Comparing the academic performance and psychological adjustment of boys with fathers and those with strong male models, Dr. Biller found virtually no differences in development on either index. In areas as diverse as cognitive performance and toilet training, a boy does better if there is a Grandpa Boyd and Uncle John or some other respected male figure in his life who can be held up as a standard for emulation.

A way the REAP program did help Angela was by showing her how to overcome her tendency to overinvest in Adam. In middle-class single families like the Boyds, often this overinvestment takes the form of overidentifying; singleness makes a woman more likely to see her child as a manifestation of herself. If his behavior is exemplary, if he is an achiever, if he's always dressed neatly, then, despite her singleness, she must be an exemplary mother.

The impulse behind this is understandable, but in their report Drs. Siegal and Ellison note that one frequent result of it is the development of what they describe as "inappropriate" maternal responses. In Angela's case an example of this inappropriateness was the great emphasis she put on Adam's dress (despite the family's small budget, his clothing was unusually stylish for a four-year-old) and on his good manners.

Both are important, of course, but they also are externals. On the whole, neither neat dress nor good deportment contribute to a child's confidence, his sense of security, or his trust. And concern about such externals does become inappropriate when, as with Angela, it so absorbs a parent's energy and attention that maternal behaviors that do promote the growth of security, trust, and other important internal qualities suffer as a result.

The most important of these behaviors is sensitivity. As we have seen throughout the book, the better a woman is at identifying and responding accurately to her child's interests and preoccupations, the more secure that child feels. Such sensitivity makes him think, "Mommy knows and understands me." In the case of a four-year-old such as Adam, one important way to encourage this thought is by demonstrating an awareness of the world he lives in. Even when his conversation begins in midsentence, as a four-year-old's often does, an attuned parent will be able to tell which of his friends the child is talking about or which of his favorite nighttime dreams he is about to discuss.

At the center we call this capacity to identify themes the "ability to track," and because of her preoccupation with Adam's dress and deportment, Angela's grasp of it was uncertain. Whenever the three of us were together, I noticed that invariably she could be relied on to spot an unbuttoned button or a missed "please" or "thank you." Often this scrutiny so absorbed her, however, that when Adam began talking about what he did yesterday in day care or about his friend Michael's father, Angela's replies would be distracted and impersonal, as if she weren't really listening. I also found that on those afternoons when she appeared especially distracted, Adam himself would become markedly less responsive to Angela, to me, and to the other parents and children he met at the center. Typically, this is how a young child behaves when he feels the environment isn't interested in his concerns.

Another example of Angela's overinvestment was the stress she placed on her son's academic achievement. Again, what I found worrisome wasn't the goal — every parent wants her child to excel academically — but that in her desire to prepare Adam to become an all-A student, Angela was in danger of confusing her own agenda with his. Seeing Adam's academic performance as a validation of her own worth as a parent, she had lost sight of whose needs were being served when she began using flash cards to build Adam's vocabulary at one, and at three enrolled him in a "special learners" class at a local private school.

In their study of single working mothers, a second characteristic that concerned Drs. Siegal and Ellison was overprotectiveness. One morning, while walking Angela and Adam from my office to the playroom, I witnessed a small but telling example of how it also had affected Angela's maternal style. Being four and eager to explore the center's still unfamiliar surroundings, Adam kept trying to run on ahead, but each time he got more than a few feet in front of us Angela would snap him back to her side with a brisk "Adam." What I found particularly striking was her tone of voice. Although Adam faced no danger, there was an edge of barely controlled panic in it.

Other staff members also were struck by Angela's overprotectiveness. For example, our play therapist, Jan Wirth, told me the most significant thing about Adam's behavior in play group was Angela's behavior. In most groups, after a few minutes a natural division normally occurs. The mothers go off to one corner to talk among themselves; the children go to another to play. Angela, however, would always remain hovering over Adam until one of the other mothers got up and coaxed her away.

Not surprisingly, Adam resented this and the other limitations that had been imposed on him. Four, as we shall see in chapter 13, is an age when the larger world assumes a new interest for a child. "What is this strange and exciting place and where do I fit into it?" he wonders. A measure of Adam's anger at not being able to answer these questions for himself as fully as he would like was the bed-wetting and food fights that had brought Angela to the center. These "misbehaviors" represented a declaration of independence for Adam. Through them, he was telling his mother, "You control most of what I do, but you don't control everything."

Developmentally, the most significant marker of change the program produced in Adam and in Angela was the cessation of Adam's bed-wetting. In clinical terms, its disappearance suggested that as Angela was growing better at distinguishing and separating her own needs from her son's, Adam's impulse to rebel against her was lessening. But in the course of the Boyds' visits to us, I developed my own, more personal series of markers to chart mother's and son's progress. They took the form of missed "thank you's" that weren't criticized, buttons that remained unbuttoned, and cowlicks that stayed unsmoothed. The day Adam appeared in my office with an exposed shirttail, I suspected a breakthrough had been achieved. And I was right. Never before had I seen Angela so absorbed and involved in her son's conversation.

Watching her watch Adam on that warm October afternoon, I was reminded of a scene, or rather two scenes, from a film about another single parent, *Kramer vs. Kramer*. The first scene occurs early in the film, immediately after the father, played by Dustin Hoffman, has become responsible for his son's day-to-day care. The two are walking to school; listening to the distracted, self-absorbed replies of the Hoffman character, a stranger might not even guess he was related to the little boy at his side. The second scene, which also involves a walk to school, occurs near the end of the film. By now, through their daily contact, the father has become so caught up in his son's world that at one point, as the boy describes an incident that happened in school the previous day, the father becomes so absorbed in his son's story that he fails to see the curb and nearly falls.

In some ways, Adam's exposed shirt was Angela's symbolic equivalent of that movie father's near fall. By freeing herself from her overinvestment and overprotectiveness, she was not only freeing Adam to be himself, but also freeing herself to begin enjoying him. Instead of being a hope to be groomed and shaped, Adam was now able to be what every child should be to a parent—a companion, a coconspirator, a friend.

Here are some of the ways Angela was helped to cope with the risks isolation poses for a single working mother:

• *Know how to recognize the signs of overinvestment and overprotectiveness.* In a relationship as close and complex as that between a mother and child, it is often difficult to identify the line that separates normal from abnormal parental concern and involvement. One of the first things Angela learned was how to recognize the signs that indicate that the line has been crossed. In the case of overinvestment, common indications are overdressing and overgrooming. The child who, in every crowd, stands out as best

The Single Working Mother

dressed is also likely to be the one who is carrying the greatest burden of parental hopes and dreams on his fragile shoulders. A second sign is constantly comparing achievements. It is normal to feel happy when a child excels, and sad when he fails, but a parent who continually compares her youngster's performance against peers is overinvesting. Perhaps the most common sign of this tendency, however, is a loss of pleasure in the child's company. Because the overinvesting parent tends to spend shared time training and grooming her child, being together becomes not the joy it should be but a duty.

Overprotectiveness, on the other hand, announces itself in unusual acts of defiance — unusual in that although all children occasionally rebel against parental injunctions, the overprotected child's rebellion is constant and ongoing. It forms a behavioral pattern. In some cases the defiance will be outright, in others it will be more subtle. In the latter case the identifying factor will be the out-of-characterness of the behavior. It will represent the only problem area in the deportment of an otherwise well-adjusted child.

• *Reach out to others for help.* This represents the best way to gain a perspective on the feelings that may be making you overinvest or overprotect. You can do what Angela did and try to involve your own parents and the people in your day-care center more intimately in your and your child's lives. Or you can join a single-parent support group. No one understands the special problems or fears of a single mother as well as another single mother, which is why such groups serve as especially good sources of perspective, balance, and reassurance. Check with your pediatrician. If he or she is unable to direct you to a group, try your local hospital, church, synagogue, or Lamaze organization. In larger cities, single-parent groups often are listed in the Yellow Pages. If there is no group in your area, you might consider organizing one. There are probably other single mothers at your office or at your child's day-care center or playground; call and see if they would be interested in joining you in a support group.

A second reason reaching out is important is that, like Angela, you can transform other important adults in your child's life into surrogate authority figures whose names can be invoked in situations of reward and punishment. If there is an uncle, aunt, grandparent, or day-care worker who is especially close to your toddler, mention how much his behavior would please or displease this other special person when he does something good or bad. One of the dangers of having to be the source of all praise and blame in a youngster's life is that it can transform a woman into a kind of Greek chorus. Occasionally transferring your thoughts to someone else is a way of ensuring that the child does not feel that no matter what he does or where he turns, you are there ready to begin reciting his strengths and weaknesses back to him. Evoking that other special person's name also adds an extra resonance to your praise or blame.

• *Make yourself (occasionally) take the long view of your child's development.* Resisting the temptation to overemphasize such externals as good manners, test scores, or an always perfect appearance is difficult when there isn't another parent there to say, "Yes, but." Moreover, because neatness, politeness, and a straight A report card are among the most commonly acknowledged signs of "good mothering," it is natural that a single mother would feel a special temptation to emphasize them. It gives her a way of demonstrating her worth to herself and to the world. The purpose of occasionally forcing yourself to take a longer view of your child's growth is that it puts this temptation into perspective.

Project yourself fifteen or twenty years into your child's future and ask yourself, "What qualities are going to be most important to my child's happiness and well-being then?" Will it be the ability to remember always to say "please" and "thank you" or to do well on tests? Yes, they will be important. But if you think about the qualities that have made an important difference in your own life, I think you will agree that a secure sense of his own worth and enough trust in others to be able to form relationships easily will be most important to that eighteen- or twenty-year-old. What is going to be most important to him are those *human* qualities, which grow best in environments where the needs and interests being served are those of the child and not the parent.

• *Think back on your own childhood.* Although there are many reasons why a child may be late to walk, talk, or be toilet trained, and although these lags occur to children in all kinds of families, when they occur in a single-parent working family a mother is quick to see them as manifestations of her family's special difference. Thinking back on your own childhood is a way of gaining some perspective on this difference.

As you think about your own past, you probably will recall times when your own growth lagged a bit or when your parents said or did something that left you momentarily upset, confused, or angry at them. The review will remind you of something every single working mother should remember at least once and perhaps twice a week: that children and mothers and fathers in two-parent families also have their own full share of difficulties troubles and setbacks. At least as frequently, you should also remind yourself that in you — in your unique spirit and courage — your boy or girl has everything a child needs for happy, healthy growth.

10

Thirteen Reasons Why You Shouldn't Feel Guilty about Working

WHY DO YOU FEEL GUILTY?

If you were able to step back from your life for a moment and see what we see from our perspective at the center, I think you would agree that the source of most of the guilt working mothers feel today lies not in their own imaginary failings but in the two standards of mothering against which they measure themselves. The first of these standards is what might be called the perfect mother (PM) model. Although this model no longer grips women's imaginations the way it did two decades ago, it continues to exert a powerful influence on today's working mothers because it was the model of maternity they saw their own mothers striving to emulate. It is embodied in those warm, wise at-home mothers of late 1950s and early 1960s television shows like "Leave It to Beaver" and "Father Knows Best." No matter how liberated, in her heart of hearts I think almost every working mother still silently reproaches herself for not being there, the way Beaver Cleaver's mother was, to dispense cookies, milk, and words of wisdom.

More recently, this image has been superseded by the superwoman model (SW). Although it represents an advance in the sense that it does acknowledge that one legitimate female aspiration is success in the workplace, by incorporating many of its predecessor's myths, it has created an even more onerous and guilt-inducing standard. Now a woman is expected to be not only Betty Crocker and Mr. Rogers but Lee Iacocca as well.

A good measure of how heavily these two models weigh on real-life working mothers can be seen in the results of a recent study by Dr. Lois Hoffman of the University of Michigan. Like a number of other investigators, Dr. Hoffman found that many of the most worrisome developmental effects associated with work are by-products not of work but of a woman's guilt about it.

In our research at the center, we have noticed the same correlation — that in most cases it is guilt, not a job, which by creating role conflicts or preoccupations siphons off maternal sensitivity. Another correlation we have noticed is that, in one way or another, most maternal guilt is linked to three beliefs about maternal perfection — shared by both the PM and the SW models — which recent research has shown to be myths. They are:

• *Belief that a mother always has to be at her best.* This notion is based on what might be called the "trauma" theory of human development, or the idea that a young child will be irreparably damaged if a mother occasionally loses her temper, misunderstands him, forgets to say goodbye, or sends him to nursery school or day care in a pair of unironed jeans or unmatched socks. Studies have confirmed what common sense has always known: children are more resilient than that.

• *Belief that a primary duty of every working mother is to shield her child from stress.* Yes, the child of a working mother probably is subjected to more minor stresses. But women who feel guilty about this overlook what we have learned recently about the beneficial effects of such stress. You can see this benefit operating clearly in the results of a recent British study. Its author, Dr. T. W. Moore, believes that the greater degree of independence and assertiveness he found among working mothers' youngsters was a direct outgrowth of the youngsters having successfully coped with the minor stresses in their environments. Dr. Moore also believes that the greater degree of conformity he found among the children of at-home mothers may have been linked to the fact that their environments lacked just such stresses.

• *Belief that a mother needs to be all-knowing.* This notion rests on a fundamental misconception about the nature of maternal knowledge. Although information about a child is important, even more important is the style used to handle it. A woman is not expected to know everything, but she does need to know how to remain creatively uncertain when she doesn't know something. For the most part, gaps in maternal knowledge are not in themselves a cause for worry; but maternal presumptuousness often is because it can lead to the kind of misinterpretations that puzzle and distress a child.

Think about my imaginary audience of infants and toddlers and the way they reacted to a shared time that was shaped to fit adult presumptions of what a young child needs and wants. Or think about Barbara Molloy and the way her insistence in laying down a developmental agenda — although well meant — put her daughter, Lisa, at risk for developing a dependent self. All of us are fallible, and the woman who incorporates this realization into her maternal style will be much more likely to display the flexibility and the sensitivity essential to the growth of a strong secure attachment.

The omniscient and omnipotent maternal figure who arose from these three beliefs continues to weigh so heavily on the heart and mind of the American working mother because of a knowledge gap — although, in this case, the knowledge gap is related not to work but to the pace of recent research. Our ideas about children and how they grow have changed so quickly over the last decade that many women still are unaware of the fact that attributes like maternal omnipotence or omniscience are now considered irrelevant to good mothering. That is why this chapter is as much about the new findings in human development as it is about maternal guilt. You will find that, although each of the thirteen points that follow addresses that guilt, they address it not in terms of exhortations or pep talks but by explaining to you, in developmental terms, why your guilt is unnecessary. You are too sophisticated to put much value in admonitions to "stop worrying"; you want something more substantial. So here, then, is the scientific case against the working mother's guilt.

1. *Guilt because you don't "measure up" by conventional standards of mothering.* As Sylvia Hewett notes in her recent book *A Lesser Life: The Myth of Woman's Liberation,* the principal reason the superwoman model has failed to provide working mothers with a sense of validation is that it has perpetuated one of the most guilt-inducing notions of its predecessor. This is the equation between good mothering and skill at, and enjoyment of, such traditional maternal functions as baking, cooking, sewing, and so on. In the mythology of the superwoman, not only does "having it all" mean having a good job, a good salary, a sensitive husband, and a BMW in the driveway, it also means being competent in the kind of nursing and care-giving chores that in the 1950s marked a woman as a perfect mother.

The carryover of this equation is usually justified on the grounds that it is in acts like making a cake or drawing a picture together that a woman most fully expresses her maternal competence and sensitivity. But there are two fundamental things wrong with this assertion. The first is that, in human terms, it is unfair. Why should a woman, especially one who is her family's sole source of support, be made to feel guilty because out of either tiredness or dislike, she assigns such functions to the caregiver or day-care worker? The second problem is that, in scientific terms, it is unjustified. We have learned a great deal about the process of human development over the past twenty years, but none of it supports the notion that a mother who serves TV dinners or leaves brownie making to others is endangering her child's emotional and psychological growth.

Security, trust, a sense of mastery and competence, humor, curiosity—all the qualities that matter to a child's future—originate not in *what* a woman does with her child but in *how* she does it; in other words, in the sensitivity of her interactional and relationship skills. Baking brownies or making valentines with a two-year-old are some of the ways maternal sensitivity can be expressed—but only some. For a woman who has no time or inclination for such activities, other options are available. She can show her sensitivity by displaying a knowledge of her child's themes, or by setting limits for him in a way that avoids humiliation, or by knowing when to act and when not to—in short, by knowing how to use the techniques I have been describing throughout this book.

The next time you come home too tired to prepare dinner, keep this in mind: what a child notices is not whether the meal placed in front of him is home cooked or a TV dinner but whether it is served with *love*.

2. *Guilt about not being there when the child takes his first step or speaks his first word.* One of the things working mothers overlook when they discuss their guilt about missing important firsts is the special nature and power of the mother-child bond. It is why, already, by the fifth day of life, a child is able to distinguish (by smell) the breast pad of his mother from that of other nursing mothers, and why, by the fifteenth or twentieth month, he has begun to experience time on two separate and distinct levels. There is caregiver time, and while it is full of important lessons and nurturing experiences, it doesn't resonate as deeply or intensely as mother time. This is why first words or first steps should properly be dated not from the moment they occur, but from the moment they are *shown to mother*. Until then, they are, in a sense, like the tree that falls in the forest when no one is listening. Achievements don't become truly real in a child's mind or imagination until they have been validated by mother's presence.

3. *Guilt about having to leave a sick child.* It is some measure of how deeply working women feel about this issue that, when we polled our program mothers on the subject of guilt in the summer of 1986, leaving a sick child not only emerged as the most common source of self-reproach, it was first by a wide margin. Nearly 90 percent of the women surveyed said they feel guilty in this situation; 65 percent said they felt guilty about losing their tempers, which was the second most common source of maternal guilt. Why this situation exerts such a special tug on working women is not hard to understand, of course, but its formidable ability to induce guilt is more a tribute to the continuing pull of the perfect mother model—in particular the almost totemic affect it assigns to a mother's physical presence—than it is a reflection of developmental realities as we understand them today.

The most important of these realities involves what we have learned recently about the mental representation of mother — the evoked companion — every child carries in his mind's eye. You can see the tremendous power this companion exerts over a child's thinking in the results of a recent study by Dr. Daniel Stern of New York – Cornell Hospital. Although most adult strangers produce wariness and uneasiness in an infant or toddler, like most mothers you probably have noticed that every once in a while your two- or three-year-old meets a strange adult with whom he clicks immediately. Dr. Stern set out to discover why these instant "fits" occur, and his results show that what gives such adults their magical powers to relax and engage a normally wary child is the way they recall his evoked companion. Because something about this stranger's set — her voice, her look, and above all, her sensitivity — reminds the child of you, his evoked companion comes to life in an especially vivid and palpable way. He is so at ease interacting with this new face because on some level he sees himself interacting with you.

Dr. Stern's study should alleviate your guilt about leaving on "sick days" because it offers you two ways of making the child's evoked companion so vivid that it will seem to him almost as if you have stayed home. The first way you can enhance its palpability is by describing to the youngster, before you leave, all the things you have told Nanny to do today to make him feel better. This will create a more direct link in his mind between the caregiver's behavior and yours. Later, when Nanny changes his sheets or puts a cool towel to his forehead or does something else the child remembers you telling him she would do, it will seem to him as if it is you who is there changing his sheets or laying that cool towel on his feverish brow. In order to further reinforce this link, make sure that, as the caregiver carries out your instructions, she reminds your youngster, "This is what Mommy would be doing if she were here now."

The second way you can enhance the evoked companion's soothing effect involves what you do when you get home. As your surrogate, the evoked companion has had a busy day healing, and it is important that you validate its healing powers now by doing all the things the child has imagined you doing: changing his sheets, reading a story to him, taking his temperature. This reinforcement, in effect, says to him, "See, what you were thinking today is right. Nothing is more important to Mommy than making you feel better."

4. *Guilt about not understanding every aspect of a child's behavior.* This is a by-product of both the superwoman and perfect mother models, since one point on which they both agree is that, like God, a good mother should have complete knowledge of her creations. Theologians call this attribute omniscience, and while it may be appropriate for the Almighty, who after all, as the song notes, is free to "roam around Heaven all day," a busy working mother who expects to exercise it is setting herself up not only for needless guilt but for depression and the kind of anger that can lead her to lash out unfairly at those around her. A story I heard from a woman in the audience of a television show I did recently in Portland, Oregon, provides a case in point.

Coming home one night, this woman said she was so upset to find her two-year-old lying silently on the floor by the side of his bed that she was about to yell at the caregiver. "I thought he was hurt or depressed, and Maryann [the caregiver] had just left him to lie there while she went into the kitchen to start dinner." When the woman got down beside her toddler, however, she discovered that his unsettling quietness had another and altogether different explanation. He was being so unearthly quiet because he didn't want to disturb the mouse who had somehow slipped under his bed and whose antics were now absolutely riveting him.

Accept the fact: some of the things a young child thinks and feels are inherently unknowable. And accept the fact, too, that as a working mother, sometimes you won't know things that you might have known if you had been there all day. There is nothing harmful or neglectful about this. What matters is not the capacity to understand and identify each and every behavior but the capacity to understand and identify behavioral patterns. Trust yourself enough to believe that if anything major does develop, you are sufficiently attuned to your youngster to spot a worrisome pattern quickly.

5.   *Guilt over imagined developmental failings.* More often than not, these failings revolve around high-profile benchmarks such as walking, talking, and toilet training. And they are usually imaginary because the woman who tells herself that if only she had stayed home, her six-month-old would be walking now, or her fourteen-month-old would be talking, or her twenty-month-old would be toilet trained, is putting the blame in the wrong place. With one major exception, there is no evidence that suggests maternal employment may be a contributing factor in developmental lags.

In the vast majority of instances, differences in development are linked to differences in central nervous system (CNS) growth. Just as some children are born with a full head of hair and others with none at all, some youngsters are born with an unusually mature CNS, which is why they walk and talk earlier, and others with an unusually immature system, which is why they walk or talk later. However, just as there is no correlation between baldness at one day or one month and IQ at age twenty, there is also no correlation between CNS maturity at birth and IQ at age twenty.

The only time work may be a factor in developmental lags is if it is overstressing the attachment bond. In environments perceived as insensitive, because they are either insecure or unpredictable, young children do have more difficulty acquiring the kind of learning that leads to developmental milestones like language acquisition or problem solving. In these cases, though, the presence of other signs of an attachment disorder, such as a pattern of clinging, regression, or avoidance, usually makes it easy to identify the true nature of the problem.

One thing a woman should not do if she suspects an attachment-related developmental lag is allow herself to become even more guilty. That will only make her responses to her child more uncertain and insecure. What she should do is go back and review the material in chapters 3, 4, and 5. Carefully followed, the advice in these chapters will help produce the kind of sensitive environment that encourages learning in a child. One other option to consider in these cases is a consultation with a child-care professional.

6. *Guilt about depriving your child of his inalienable right to a Golden Childhood.* This is a facet of the perfect mother myth in that the myth holds it a duty of every mother to provide her youngster with an idyllic youth. For the most part, the models for this childhood were established by the situation comedies today's working mothers grew up on, such as "Father Knows Best," "The Brady Bunch," and, of course, Paradise Lost itself, "Leave It to Beaver." None of the children in these shows was ever seen being rushed through breakfast by a busy mother or being dropped off at a day-care center or being put to bed by the caregiver because Mother was in Seattle on a business trip. And of course, whenever there was a special moment in one of their lives, like a school play, Mrs. Anderson, Mrs. Brady, and Mrs. Cleaver could be depended on to be there.

The impression left by these shows — especially on younger female viewers — was that whatever happened to be true in their own homes, what a mother really did all day was to interact with her child in ways that were always wise, insightful, and imaginative. Rarely was one of these television mothers seen preoccupied by a broken vacuum cleaner, an empty refrigerator, or a dirty floor. When researchers actually studied the behavior of real at-home mothers, however, they found not only that a great majority of their time was devoted to such chores but that doing them was so time consuming that, in terms of direct one-on-one exchanges with their children, at-home mothers spent roughly the same amount of time, ninety minutes per day, as working mothers.

The next time you are sitting in your office feeling vaguely guilty because you think the caregiver has put your two-year-old in front of "Sesame Street" again or has left him alone in his room to play while she starts dinner, remind yourself of this statistic. Also remind yourself that if you were at home, you probably would be doing the same thing. With the cooking, cleaning, and marketing to get through, you would be grateful if the television could preoccupy your toddler for an hour.

7. *Guilt over becoming angry, forgetting to say goodbye, or committing some other perceived maternal error.* One reason this kind of guilt is more common among working mothers is that they feel

they have less margin for the kind of normal and inevitable parental missteps that at-home mothers allow themselves. This is a
reflection of each group's different perception of time. While
at-home mothers believe in tomorrow and all the tomorrows after
that, on some level every working mother believes that she and her
child are involved in a kind of developmental countdown and zero
hour is only minutes away.

Adding further to her urgency is the sense that, once made, the
missteps will leave an indelible impression. This is a by-product of
what I called earlier the "trauma" theory of human development,
or the notion that the woman who loses her temper, or leaves a
tearful three-year-old on the doorstep the morning of a business
trip, is irreparably harming him. Infants and toddlers are remarkably resilient creatures; it is important for a working mother to
remind herself of that from time to time. Indeed, often, if a child
feels himself in a loving, sensitive environment, he won't even
notice an occasional misstep — like forgetting to say goodbye on a
hectic morning — and even if he does, it will be quickly forgotten.

8. *Guilt because the caregiver is more competent than you are.* On
the issue of caregivers, working mothers tend to be of two minds.
Although they want a person who is imaginative, lively, compan-
ionable, and skilled in the essentials of child care, great competence in these areas often produces profound maternal ambivalence. This is why a caregiver who turns out to have the magic
touch with chores like toothbrushing or hair combing often is as
likely to be a source of self-reproach as self-congratulation. "Why
can't I do that as well?" a woman wonders guiltily as she marvels at
the ease with which the new caregiver is able to get her youngster
to do something that normally gives her great trouble.

One thing not to do in such cases is allow this guilt to goad you
into a contest. This serves neither the caregiver, who will feel
herself undermined; the child, who won't get the care he otherwise
might because the caregiver will be afraid of intimidating you; nor
yourself, since it may lead you to overreact — turning a minor
issue like toothbrushing into a major contest of skill and will.
Remind yourself that in the world in which you and your child
live, the most appropriate measure of maternal competency is a

woman's ability to choose, oversee, and shape the care of her child, not her own skill at individual facets of it. You should remind yourself that, in choosing wisely and well for your youngster, you have exercised a competency far more important to his long-term growth than your ability to part his hair evenly.

Realizing this not only will make it easier to put your feeling about the caregiver into perspective but will make it easier to accept her as an ally, even a teacher. Caregivers have a great deal of expertise about the nursing aspects of child care, and guilt or jealousy shouldn't be allowed to stand in the way of a working mother's taking advantage of that expertise.

9. *Guilt because the caregiver is less competent than you are.* When a woman tells me she is concerned about her caregiver's competency, the first question I ask her is, "How are you defining competency?" What you should expect — indeed, demand — from a caregiver is competency in nursing chores like dressing, feeding, and toothbrushing. What you should also expect (and demand) from her is competency as a human being. She should make you feel that she can be trusted, and she should make your child feel that she understands him and is responsive to his needs. The best way to determine whether she possesses these qualities is by checking with the other families she has worked for and by insisting on a trial period before you hire her. If you are there with her, you will be able to judge firsthand how patient, flexible, and sensitive she is to your child and how competent she is at things like dressing or nap times. If you are not, observe your child's behavior closely in the evening. Does he make a smooth transition from the new caregiver to you? Is he alert and focused when you come home? Is he easy to interest and keep interested during your shared time together in the evening? (What not to pay attention to are his leave-taking protests; they will be sharper, and under the circumstances that is quite normal.) A child who is able to do all of these things is telling you that he likes the "fit" of his new care-giver.

What you should not expect from a caregiver is competency in those areas where you and other middle-class parents usually are very competent — such as language and problem solving — not only because you are unlikely to find a caregiver who can match you in these areas, but even more important, because in the first four years of life these abilities are directly flowing from the sense of belonging only a parent and child can have with each other.

10. *Guilt because you find some things more interesting than mothering.* Can you imagine a man rebuking himself because he found more pleasure in winning a new account than in diapering his ten-month-old? It is some measure of the depth of the double standard that continues to operate in American society that women often do. A great deal of child care is unexciting, even humdrum, particularly in comparison to the rewards of an exciting job. To deny this is to deny simple common sense. Adults need adult stimulation, and it is no reflection on your love for your child or on your maternal sensitivity to admit this. Adults also need, and are entitled to, a sense of validation. One of the best things about the recent growth of employment among women is that it has given millions of mothers an opportunity to validate themselves as human beings as well as parents. Certainly, that is nothing to feel guilty about.

11. *Guilt about returning to work too soon.* This is such a frequent source of guilt because, not having the superwoman's infallibility or the perfect mother's omniscience, most working women are unsure about just what constitutes the 'ideal time' to return to the office or factory. And all the conflicting advice they have received on this issue has only deepened their uncertainty. Should a mother listen to her company, which is so sure six to eight weeks postpartum is the right time to return to work that it usually cuts off paid maternity leave at that point? Or should she listen to the "experts"? And which experts? Those who advocate a return to work in the fourth month before the stranger anxiety, which can make a child's adjustment to a day-care setting more difficult, sets in? Or those who say wait until the fourteenth month, when the anxiety begins to abate? Or those authorities who ignore the issue of stranger anxiety entirely and declare the twelfth month the ideal time for a mother to begin thinking about going back to work?

The most objectionable thing about this is that it completely ignores the basic issue of economic need and the competition for jobs and job security. The primary duty of every parent is the maintenance of the family's security. If, in order to ensure it, you have to return to work in the fifth, fourth, or even third week postpartum, pride, not guilt, would be the appropriate maternal emotion.

I'm still not sure Nadine Robinson believes me, though. The most distressing thing about the finger pointing produced by the numbers game is what it does to a mother like Nadine. She works for a small clothing manufacturer, and like many small firms in the competitive garment industry, Nadine's company does not look favorably on work absences for any reason. Nadine was told to be back at her job within three weeks . . . the "or else" being left for her to fill in. Because Nadine is a single mother, and because she lives in one of the few major industrial nations that fail to completely protect their female citizens' job rights, Nadine felt she had no real choice. She was back at her cutter's bench three weeks, to the day, after her daughter, Dothlyn, was born.

We talked the day before her return. "I want Dothlyn's life to be better than mine," Nadine said. "Mine has been so hard. But now I'm not even going to be there to help give her the start I want her to have."

I told Nadine she was being unfair to herself. "Between nights and weekends, you will find you do have the time you need to be there, and be there in a way that will make an important difference to Dothlyn." As Nadine put on her coat, I also told her something else. "Someday," I said, "I'm sure Dothlyn will tell you herself how she feels about what you are doing now; but in the meantime, let me be her surrogate and tell you what I think she is going to say: 'I am very lucky to have a mother who is as brave, responsible, and resourceful as you are.'"

For women who, unlike Nadine, do enjoy the luxury of choice (however limited), the other major factor to be weighed in deciding when to return to work is the child's ability to stretch — the ability to master unfamiliar experience and stress without losing equilibrium. Our experience shows that the best measure of stretchability is whether growth is what we call *stage appropriate*. Is the child's behavior on target for the position he occupies in the growth cycle, including developing appropriate elements of humor, empathy, curiosity, and competence?

For example, you needn't and shouldn't feel guilty about leaving:

- *A three-month-old* who has developed a predictable daily cycle of feeding and nap times, shows an increasing ability to remain alert in interactions with you, and is easily soothed.
- *A six-month-old* who turns when his name is called, tries to imitate your facial expressions, has begun to develop preferences for particular foods and forms of play, sleeps throughout the night, and smiles predictably.
- *A nine-month-old* who cries when feeding time approaches (this shows the child is aware of the day's schedule), initiates play, chooses toys deliberately, and is able to hold his bottle and feed himself simple items such as crackers.
- *A one-year-old* who has developed sufficient understanding of body language to be able to communicate his thoughts and feelings to you through his smiles, frowns, hand gestures (pointing, for example), and body movements.
- *A two-year-old* who is able to tolerate the kind of minor stresses and frustrations that result when there is a short delay in dinner or at the door while you fumble for your keys, without breaking into tears or collapsing on the floor in anger. Another marker of normal development at this age is language; every month or two there should be a noticeable expansion in the two-year-old's vocabulary, new discoveries keeping company with a feisty stubbornness.
- *A three-year-old* who displays an increasingly well defined and assertive personality. By this stage, the child's awareness of his likes and dislikes should begin to be reflected in his behavior. For example, he should be asking you to read a particular book or to sing a favorite song. He should be trying to comfort you.
- *A four-year-old* who shows a growing interest in the world around him. One sign of this is that the preschooler will have

developed a circle of real friends. Also important is his ability
to self-comfort. By age four, every minor stress should not be a
source of tears, whining, or other forms of regressive behavior.

These stage-appropriate markers indicate that normal development is not being impeded by deep-seated or unresolved conflicts.
A child who is free of such conflicts will find it easy to make the
stretches his mother's work requires, whatever his age.

12. *Guilt because you are missing the "best years" of your child's
life.* The next time you find yourself sitting on the bus on a Monday morning feeling guilty about this, remind yourself of one
thing: without the satisfactions work provides for your adult side,
even the delights and charms of your two- or three-year-old would,
in time, begin to lose some of their specialness. Another thing to
tell yourself on such mornings is that your work — even if you do
it because you have to do it — represents a form of insurance for
your future. One day your child will, as all children do, grow up
and leave. What you are doing now ensures that on that day you
will still have an important source of validation and stimulation in
your life.

13. *Guilt about leaving your child behind when you go on vacation.*
Maternal myth and maternal reality also clash on the issue of
parental vacations, but in this case it is the myth in the form of the
superwoman model that whispers reassuringly, "Don't worry, the
child won't mind if you and your husband take off time alone."
Maternal reality, on the other hand, speaks with a less reassuring
voice on this point. While it concedes that a young child is capable
of a great many stretches, it points out that adding a week away to
the daily stretches work imposes can bring him to the absolute
limit of his endurance.

Does that mean parents should never vacation alone? My own
feeling is that during the first four years, except for two-day vacations, a child should always be taken along. Not only does this
avoid the risk of overstressing him, the time alone with Mother
and Father helps to instill what children with two working parents
may sometimes lack — a firm sense of family. Swimming, eating,
playing together — doing all the things families typically do on

vacations — encourage the infant or toddler to see himself as part of a larger unit. A way to ensure that there is also time for you and your husband is to bring along the caregiver. Her presence will enable the two of you to have a few nights out together or a few days alone on the beach.

To those readers who feel the vitality of their marriage requires occasional time alone with a spouse, I would advise two things. First, don't start with a seven-day vacation. That is too big a stretch to ask a young child to make all at once. He needs time to adjust to the idea of prolonged parental absences, and the best way to provide it is by beginning with two-day minivacations. Another way to help him adjust to prolonged separations is by having the caregiver, grandmother, or whoever will be looking after him stay at your house. The familiarity of the surroundings will provide an important form of reassurance at a time when the child needs it.

This, then, is the scientific case against the working mother's guilt. And if it can be said to conatin a single, clear message, it is that in developmental terms there is nothing about work that interferes with a woman's ability to give her child everything that child needs for healthy, happy growth. To put it in more colloquial terms: relax; you're okay; your child is okay — and so is your work.

11

Fathers
Your Support Team

GARDNER HALSEY stands six foot three and three-quarter inches in his L.L. Bean duck hat. The reason I happen to be in possession of this vital statistic is that one snowy February afternoon, Gardner and his duck hat measured themselves in my office. "This is only going to take a minute," Gardner assured me as he began peeling off his Wellington boots. I wanted to tell him that he needn't take off the slippers underneath but by that time Gardner already had the slippers off and the two pairs of socks underneath them. Instead I said, "I can see you want to be very accurate about this," as I watched the melted snow from Gardner's boots begin to form a puddle on my Persian rug. "Sorry about the mess," Gardner said, giving me his most solicitous smile. "Why don't you go over to the wall now so you can measure me in my hat?"

Actually, the incident was my fault. Knowing Gardner, I should have known that a remark about his new duck hat could lead anywhere. As my secretary, Jane, says whenever anyone tells her a new Gardner story, "Gardner is like that."

Jane, I should point out in fairness, usually is very discreet. I have known her for twelve years, and the only time I've ever heard her comment on a client was after her first encounter with Gardner. "You know," she said, wide-eyed, "he actually went, 'Harrumph.'"

John Nicholson, the child psychiatrist who works with Gardner and his wife, Sarah, describes Gardner as Dickensian. And there is a good deal of truth in John's observation. Gardner stays in mind for much the same reason Mr. Pickwick and Martin Chuzzlewit do. Whether it's the length of the stories he tells, the way he cocks his left eyebrow like a Victorian paterfamilias, or the unbridled enthusiasm he brings to everything he does — even measuring himself in a duck hat — Gardner has that larger-than-life quality that make so many of Dickens's creations memorable.

Sarah Halsey is as quiet as her husband is ebullient. She is also an unusually thoughtful woman, and if you watched her and Gardner together for any length of time, I think you would understand why I use that word. Around Gardner, Sarah functions as a good editor. She has thought a great deal about her husband's personality, and she knows how to help Gardner display his best self. Her touch shows up in the little things. If Gardner's stories always attract a large audience at our parenting gatherings, for example, it is because Sarah always is there hovering in the background, ready to interrupt unobtrusively when her husband's stories go from entertaining to overlong. Sarah Halsey's touch also is apparent in the larger things. I'm sure Gardner would be surprised to hear himself described as "sensitive" and "supportive"; those adjectives usually are applied to the New Man, and I'm not sure Gardner is even aware there is such a thing. Nonetheless, he is one of the most sensitive and supportive husbands and fathers I have met.

Usually, these qualities are defined in terms of the contributions a man makes around the house, and Gardner is unusually mindful about household chores. He washes the dinner dishes every night, does the laundry on Tuesdays, and takes care of the family marketing on Saturday. But the best measure of Gardner's sensitivity and support is the contribution he makes to Sarah's mothering. Sarah never feels herself undercut or cast in the role of the disciplinarian the way some women do because their husbands don't share their concerns about things like bedtime schedules and proper diet. Gardner knows how hard Sarah has worked to establish a regular eight-thirty bedtime for three-year-old Peter Halsey. And so in the hour leading up to that bedtime, he avoids roughhousing or other forms of physical play that will leave his son too stimulated to fall asleep.

Gardner is as staunch in his support of Sarah's dietary concerns — not so much because he thinks an occasional ice cream, brownie, or Coke will harm his son (as, I suspect, he secretly believes his wife does), but because he knows that if he gives in and buys the occasional ice cream, in time Peter will divide his parents between the Good Guy who buys him treats and the Bad Guy who makes him eat his carrots and peas. As much as Gardner wants to be seen as a good guy by his son, he doesn't want to do it at his wife's expense.

Gardner is an example of what we call a "willing father." What distinguishes men like him isn't that they are especially attuned to the new feminist consciousness, but simply that they are open to change and growth. Three years ago, Gardner Halsey knew very little about how to be a supportive husband, but what he did possess was a desire to do everything he could to help his working wife. Larry Cruickshank, the other man you will meet in this chapter, is an example of a "reluctant father." And what distinguishes men like Larry isn't that they are more wedded to a swaggering macho ethic or that they love their wives less, but that they find the challenges of parenting so threatening to their self-image that they withdraw into themselves.

What gives the stories of these two different individuals a wider resonance is that as with the mothers we met in chapter 8, Gardner and Larry are representative types. Like them, most of the men we see at the Early Care Center can be categorized as either willing or reluctant fathers. The purpose of presenting their stories here is to acquaint you with these two types and, more important, to show you how to shape your requests for assistance in ways that will appeal to the willing or reluctant father in your spouse.

GARDNER HALSEY: THE WILLING FATHER

Gardner knows that Sarah is as forthright in assessing her own strengths and weaknesses as she is in assessing his — and is as shrewd in dealing with them. That's why he became so concerned when, during her sixth month of pregnancy, Sarah began expressing doubts about being a working mother — and also why, after Peter's birth, he agreed so readily when Sarah suggested that they join REAP.

I think Sarah's concerns about her ability to cope with the demands of working motherhood were, to an extent, justified. Stylistically, she is a worrier, and, without the help she received in the program, the proneness to guilt and tunnel vision inherent in that style might have made her transition to the role of working mother a difficult one. I also think, however, that being in the program benefited her in another, more subtle way. I suspect a good deal of the confidence we began to see in Sarah as the months passed grew out of her realization that while REAP might have much to teach her in other areas, in one area she had already achieved mastery on her own.

The term *willing father* may have been new to her, but well before joining the program Sarah had sensed that this was the category her husband belonged in, and — more centrally — well before joining the program, she also had sensed that one of the few things that will make a willing father less willing to help is subtly imposing conditions on his offers of assistance. So immediately after Peter's birth, Sarah had made a promise to herself: before asking Gardner for help, she would sort through her own feelings and try to identify any needs and conflicts in her that might make her resist that help.

One potential trouble spot, she decided, could be her jealousy about sharing parental authority. "My mother had been the authority figure in my family, and a part of me always wanted to be like her," Sarah told me one afternoon. "But I knew that if I tried to exercise the kind of control over Peter that my mother had exercised over my brother and me, Gardner would react the same way my father had — he would withdraw into himself. You can't ask a man to share the responsibility of raising a child and not also allow him to share in the decision making."

On joining the program, Sarah discovered that we have a formal name for the self-examination she had conducted in the hospital. We call it *examining ambivalences,* and usually it is the first thing we suggest when a woman complains to us that her husband isn't doing enough. If you ask a working mother, "In what areas could your husband be contributing more?" most often she will reply, "In every area." But frequently, when we sit down with a woman and her husband and examine the nature of her wants carefully, we find that one reason her husband isn't doing more is that her behavior is full of mixed messages. And mixed messages will drive even the most willing fathers away.

Sam Ratner is a case in point. One Saturday, not long ago, his puzzled wife, Deborah, spent half an hour in my office describing Sam's change of heart to me and to John Nicholson. "For the first six months after Anna's birth, Sam was a dream," Deborah said. "I didn't have to ask him to do a thing. If Anna's diaper was wet, he would change it without being asked to, or if the dishes needed to be done, he'd do them, even if he knew I wasn't busy. Then one day, suddenly, Sam just stopped. Now, no matter how much I complain or threaten, I can barely get him to lift a finger."

Sam Ratner, who was sitting next to his wife on the couch listening, interrupted at this point. "Deb," he said with some heat, "the reason I stopped helping is that it became very clear to me that you didn't want my help. Taking out the garbage was all right, but when it came to decisions about Anna and her care, you were very territorial. Look at the way 'we' decided on a day-care center for her. You came home one night and announced that 'we' found the perfect center. I didn't even get a chance to offer an opinion. You just laid the decision out in front of me and said, 'Here it is, pal.' That's not fair."

"Oh, I see," said Deborah. "How stupid of me. I should have realized it was my fault that you don't get up when Anna starts crying in the middle of the night. Poor, brave you. I don't know how you've managed to put up with me."

This time I thought I had better interrupt. I told Deborah: "I don't think Sam is trying to criticize you. I think he's just trying to tell you that he's been made to feel his help really isn't wanted. I know there are certain areas of parenting that are very important to you; they are to every mother. But the only way a woman is going to receive the support she needs is by making her husband want to give it. And one of the ways she creates this desire is by making him feel that *all* his contributions are welcome. The husband who is told, 'You can help me here, but not here,' is, in effect, being told he has second-class parenting rights. Imagine how you would react to this message. Men aren't any different."

The reason the Halseys have avoided such conflicts, and the reason each feels deeply invested in the decisions that have been made about Peter and his care, is that Sarah and Gardner have developed a democratic way of presenting problems to one another. Often, when a husband or wife feels strongly about a problem or issue, he or she will describe it and a solution all in the same sentence. Gardner and Sarah are more open with one another. Even when they do have a deeply felt opinion, each Halsey is careful to put aside that opinion when they describe the issue or problem under consideration. They describe the facts of the case as clearly and objectively as possible, and then ask the other, "What do you think?"

Usually, Sarah and Gardner find themselves in agreement, but even when they don't, this democratic style always gives their discussion an open, give-and-take quality. A good example was the issue they faced of whether Peter should be put on antihistamines. In reporting why Dr. Levin, Peter's allergist, felt the antihistamines were needed, Sarah kept her own reservations about this recommendation in abeyance. She told Gardner what the allergist had said and then, when she found that Gardner didn't share her concern that the side effects of the drugs might be worse for Peter than the hay fever itself, she listened to his arguments for supporting Dr. Levin. The reason Gardner left the discussion that evening feeling validated had less to do with the decision that was finally reached — a compromise: Peter would stay off the antihistamines for now, but go on them if his hay fever worsened — than with the fact that everything about Sarah's behavior had said to him, "Your opinion is welcomed, valued, and respected."

John Nicholson, the REAP staff member who has worked most closely with the Halseys at the Early Care Center, believes Sarah's openness and receptivity are an important reason why Gardner has been so supportive of her on issues like Peter's bedtime and diet. "I don't think Gardner worries particularly about Peter's ice cream consumption or his bedtime," John said at a staff meeting one day. "But I do think he sees these concerns as part of a larger network of family goals. And he feels very proprietary about that network because he has had an important voice in shaping it."

John, who probably comes closest to being our resident expert on fathers, believes that when it comes to actually enlisting the aid of a willing father in household and child-care chores, the best method is to encourage and build on the gestures of support the man offers on his own. "There are certain instances where preparing a list of formal duties may be appropriate," John notes, "but in the case of men like Gardner, demands are usually counterproductive." I agree, and I think you might, too, if you imagine how unappreciated you would feel if, on coming forward to help, you were immediately handed a list of duties instead of being thanked.

I also agree with John that the best way to build on the gestures of support a willing father offers is through your *praise*. Compliments provide a way of gracefully easing a man from a general eagerness to help to a specific commitment to help with clearly defined chores. Betsy Farley, one of our REAP mothers, was especially skilled at using her praise this way. After the birth of the Farleys' daughter, Eleanor, Betsy was touched and pleased by husband Michael's efforts to aid her; but the efficiency expert in Betsy also felt that Michael's efforts would be of a lot more value if, instead of flitting from chore to chore each night, he committed himself to certain household duties.

Betsy briefly entertained the idea of trying to obtain this commitment via a formal division of the family's child care and domestic chores, but after giving it some thought she decided the best medium for harnessing Michael's eagerness and energy would be her praise. So gradually, through her compliments, she began to focus Michael's attention on the two areas where she felt his help would contribute most: clearing the dinner dishes and giving Eleanor her nightly bath. Whenever Michael took the initiative in either area, Betsy would go out of her way to praise him, and whenever there was more than a two- or three-day lapse between shows of initiative, Betsy would make it a point to tell Michael what a big help it had been last Thursday when he removed the dinner dishes from the table or bathed Eleanor. It has been nearly a year since Betsy last had to use one of her compliments as a reminder, however. Between the Farleys, there is now an understanding that these two tasks are Michael's responsibilities, and, as Betsy notes, the best thing about the understanding is the way it has developed.

Since even willing fathers like Michael and Gardner tend to have a narrow idea of the different forms love can take, praise also can be used to educate and enlighten. From childhood on, men have been taught to think of their work and the money it provides as a way of saying "I love you" to a wife, but often what has to be pointed out to even the most eager and supportive male is that picking up after a child or taking out the garbage also says "I love you." Compliments are a way of acquainting a man with this fact.

I don't know if Gardner Halsey would describe Sarah's praise as a form of education. But if Gardner were asked, "Have you always checked the refrigerator before leaving for work in the morning?" I'm sure he would say no. Gardner would probably even admit that the idea hadn't occurred to him until the night he came home with a quart of milk and found himself praised to the skies for his thoughtfulness because Sarah had meant to pick up some milk on her way home but then had forgotten.

I'm also sure that if Sarah were asked if there was any one thing she said or did that was instrumental in inspiring her husband's morning refrigerator checks, she would point to a conversation the Halseys had had the following night while they were sitting on the living room couch deciding whether or not to stay up and watch David Letterman. "I mentioned the milk, and told Gardner it had been very sweet of him to check the refrigerator the morning before to see if we needed anything for dinner. I don't know whether it's just that we're both more relaxed or that things sound different when we're snuggled up together in front of the TV. But I have found that in intimate moments Gardner hears me in ways he doesn't hear me at other times."

Another conversation also stands out in Sarah Halsey's mind with a special clarity. It occurred one hot summer night in the middle of Peter's thirteenth month, and the reason it remains so vivid to Sarah two years later is that she believes it changed the way

Gardner sees Peter and the way he sees his own role in Peter's life. Most of the deeper pleasures of parenting arise from its nurturing aspects. The satisfaction of knowing you can soothe a child in a special way or please him not only is deeply validating, but also exercises an elemental pull on a parent. The more parents find that they can do for a child, the more they want to do. Because of the different ways they are socialized, women know this but men don't. They have to be helped to discover it. This particular conversation stands out so clearly in Sarah's mind because she thinks of it as the turning point — the moment that Gardner first began to discover the deeper joys of being a nurturer.

Sarah is modest in describing her role in facilitating this discovery. She says that it was more out of desperation than anything else that she handed Peter over to Gardner on that summer night. "He was very colicky, and nothing I did seemed to help. Peter just kept crying and crying." Sarah also says the praise she lavished on Gardner ten minutes later when Peter fell asleep in his arms was entirely free of ulterior motives. "I really was honestly delighted to find that Gardner had been able to comfort Peter in a way I couldn't." But Sarah does admit that the special look of pride she saw on Gardner's face when she told him this made her stop and think. So a month later, when she noticed that Peter responded more readily to his father's "no" than to hers, she mentioned this to Gardner. And three weeks after that, when she noticed that Peter also put up less of a fuss when he was dressed by his father, this difference was mentioned. Thereafter, what Sarah calls a "multiplier effect" developed: the more Gardner found he could do with Peter, the more he wanted to do.

Often, when a man becomes as deeply involved in his child's life as Gardner is involved in Peter's, he is responding not only to what he sees, hears, and is told but to what he remembers. Part of the deep satisfaction of succoring a hurt, confused, or upset child is that a part of us remembers how good it felt when, at three or four and in distress or pain, we were held and comforted by a loving parent.

One of Gardner's most cherished memories of his boyhood is the night his father arrived in his hospital room with a chocolate ice cream soda. "The doctor had taken out my tonsils that morning and I still remember how cool and smooth the ice cream felt in my throat," Gardner said the afternoon he told me his story. Gardner usually isn't physically affectionate with Peter in front of me, but as he began describing his father's visit, he reached down and picked up Peter, who was playing on the floor, placed him in his lap, and began to stroke his forehead. I'm not sure Gardner was aware of what he'd done — he seemed suddenly to be in another moment, one that had happened long ago and far away — and at three, Peter couldn't be expected to understand the reason for his father's tenderness. But on some level, conscious or unconscious, the memory of that tenderness is going to stay with Peter just as the memory of his father's visit has stayed with Gardner.

Every man has memories like this one, and they also can be used to put him in touch with his nurturing side. Protests about not having enough time to drop Margaret off at school or take her to the dentist's office on Saturday often will vanish when the protester is reminded of how proud he felt on the days when *his* father accompanied him to school, or how much more bravely he had faced the dentist's chair when Dad's hand was there to hold.

From our perspective, the most remarkable thing about Sarah and Gardner Halsey's story is that it really isn't very remarkable at all. Most of the men we see at the center love their wives and, we find, with a little encouragement and a little learning most of them will readily translate that love into the kind of effective practical support a working mother needs. Admittedly, there are some exceptions to this rule, and although some of the exceptions are rooted in the kind of marital difficulties that require professional guidance, more often when openness and praise don't work the reason is simpler and more easily remediable. The man feels threatened by the emotions fatherhood produces in him. Larry Cruickshank is a case in point.

LARRY CRUICKSHANK: THE RELUCTANT FATHER

You know Larry. He was the boy you sat next to in sixth grade who awed you and your friend Mary Ann Donahue by building a television set for the class's science project and who, by high school, had

advanced to building home computers. The years haven't changed
Larry much. He still is thin, still wears short-sleeved dress shirts
with a plastic pencil holder clipped to the breast pocket, and still
has one of those pleasantly bland faces that would make it easy to
mistake him for the manager of the local K mart. You won't be
surprised to learn that Larry has grown up to be an electrical
engineer or that he waited until relatively late, thirty-six, to become a father. As you recall, in his own quiet, methodical way
Larry always was ambitious. I am also sure you won't be surprised
to learn that Larry approached fatherhood in the same spirit he
approached the building of the television set he made for your
class's science project — as a problem to be solved.

The story of how Larry Cruickshank became a reluctant father is
the story of the limitations of this problem-solving approach. That
Larry's is a fairly common story also says something about how
poorly many of the values and qualities we stress in males equip
them for fatherhood. One of these qualities is a mechanistic cognitive style. Larry may be an extreme example, but men generally
are taught to approach a task, a person, or a problem with their
minds and not their hearts. This approach may be useful for analyzing the rights and wrongs of a football play, but it doesn't get a
man very far with a four-year-old who is carrying on about a minor
bump or scrape.

Having a more emotionally attuned style, a woman usually
knows what is behind the four-year-old's operatic behavior. She
knows that it isn't pain but a desire for an extra, reassuring hug.
And she also knows that, even from a strictly utilitarian point of
view, the quickest way to bring his tears to an end is to give him
that extra hug. A mechanistic style often blinds a man to this
simple emotional truth. He can see that his son's cut is minor, and
he has already given him one hug. In his mind, that should be that.
When it isn't, he begins to get angry and frustrated, and a vicious
cycle of misunderstanding develops. "Stop that; you are carrying
on like a baby," the man snaps, which of course only makes his
four-year-old cry all the harder. And that, in turn, increases his
own frustration and anger.

Male notions of mastery often don't translate well into fathering skills, either. Above all, what a young child needs is a notion of parental mastery that is flexible enough to realize that sometimes a young child can't be mastered. A case in point is the cranky six-month-old who usually can be lulled back to sleep with a bottle, some gentle rocking, or a soft song, but who tonight for some reason resists all these usually effective remedies and continues crying. One of the reasons men are so quick to give up on nursing chores like soothing, feeding, and bathing is that male expertise-oriented ideas of mastery don't allow for such lapses. Once mastered, a person, place, or thing is supposed to stay mastered. When it doesn't, a man feels more than upset — he feels incompetent. And there are few emotions more threatening to a male — particularly to a middle-class male — than incompetence.

Harvard psychologist Samuel Osherson believes that if you scratch a reluctant father, often you find underneath a confused, insecure man who can't understand why the skills and attitudes he had been taught since boyhood and that work so effectively in other areas of his life don't work when he applies them to parenting. "This breakdown is deeply threatening to a man's idea of himself as a competent, masterful individual," says Dr. Osherson, "and the way many men deal with it is by withdrawing into those areas like work where their skills continue to be effective."

I agree with Dr. Osherson's analysis, and I think Maggie Cruickshank would as well. Knowing Larry as well as she does, it didn't particularly surprise Maggie that, at first, he was a bit stiff with their new daughter, Suzanne. Maggie even found it funny when Diane Somers, one of the other copywriters at her ad agency, joked that, watching Larry hold Suzanne, Diane understood why Richard Nixon stopped having his picture taken with babies. Larry's manner might be mechanical, but underneath Maggie knew what a tender and loving man her husband was. And she imagined that in his own methodical way Larry would set out to win Suzanne over as determinedly as he had set out to win her over.

Things didn't work out quite the way Maggie had anticipated, though. The first hint of trouble came in Suzanne's sixth week, when Larry began making jokes about his competence as a bather and diaperer. Maggie had never heard him do that before; prowess in any endeavor was not a subject Larry tended to treat lightly. So Maggie wasn't altogether surprised when, a few weeks later, Larry began to back away from his commitment to help with nursing chores like bathing and feeding. Maggie told me later that her first impulse had been to protest this withdrawal, but after thinking about it she decided to say nothing. "I felt these weren't the kinds of tasks you could reasonably expect a man to like," she said, "and I suppose a part of me believed that when Suzanne got a little older and came to seem more like a real person to Larry, he'd begin to take a more active part in her care again."

Instead, as the months passed, Larry grew increasingly remote. Work had always been an important part of his life, but now it seemed to occupy every moment. "I feel like I've become a single parent," Maggie complained to him one night in Suzanne's tenth month. Larry shrugged noncommittally, which she knew was his way of saying, "I don't want to talk about it."

"I think I could have learned to handle Suzanne pretty much on my own; I even think I could have put up with the awful sulk Larry went into," Maggie said, the afternoon she talked about this difficult time with me. "But what I decided I couldn't and shouldn't put up with was Larry's criticisms."

These began shortly after Suzanne's first birthday, and initially, they puzzled Maggie. "It was very out of character for Larry," she said. "He had never criticized me before. Now, suddenly, I couldn't do anything right in his eyes — especially with Suzanne." Gradually, Maggie realized that it wasn't her diapering style ("You pin them too tight," Larry complained) or the toys she bought ("Suzanne won't learn anything from them," Larry said) that was troubling her husband, but something more fundamental. Suzanne's birth had reversed the roles they played with one another. "For the first time in our relationship," Maggie said, "I was the authoritative, competent partner who knew how to do things right, and Larry was the uncertain one who had to turn to me for help. He was criticizing me because he was resentful — even a little jealous of me."

A generation ago, a story like Larry Cruickshank's very likely would have ended in one of two ways — each of them equally sad. Either Larry would have reverted to his earlier, joking pattern, turning himself into one of those bumbling, inept sitcom dads so beloved by television writers or — more likely in Larry's case — he would have continued retreating into himself until he became a remote, forbidding figure to his wife and daughter, someone they had to learn to "handle" rather than simply love. Earlier generations of men have made both stereotypes almost synonymous with the word fatherhood. But thanks largely to the influence of the women's movement, over the last fifteen years men have grown as unhappy with these images of themselves as parents as women have always been. Today, even reluctant fathers like Larry aspire to be a part of what writer Bob Greene *(Good Morning, Merry Sunshine)* calls the "New Order of the Snugli."

Larry's induction into this order was a twenty-month process, and it began one June morning when he and Maggie visited the center for a consultation. Rarely do support system problems alone bring a family to REAP, and the Cruickshanks were no exception. As she talked that morning, it was clear that Maggie was as concerned about structuring and shaping her own optimistic style as she was about Larry's lack of support. So the variation of REAP that we created for the Cruickshanks focused on two goals. While we showed Maggie how to add a measure of predictability and order to her behavior, we helped Larry liberate himself from those aspects of his style we felt were interfering with his ability to be a happy, confident father.

Not long ago, Dr. Ron Levant, director of the Fatherhood Project at Boston University, noted that men tend to take an expertise-oriented, problem-solving approach to parenting by default. "It isn't that males are blind to the part that qualities like tenderness and nurturingness play in good parenting," said Dr. Levant, "but very little in a man's upbringing teaches him how to draw on these sides of himself." Other fathering experts agree, and they also agree with Dr. Levant that one of the best ways for a man to learn how to begin tapping the more emotional aspect of his persona is by sitting and observing his wife with their child.

Larry was skeptical when I pointed this out to him. "What good will it do?" he asked, almost annoyed the Saturday morning I said I wanted him to start devoting a half hour three times a week to observing Maggie with Suzanne. "One important thing you will learn from your watching," I said, "is how to just be with your daughter. Some of the most magical moments a parent and child share occur when they are simply gazing into one another's eyes or holding hands. Maggie's very good at creating these moments with Suzanne because she enjoys their intimacy and tenderness. But you are missing out on them because these emotions make you feel uneasy. Like most men, you tend to get uncomfortable when you're required to feel instead of do."

To illustrate my point, I reminded Larry of an interaction I had observed between him and Suzanne, who was sixteen months at the time, several weeks earlier. "As long as you had a book to read or a toy to play with, you were reasonably relaxed with her. But when Suzanne pushed aside the Busy Box the two of you were playing with and began gazing into your eyes, you suddenly became very uncomfortable. Instead of enjoying the moment with her, you began looking around for ways to distract her." For a moment Larry was quiet, as if he was trying to decide how incriminating it would be to admit his culpability. Then he gave me a half-embarrassed smile and said, "You're right. Suzanne's staring did make me uneasy."

"Not staring," I said, "gazing. There is an important difference, you know."

"Yes, I suppose there is," Larry replied. "I guess that's one of the things watching Maggie can teach me."

I told him another important thing I thought he could learn from observing her is how to read and respond to Suzanne more sensitively. One of the principal drawbacks of the man's mechanistic cognitive style is that it can blind him to the emotionally complex messages behind a child's behavior. A case in point is the way Larry responded when Suzanne deserted his lap during the exchange I just mentioned. Such temporary desertions are common among toddlers who are taking their first tentative steps toward independence, but these desertions are governed by an important ground rule. No matter what, the parent is never supposed to break visual contact with the child. The reason Suzanne burst into tears midway through her journey to the slide is that, when she looked back, she saw her father was ignoring this rule. Instead of following her with his eyes as Suzanne had expected, Larry was absorbed in a newspaper he had found lying nearby.

There was nothing malicious in Larry's behavior, of course. Indeed, from the analytical male perspective his response was commonsensical. Suzanne was off, absorbed in her exploration; therefore, he could read the paper. Similarly, from a female perspective, it was equally commonsensical for Maggie to continue following Suzanne with her eyes when confronted with a similar desertion in the playroom an hour earlier. Having been taught, as women are, to pay as much attention to the emotions behind a behavior as to the behavior itself, Maggie knew that Suzanne would expect her explorations to be covered by a visual safety net, and so Maggie had provided it.

Besides watching his wife, another way a man can enhance his parenting skills is by spending more time exercising them in direct, one-on-one exchanges with his child. "But it's nearly impossible to get Larry to spend ten minutes alone with Suzanne now," Maggie protested when I said we wanted him to start setting aside half an hour a day for time alone with Suzanne. I told her I realized that. But I also told her about some interesting research that had been done several years ago by Dr. Levant and his colleagues at the Fatherhood Project. They had found that a man's receptivity to the idea of increasing one-on-one time with his child was largely determined by the way this proposal was put to him. If it came in the form of a warning or if the proposal was put in the kind of highly emotional language men feel uncomfortable with, a father usually resisted. But if the proposal was presented as a kind of exercise in skills training, not too different from the kind of skills training he underwent when he learned a new sport or job, the father agreed willingly.

I told Maggie that this is how John Nicholson and I had presented the idea of spending more time alone with Suzanne to Larry. We had described the one-on-one time as part of an exercise in skills training. I also told her that to emphasize further the masculine style of our proposal we had suggested that after each session, Larry should write down his impression of the exchange in a notebook the way he might write down his impressions of a talk by a colleague.

"You mean you gave him a security blanket to hold onto in case Suzanne touches an emotion he's uncomfortable with?" asked Maggie.

I conceded that that was one possible construction that might be put on the use of the notebook. But I said that, like the investigators at the Fatherhood Project who had pioneered this technique, we had found that note taking also had the practical benefit of helping to enhance a man's sensitivity. Reviewing his notes later, often a father will identify emotional messages that he missed during the exchange, so he will be more alert to those messages the next time. "The notes will also help him make more effective use of your advice," I told Maggie. "I'm sure that there have been many times when Larry has been puzzled by Suzanne's behavior and would have asked you about it if he hadn't forgotten. Writing his thoughts and impressions in a notebook is a way of ensuring he won't forget anymore."

"It sounds like I'm being appointed Larry's parental adviser," Maggie said.

"In a way, you are," I replied, "but a very special kind of adviser. Larry already has all the tenderness and sensitivity he needs to be a loving father. The purpose of your counseling and example-setting with Suzanne is to help him *discover* these qualities in himself, not to teach him how to parent more like you. You're going to find that he will do things with Suzanne you wouldn't do. Some of the things he does might even upset you. For example, he is probably going to play more roughly with her than you would like. You can suggest he be a little more gentle, but don't put your suggestion into the form of criticism or instructions. Larry's insecurities about his parenting skills are what made him withdraw from Suzanne in the first place; criticizing those skills will only make him retreat again. Only when he finds a parenting style that feels comfortable to him is he going to become an important presence in Suzanne's life and a help to you."

One other recommendation we often make to the wives of reluctant fathers is that they increase their spouses' exposure to men they think will serve as good role models of a willing father. And, indeed, those of us who worked with the Cruickshanks at the center feel that many of the dramatic changes we began to see in Larry had as much to do with his growing friendship with Gardner Halsey as with the strategies we had shown him and Maggie. The idea of bringing the Halseys and Cruickshanks together originated with John Nicholson, who brought it up one Wednesday morning at a staff meeting. Knowing how different Gardner and Larry are from one another, I have to admit I had some doubts about this suggestion. And from the number of "Odd Couple" jokes that were heard around the table that morning, most of the staff shared my skepticism.

Nonetheless, John persevered and arranged a date between the Cruickshanks and the Halseys. The reports that came back to me in the months that followed were encouraging. At another staff meeting seven weeks later, John reported that the couples had seen one another several times. He also said that Maggie believed Gardner's influence was having an effect. She felt Larry was becoming more attentive to Suzanne, and more sensitive to the meanings behind Suzanne's behavior. At a parents' meeting a few weeks after John's report, Sarah also told me she thought Gardner was having a good influence on Larry. But not having heard from the most central figure in the arrangement, I still wasn't entirely convinced. Then one evening on the way to my health club, I ran into Larry on the street. Even before he spoke, I knew John's idea had been a huge success.

Larry was wearing a duck hat.

12

Caregivers
Your Other Support Team

IT DOESN'T TAKE A new working mother much more than a week of interviewing potential candidates to understand why the other working mothers she talks to devote so much time, attention, and concern to the issue of caregivers. Occasionally, in the course of her interviewing, this new working mother may discover the Mary Poppins ideal she has been dreaming about since the moment she learned she was pregnant. But if her experience is typical, usually what she is going to meet in her interviews are young women who, although often willing and eager and sometimes possessing great potential, are far from the wise, experienced, and articulate ideal she has been envisioning in her mind's eye.

The caregiver dilemma — or as some of our mothers have described it, the caregiver crisis — is why we decided to add a new component to REAP in 1983. The Mary Poppinses may be few and far between and, when found, often prohibitively expensive, but a woman who knows how to hire and, even more important, how to manage and train her child's caregiver can create her own Mary Poppins. And that is what the caregiver component of the program teaches our REAP mothers to do.

At the center, the tools we use to foster this skill are a battery of psychological tests and videotape and training sessions, but the key to helping a caregiver grow and learn lies less in technology or special tests than it does in patience, empathy, articulateness, understanding, and the other human qualities you and millions of working mothers like you already possess in abundance. In this chapter, we will show you how to organize these skills into a plan of caregiver orientation and training. The plan is designed primarily for the woman with an inexperienced caregiver, but it also can be used to help a good caregiver become even better.

The plan's starting point is the criteria we have developed for selecting a caregiver. No amount of skill on your part will be of use unless the person you hire possesses the potential to grow in her job. And one important source for gauging this potential is the recommendations she brings with her. Most mothers use these recommendations as a way of checking an applicant's honesty and reliability, but in talking to her last employer, you should also ask about the applicant's imagination. How creative and inventive a playmate is she? Her nimbleness in emergencies and ability to describe problems clearly also should be carefully explored, since quick-wittedness and articulateness are reliable benchmarks of a person's native ability.

Equally important, ask the applicant's last employer if she was sometimes made to feel shut out or excluded from her child's life by the caregiver. Surrogates with a history of this kind of overprotective behavior usually see themselves as saviors whose primary mission in life is to rescue their neglected charges from their thoughtless working mothers. Technically this syndrome is known as "rescue fantasizing," and not only will an applicant with a proneness to it be incapable of the kind of growth and development you will want to foster in your child's caregiver, but very likely she will be a problem — possibly a big problem. Cross her off your list of likely candidates.

Applicants who evidence a deep commitment to authoritarian child-rearing values also should be dropped from your list. Coming from more rigid, tradition-oriented cultures, many of the women you interview will have a more authoritarian outlook on child rearing than you do. A certain degree of authoritarianism is permissible — even beneficial when it comes to things like struc-

ture and scheduling — but a caregiver with a deep commitment to
an authoritarian style is not going to be capable of the kind of
growth that will allow her to master the more open, democrati-
cally oriented style you want to use in raising your child.

The best way of measuring an applicant's potential for growth
and change is by observing her over an extended period of time.
Most of the women you interview will resist the idea of a trial
period. And if the applicant you have in mind has had extensive
experience as a caregiver and comes to you with a box full of
glowing recommendations, you can probably safely waive this
requirement. But if this is the candidate's first, second, or even
third experience as a caregiver, you should make her employment
conditional on a two-week trial period.

What you should be looking for in these weeks depends on
where you are. If you have taken some vacation time to be at home
or you haven't yet returned to work, pay particularly close attention to how fast — or slow — the candidate is in getting down
your child's day and its routines, how good she is at amusing and
stimulating him, and, most important of all, the degree of insight
she displays when she talks about him. After a week and certainly
after two, she should be evidencing some knowledge of his personality, moods, and likes and dislikes.

One way of assessing the competency of a candidate who will be
at home alone with your child during the trial period is via the
evening reports she provides on your return from work. Are her
reports detailed and factual? More important, do they seem true to
your child's personality? If the two-year-old you encounter in her
nightly briefings seems to bear little relation to the two-year-old
you know, the candidate probably is having trouble understanding your youngster. Another way of assessing an applicant's competence if you will be working during the trial period is by noticing
how hard or easy she makes it for you to leave in the morning. One
distinguishing characteristic of a very good caregiver is that she
can sense when a child is about to succumb to a case of leave-taking blues and distracts him before those blues lead to tears. The
homecoming greeting you receive — from the candidate and from
your child — also can be revealing. If the two of them are involved

in a game when you walk in the door, does the caregiver ask you to join them or does she seem to shut you out? A caregiver who does the latter probably is harboring rescue fantasies and should not be hired. Also, how alert is your infant or toddler during the transition? As I pointed out earlier, one other mark of a skilled surrogate is that she always hands over a focused and alert youngster.

Once you have settled on a caregiver, the next step is helping her grow into the warm, sensitive, loving companion you want for your child. One element that is absolutely essential to facilitating this transformation is knowledge. Your choice should have a thorough and complete understanding of your child and the behavioral principles and values you consider most important to his upbringing. During the interview process and in the trial period, you probably will have thoroughly briefed her on your youngster's likes and dislikes, identified the kinds of soothing he responds to, and described how he acts when he is especially pleased or displeased. But your new caregiver will be much quicker to understand and begin applying these important pieces of intelligence if you also take the time to demonstrate behaviorally the points you have made to her verbally.

We call this technique *active demonstration*. To illustrate how it works, let me tell you a story I was told recently by Rhoda Salmons, one of our REAP mothers. It concerns Rhoda's thirteen-month-old daughter, Micheala, and Micheala's best friend, True Heart (one of the Care Bears). Over the months, Rhoda has learned that one nearly foolproof way to soothe a cranky or whiny Micheala is to animate True Heart into a song and dance. Seeing her best friend suddenly spring to life so delights Micheala that she usually can be relied on to forget whatever is upsetting her.

Before going back to work, Rhoda was careful to describe the soothing effect of True Heart's songs and dances to Micheala's new caregiver, Fina Santos. So initially Rhoda was puzzled when Fina complained that True Heart's vaudevillian routine didn't work for her. No matter how actively she animated the bear, Fina said, it had no effect on Micheala. Rhoda thought a great deal about this discrepancy but was at a loss to explain it until one afternoon, coming home early from work, she found Fina bouncing True Heart back and forth across the living room rug like a jumping bean.

That this hyperactive True Heart was having no effect on Micheala, who was sitting in a corner under a window, quietly sad, didn't surprise Rhoda. One of the things she had noticed about the bear's performances is that the slower his dances and the softer his songs, the more soothing his effect on Micheala. Rhoda thought she had explained this carefully to Fina. "I had made a point of telling Fina that if True Heart's song and dance routines became too raucous they upset Micheala," Rhoda said when she described this incident to me.

Not wanting to undercut Fina in front of Micheala, Rhoda also told me that she was reluctant to intervene on that afternoon. But seeing that True Heart's antics were making Micheala more and more upset, she decided she had to do something. As gently as possible she said to Fina, "Why don't you give me True Heart for a moment? If we slow him down a bit I think Micheala will enjoy him more."

"Fina wasn't exactly thrilled by my suggestion," Rhoda noted. "But as she watched me put True Heart through a series of slow pirouettes that landed him up onto Micheala's lap, and then saw the expression on Micheala's face when I made him begin serenading her, with some soft songs, Fina's attitude changed. By the end of True Heart's performance she was smiling as happily as Micheala."

Often, when a mother like Rhoda Salmons asks us for help with a new caregiver, one other recommendation we make is that she encourage a friendship between her caregiver and an older, more experienced surrogate, who can act as a mentor and role model. The best candidates for this mentor's role will be your friends' caregivers. If one of them has a woman whom you especially admire for her maturity, skill, and knowledge, try to arrange a series of play dates between her and your new caregiver. Just sharing a park bench with a woman who has spent ten or fifteen years looking after infants and toddlers can have enormous educational value for a young woman who is looking after her first or second child.

One thing experienced caregivers are especially good at, for instance, is exercising authority. Years of experience have taught them how to bring a tussle about a toy or a wrestling match to an end with a few quiet words or a stern look. If you have ever seen a veteran caregiver bring two sand-throwing four-year-olds to heel with a withering glance, you know what I mean. The moral authority in the veteran's look, posture, and attitude says all that needs to be said to the four-year-olds. Lacking this experience, new caregivers often tend to rely on shouting and threats in such situations. So one important lesson a mentor can teach your novice is how to deal with disciplinary infractions in ways that bring them to an end but still leave your child's dignity intact. The experienced caregiver also can teach the novice the difference between the child who has a legitimate complaint and needs to be heard and the child who is merely cranky.

A mentor can also be of help in dealing with you. There may be things — important things — your new caregiver notices about your child that she would like to discuss with you but is afraid to bring up. She may think you might feel she is overstepping the bounds of her authority or — worse still — that she is criticizing you or your youngster. A mentor can act as an advisor in such situations. Veteran caregivers usually have a very thorough understanding of the etiquette and diplomacy of employer-employee relations, so they can advise the novice on how to raise and phrase her concerns in a way that will make them sound like helpful suggestions and not accusations.

Nora Kennedy's experience with Daphne Holmes illustrates a third way a new caregiver can be helped to learn and grow. It involves the use of a technique we call *individualizing,* although you would probably describe it as putting your best foot forward, and is based on a fundamental principle of human psychology. We all do best in new environments, if — initially, at least — they allow us to emphasize our strengths.

In Nora's case, it didn't take more than the two-week trial period to identify Daphne's two principal strengths. The first was Daphne's remarkable facility with two-and-a-half-year-old Megan Kennedy. Indeed, watching Megan and Daphne play together on the third day of the trial, Nora had to remind herself that their relationship was barely seventy-two hours old. Daphne was considerate, funny, and patient, and displayed an almost intuitive grasp of Megan's moods. Nora also found Daphne to be unusually creative. This talent showed up in little ways (Daphne was especially good at inventing amusing games for Megan) and in big ways (by the end of the trial period she had sold Nora on a new color scheme for Megan's room).

Daphne's weak points were a bit slower to emerge, but by the end of her second month with the family, Nora knew that there were a number of relatively simple household chores and responsibilities Daphne could not be trusted to perform. One was reporting the phone messages Nora got during the day; Daphne either forgot to write the caller's name down or got the name wrong. Another problem was Daphne's shopping skills. On a seven-item shopping list, Daphne's average score was between three and four. What troubled Nora most, though, was Daphne's attitude toward authority figures. In Daphne's mind, bank tellers, carpenters, electricians, and every other variety of repairman represented a strange and intimidating breed and she refused to have any dealings with them. If money was needed for shopping that day, Nora would have to make extra time in the morning to cash a check at the grocer's for Daphne before leaving work. It also meant that the Kennedys' television stayed broken for seven weeks, because each time the television repairman arrived to fix it, Daphne sent him away with the admonition she used for all repairmen: "You please come back when Mrs. Kennedy is home."

By the end of her third month, Nora was so upset by Daphne's deficiencies that she was thinking of firing her, which is why she came to see me. "Daphne's so good with Megan, I hate to let her go," Nora said. "But she's also slowly driving me crazy. I'm continually late for work because I have to stop off at the grocer's every morning to cash a check, and half my friends think I'm snubbing them because I haven't returned their phone calls. Do you think I ought to fire her?"

I told Nora no, I thought there was a less traumatic way of solving her Daphne dilemma. "Daphne's problem isn't ineptness, but insecurity. She's never dealt with a bank teller before or supervised a repairman and, understandably, she finds the thought of doing these things intimidating. What you need to do is build up her self-confidence. Start by praising the things you know she's good at. Tell her how much you admire the inventiveness of her play with Megan. You also said she made some imaginative suggestions about redecorating Megan's room. Why don't you ask her to help you select some pictures and wallpaper for the room?

"In time," I said, "I think you will notice that these little votes of confidence will begin to produce a spillover effect in Daphne's mind. Finding herself praised and admired for her skills as a caregiver and decorator, Daphne will begin to think, 'If I'm good at these things, maybe I can also be good at other things like marketing and banking.'" I also told Nora one way she could help to foster this connection in Daphne's mind was by pointing out that the aspects of her work she already excels at, such as taking care of Megan, are much more difficult than dealing with a bank teller or doing the family shopping.

"You were right, the praise worked," Nora announced when I ran into her at a parent's meeting at the center five weeks later. Before I had a chance to take a bow for my sage advice, however, Nora added that Daphne's newly developed efficiency and self-confidence also owed something to several steps she had taken on her own. One was bringing Daphne to the bank and personally introducing her to the two tellers and officer who handled most of the Kennedy family's banking. Another was to pick up one of those pink PLEASE CALL pads at a local stationery store; just by rotely following the instructions on the pad, Daphne could take reliable phone messages. Nora also told me that Daphne's shopping skills improved dramatically when she began making out the marketing list in front of Daphne.

Daphne's transformation into a competent, responsible household manager also illustrates another key point of caregiver management: the important role simple respect plays in helping a novice caregiver learn and grow. In taking the time to pick up a phone message pad and the trouble to go over the weekly shopping list item by item with Daphne, Nora was doing more than just trying to help her master her job. She was telling Daphne, "Our family cares about and respects you and the work you do." Asking a caregiver about her ailing mother, how her sister's new job is working out, or how her son did on his college boards conveys the same message and produces the same effect. They make the caregiver want to give your family her best self.

The more personal empathetic style we advise our REAP mothers to adopt toward their caregivers doesn't, however, mean we believe a family caregiver should be given a special dispensation from all the rules that normally govern employer-employee relations. Like all jobs, caregiving involves certain duties and responsibilities. And like all employees, a caregiver should, first and foremost, be judged on her ability to meet the duties and responsibilities of her work. At the same time, a caregiver also is an employee with an unusually intimate relationship to her employer — she is entrusted with the care of her child — and the special nature of this intimacy should be reflected in the relationship you develop with her. It should be personal, supportive, and concerned.

I don't think competent, responsible caregivers can be mass-produced according to a simple standard formula. But if there is one element essential to the shaping of such a caregiver, it is the adoption of the kind of personal, involved style that says, "Our family respects you and will always treat you and your work with dignity." Almost as essential to the making of such a caregiver is patience — sometimes great patience. Daphne Holmes's transformation into a mature, competent, responsible manager took nearly two years. And if you asked Nora Kennedy, I'm sure she would tell you that facilitating that transformation was one of the most difficult things she has ever done. But I'm equally sure that if you asked Nora, "Was it worth the effort?" she would smile, point to Megan, and reply, "Yes, it was — every bit of it."

13

The New Developmental Guide to the Preschool Child

MOST DEVELOPMENTAL GUIDES focus on changes in the child's growth. They tell you which month you should expect his first smile, when he will be able to sit up by himself, and at what point his crawling will turn into walking and his babbling into talking. The guide in this chapter takes a somewhat different form. For one thing, it focuses as much on you as on your child; and for another, it looks at development through the prism of your work.

Is work such a major developmental force that a working woman requires her own special guide? If you think about the questions your child asked about your work at two, and the much more probing questions he asks about it now at four ("Why don't you stay home like Tommy's mother?"), or about how greatly the fears and concerns it inspires have altered between his second and fourth birthdays, I think you will agree a working woman does need her own developmental guide. As her youngster changes and grows, his feelings about her work, the new demands and fears it creates, and the developmental issues it raises for him also change. To maintain her sensitivity a woman needs to be aware of these changes, and she also needs to know how to respond appropriately to them.

One way our guide will help you to do this is by introducing you to the major developmental themes of the first years of life. You will be a much more sensitive helpmate to your child if you know how the priorities of his developmental agenda shift from year to year. Another way the guide will help you maintain your sensitivity is by showing you how to help your child deal with the new concerns and fears that arise as his awareness of your work expands. A third way the guide will help is by showing you how to keep your hopes and dreams for your child realistic. One distinguishing characteristic of the sensitive mother is that her expectations for her infant or toddler are always appropriate to the developmental stage he occupies.

Here, then, is a working mother's guide to the first sixty months of her child's life.

INFANCY

If this year can be said to have a byword, it is "joy." Put aside concerns about limit setting and self-regulation for now. During infancy, the rule of thumb to follow is: do more of whatever produces a smile in a child, and stop whatever leads to a frown.

Birth to Two Months

Eating, sleeping, and bathing are the primary activities of the first five to six weeks of life, so enhancing the baby's joy in the first part of this period is largely a matter of making these events as pleasurable as possible. In addition to the ways parents usually do this, such as ensuring that the bathwater is just the right temperature and wet diapers are changed regularly, you can help make activities more enjoyable for an infant through proper timing. The shorter the waiting period between a child's first hunger pang and feeding, and his first yawn and the feel of the crib mattress under him, the more he will enjoy his feeding and nap times.

Increasingly, toward the end of the second month, however, a baby begins to seek joy in a new and distinctly more human way. He looks to his social contacts with his father, his caregiver, and most of all with you to give him pleasure. In the parlance of developmental theory, these social contacts are known as interactions; one of the most important discoveries to emerge from the recent research is the important role these interactions play in development during the first year of life. A baby is born with a large number of innate potentials, but the degree to which he is able to tap these potentials depends on how sensitively his interactive partners respond to him.

To illustrate the point, take the two-month-old's ability to remain alert. In some ways this is the most important of the child's innate capacities — if he can't focus in exchanges, he can't learn the things he needs to learn to tap other innate abilities, such as how to communicate and how to cooperate. The way a sensitive, interactive partner helps that two-month-old to stretch his concentration span is by noticing his special likes and interests (for an explanation of how to do this, consult chapter 6) and by including those preferences in their exchanges. Encountering a favorite song or funny facial expression or a hand trick does more than just please a twelve-week-old; they make him want to try to stretch himself a bit. He is having fun, and since Mother may be offering still more fun ahead, he makes a special effort to concentrate a little longer in this interaction. The correlation is almost unvarying: the more alert a baby is in this exchange, the more alert still he will be in the next one.

This is why the working mother, whose paid maternity leave covers most of the first eight weeks, should use these weeks to identify her newborn's special likes. Interesting, easily tolerated sights and sounds will rivet an infant; ones he doesn't like or finds overstimulating will produce either a glassy-eyed look or tears. Knowing what works for her child is important not only because it allows her to please and help him grow but also because once she returns to work, she can pass this information on to those who will be caring for the child.

Three to Nine Months

In these months, the principal tools for enhancing a baby's joy are the ones you might imagine: tickling, rolling, mutual babbling, and peek-a-boo. Providing an infant with the colors and shapes (in the form of toys and crib mobiles) you noticed catch his eye also can do much to enhance his enjoyment. Ensuring that all the playthings you give him are safely mouthable, so you won't have to keep taking away the things he likes, helps as well.

Toward the end of the sixth month, however, you should begin concentrating more and more on the role of *facilitator* in interactions. In developmental theory, the facilitator is the person who helps the child begin tapping his innate potentials. Translated into day-to-day behavior, the facilitator does what I saw Deirdre Ryan doing one afternoon with her eight-month-old, Patrick. Mature as he is in comparison with his two-month-old former self, an eight-month-old still can't remain alert and engaged in an interaction without help. Deirdre's behavior the afternoon I came across her and Patrick in the playroom offers a good example of how a facilitator provides that help.

Having noticed that the sound of a favorite song or the sight of a favorite toy always enhanced Patrick's alertness in exchanges, Deirdre had deduced that the sound of a favorite song followed by the sight of a favorite toy followed by the playing of a favorite game would keep Patrick alert and focused even longer. The afternoon I watched her and Patrick, she was testing this theory. Finding himself in the presence of so many favorite things clearly excited Patrick. I have never seen him smile so much in an exchange. Even more important, encountering a string of favorite things, one after the other, was increasing his alertness. Not wanting to miss anything, Patrick was making himself stay focused and engaged. I am sure his pleased mother would be surprised to hear herself described as a facilitator. If you asked Deirdre what she was doing that Friday afternoon, she would have simply said, "I'm just playing with my baby." Nonetheless, in developmental terms, that was the role she was playing: by stringing together Patrick's preferences into a single play sequence, Deirdre was facilitating his ability to remain alert and focused in an interaction.

What makes facilitator such an important role for a working mother to stake out for herself is that it is a way for her to establish her primacy. Her youngster comes to see her as the person in his life who is most interested in helping him grow. One consequence of this is that a working mother has to gradually lessen her association with the nursing aspects of her child's care. More and more, as the baby matures, chores like bathing and feeding should be left to the caregiver.

As the infant's social contacts begin to grow in this period, also important is ensuring that his meetings with new faces are always comfortable. One way of doing this is by promoting a distal style of information collection (see chapter 8). Another is by making sure that strangers *always* follow the baby's rules of introduction, of which there are two: "Don't get too close to me," and, even more important, "Don't touch me unless I invite you to with a smile or an extended hand." Usually it takes two or three encounters with a new person before an infant feels comfortable enough to signal a desire to be touched or held. In introducing him, make sure that both you and the caregiver tell the new person that "while the baby would love to be picked up and cuddled and kissed, he would like to get to know you a bit better first."

Nine to Twelve Months

While joy remains important, the baby's growing awareness and sense of "personhood" will raise new issues for you in these months. A case in point is the ten-month-old's recently developed desire never to let you out of his sight when you are home. The best way to respond to this desire is to position his infant seat in a manner that allows him to keep you in visual range no matter where you are or what you are doing. Being something of a gourmet chef, Joan Gleason, one of our REAP mothers, spends a lot of her weekend time in the kitchen preparing meals. But she is always careful to place her eleven-month-old, Kimberly, at the kitchen door in her bounce seat. "That makes Kimberly happy because I am right there in front of her," says Joan, "and it makes me happy because I have what every great chef dreams of, an appreciative audience."

Another way of displaying sensitivity to the older infant's concerns is by not allowing yourself to become too distracted when you run into a friend at the supermarket or dry cleaner. No matter how engaging the conversation, it shouldn't be so absorbing that eye contact is lost. This will disappoint the infant, who will be left wondering, "Why isn't Mommy paying more attention to me?" It will also upset him because without the reassurance of mother's glance, the unfamiliar person seems more intimidating to him.

TODDLERHOOD
Twelve to Eighteen Months

A predominating theme of early toddlerhood is mastery. The child wants and needs to feel that he is in growing control of himself and his environment. Walking, talking, holding a spoon — all the important developmental breakthroughs that mark these months — are in one way or another, manifestations of the toddler's quest to feel himself a competent, capable human being. One important way a working mother can support this quest is by learning to be a good follower. While, no, this doesn't mean that the seventeen-month-old who offers to help out in the kitchen should be given carte blanche, it does mean his desire to initiate actions should be supported — even if, on occasion, those actions conflict with your own agenda. A case in point would be that seventeen-month-old's desire to help you help him get dressed. His help is going to add a few extra minutes to the dressing process, but the sense of doing it himself that he gets from wrestling with his T-shirt is well worth the delay his aid may produce.

Eighteen to Thirty-six Months

During these months, the toddler passes through the terrible twos. And behind the confrontations that give this developmental phase its well-deserved reputation lies a curious imbalance. Physically, there is little a child can't do now. By two he can walk, talk, run, jump, and climb; and he can hold and reach for things with a new — and when you consider his awkwardness of just a few months ago — dazzling agility. Emotionally, however, his growth hasn't quite kept pace. Still lacking are the cognitive skills and self-regulatory mechanisms that by three at least will make him look before he leaps, and by four will have begun to produce the beginnings of recognizably responsible behavior. In a way, a two-year-old is like a teenager who, having received a high-powered new car for his birthday, insists on driving it, even though he hasn't learned how to drive yet. All those new physical skills are the two-year-old's equivalent of the high-powered car; confrontations characterize this year because while you know he can't drive his new car, he knows he can.

Trying as this makes life for a woman who is at home, it is next to nothing compared to the terror the terrible twos can hold for the woman who works. Having the language to state his feelings and the physical strength to do something about those feelings, a two-year-old can turn events like leave-takings into a nightmare. His newly developed assertiveness also can create conflicts with the day-care center or caregiver, imperiling his mother's support system.

Ginny Ginzburg-Levinson can attest to that. In many ways her two-year-old, Alexander, is a delightful child. He is intelligent, inventive, and charming. Unfortunately, what Alex does not have to go along with his charm is a tolerance for stress and frustration. This was evident in his first year, but it didn't become a serious problem for Ginny until his second year. That was when the now very mobile and physically active Alex began expressing his frustrations and upsets not only through tears, as he had in his first twelve months, but also by biting, hitting, and throwing things. After the family's first caregiver walked out, Ginny had to take a three-week leave of absence from her teaching job. After the second caregiver walked out four months later, Ginny had to take another three-week leave of absence. That was when, on her pediatrician's recommendation, she came to the center for a consultation.

Stories like Ginny's illustrate why, if the byword for the first year is "joy," the byword for the second and third is "self-control." As quickly as possible, the two-year-old needs to be taught how to

drive his new car. Here are some of the ways we showed Ginny how to help Alex drive his:
• *Create minor delays.* This strategy reflects an important feature of stress and frustration tolerance. It grows best in increments. Having successfully absorbed this stress leaves a child that much better equipped to overcome the next, slightly larger stress. The advantage of promoting such tolerance via deliberate minor delays—in eating, playtimes, and other looked-forward-to activities—is that such delays can be edged upward with great precision. Having developed the ability to absorb the frustration produced by, say, a one-minute delay in feeding, a twenty-month-old now can be moved up to the two-minute level.

Minor delays build stress tolerance because they introduce that twenty-month-old, in a way he can understand, to the entirely novel concept of "future time" and the often happy endings it holds. Alex is a case in point. What made something so minor as a thirty-second delay at the doorway, while Ginny fumbled for her key, intolerable to him wasn't the delay but his ignorance of the future. If Mommy didn't have her keys now, Alex thought she would never have them and they would be left standing out in the cold forever. Although Alex's reaction to this situation was extreme (collapsing to the floor in tears), the thought process that led him to the reaction was not unusual. Present-minded toddlers are not aware of the concept of future time. And if you are not aware of the future, it is understandable why you might think you were going to spend the rest of your life waiting in the cold while Mommy searched for her key. That you might find it difficult to cope with the anxiety that thought produced is also understandable.

The minor delays Ginny created at dinner taught Alex that, although the things you want sometimes may be late in arriving, they do arrive if you are just patient and wait. Ginny found Alex was very quick to extrapolate this lesson to other areas of his life. While he would still be upset if there were a delay at the doorway, for example, Alex no longer flung himself on the floor. He now understood that after this moment there was another moment and another moment after that. And in one of those moments Ginny would find her keys and they both would be safe and warm inside the house.

• *Emphasize language.* This strategy is based on a second important fact about emotional self-control: language enhances it. One reason is that words force a toddler to begin defining what he really feels. Is he slightly, moderately, or very upset? And this process of self-definition provides its own form of self-control, since it encourages a youngster to keep what he is expressing behaviorally in tune with what he is saying verbally. Having declared himself "a little hurt," he will be less likely to express that little hurt by screaming, the way a child who is unable to put his feelings into words often does. Another reason for language's restraining effect is that the ability to articulate upsets is healing in itself. Two-year-olds, like thirty-year-olds, feel better once they have had an opportunity to get it "off of their chests" and into the mind of someone significant.

The best way to facilitate language learning is by being gently directive. In exchanges, make it a point to identify every object the two of you are playing with by name. You should also encourage the toddler to acquire a multimodal knowledge of these objects (in other words, a knowledge of the way they sound, taste, and feel as well as look). Also important is to make him express himself as clearly as he can — even if that means stressing him a bit. For example, if you see your son's eye go to a toy, don't immediately pick it up and hand it to him. Wait until he points; better still, wait until he points and gurgles. This extra effort will sharpen his memory of the object. It will also teach the child a more general lesson — that clarity is essential in communication.

• *Be response-specific.* A principal way a child defines how good, bad, competent, or incompetent a behavior is, as well as how frightening, sad, happy, or stressful an event or situation is, is by noting how *you* respond. One other reason Alex tended to overreact to minor stresses and frustrations, for example, was that Ginny tended to overreact. Alex's minor bumps and bruises were treated as major life-threatening injuries. Although the impulse that produced Ginny's alarm over these minor mishaps was understandable, it did not serve her son. If Alex were old enough to be asked why every minor delay made him so upset, he might fairly point out, "Well, I'm only behaving the way Mommy does."

Seeing you respond accurately and appropriately to a situation, event, or feeling makes it easier for the child to define the true meaning of that circumstance to himself. Like precision in language, precision in understanding is a key building block of self-control. To illustrate why, take an everyday incident like a scraped knee. Seeing your sympathetic but mild response to this minor, slightly painful injury makes the child think, "Mommy's right, this cut hurts, but it doesn't hurt that much." Better still is to do what we taught Ginny to do when Alex got a bump or scrape: delay your response for a moment. This gives the toddler time to sort out his own feelings, and then if he says it hurts, you have an opportunity to make your words something more than just an expression of sympathy (important as that is). A statement such as, "Yes, I know it hurts, but I'll bet it doesn't hurt as much as when you bumped yourself on the head last week," gives an eighteen-month-old a yardstick against which he can measure his upset about this scrape more precisely.

No one has polled day-care workers and nursery school teachers on the attributes they consider most important, but I have no doubt if someone does, this capacity to define feelings accurately will emerge as among the qualities they value most in their young charges. Not only is such a child better able to be comforted by others, but he is better able to comfort himself. Knowing what does and doesn't hurt, he is able to tell himself, "Well, that bump hurt but not enough to make me want to cry."

Precision in praise also is important, but, for a different reason. Unlike the woman at home, who with more free time available can promote the skills she targets as most important in several ways, a woman who works has one principal tool — her words of praise. This isn't to say you should be parsimonious in your use of compliments, but you should be discriminating. One way a fourteen-month-old learns that it is always better to attach a sound (even if it is only a babble) to an object rather than just to point at it is by the level of maternal praise each of these acts earns. The same is true for the twenty-month-old who sometimes uses her hand when eating, and sometimes a spoon. Unless these triumphs are praised in ways that reflect their various levels of accomplishment, the child is not going to know which represents the greater triumph.

PRESCHOOL YEARS
Thirty-six to Forty-eight Months

In developmental texts, discussions of these months usually center around a process that, although ongoing from birth, now becomes overt — the formation of self. In the fourth year especially, new energy and attention are devoted to the shaping of the "I" that will mark the child as an individual personality. As part of this process, he begins to look at mother in a new light, not only as a facilitator and playmate, but also as a role model who can help him answer the all-important question of "Who shall I be?"

This is why the fourth year is also a year of decision for a working mother. She must decide which of the various maternal models available to her will best foster the qualities she wants to promote in her child. Should she present herself in exchanges as the all-knowing, perfect mother, the supercompetent superwoman? Or should she present herself as a more complex, fallible, and three-dimensional figure, someone who uses her own mistakes and uncertainties to teach her boy or girl about the importance of such characteristics as tolerance — of oneself and others — and flexibility?

There are two reasons why the three-dimensional model represents the best choice. On the immediate practical level of adjustment to work, the model puts inevitable events, such as a missed check-in call, into context for a child. This is one of the ways Leah Rank's predictable unpredictability serves her. Leah's proneness to mistakes and forgetfulness make her a very three-dimensional figure to her son, Jeffrey. So, at five, Jeffrey will know what to think if one morning Leah's check-in call is late in coming. Jeffrey won't like that lateness, of course, but he will know enough about his mother to know that the reason for it is her forgetfulness, not her anger or indifference. One of the dangers of being a superachiever like Barbara Molloy is that, often, the superachiever's child will react to lateness in calling or in arriving at the day-care center with surprise and confusion. How could Mommy be late? It doesn't make sense.

The other reason that the three-dimensional model is preferable is even more important. By allowing a child to see all sides of you — your weaknesses as well as your strengths, your inconsistencies as well as your consistencies, your bad points as well as good points — and by exhibiting an unself-conscious ease in being who you are, you encourage the growth of two qualities that will serve a person as well at thirty as at three: tolerance and flexibility. The difference will be apparent in his ability to accept and like both himself and others — even when those others occasionally do something he doesn't like.

Here are three examples of how to promote tolerance and flexibility.

1. *Let the child see you be wrong as well as right.* The goal of this strategy is to provide a child with a model of tolerance — to show him that while mistakes are an inevitable part of life, they do not diminish the person who makes them. And it can be implemented in two ways. One is by calling attention to the errors you make in the normal course of things; the other — since the first is sometimes impractical or inconvenient — is occasionally to do something wrong deliberately in front of the toddler, for example, spill a glass of water or announce that you have misplaced a shoe or hat. What matters isn't so much the route you choose as the style you display in making, noticing, and correcting the error; it should be relaxed, casual, and humorous.

The child who sees you smile wryly at your own clumsiness or dismiss it with a humorous, self-critical remark such as "Oh, silly me," is being taught something very important: that errors are not a reflection on the person who makes them. The three-year-old who learns this lesson is going to be kinder to himself, kinder to his playmates, and kinder to you.

2. *Draw attention to it when you are doing something you don't want to do.* It may seem simple to us, but it comes as a revelation to a three-year-old to hear his mother say, "I'm so tired," and then see her walk into the kitchen and cheerfully begin preparing dinner. It

also comes as a revelation to hear her announce, "I'd rather be sitting watching TV with you," and then see her continue to vacuum the floor. At thirty-six or forty months, it is all but unimaginable to a child that one can do a thing one doesn't want to do and still smile. And it *is* unimaginable for him to conceive that a smile might actually make an unpleasant task easier to do.

This is why you should go out of your way to point it out when you are engaged in tiresome or demanding chores, and why you should also make sure that your child sees how effectively you attack even unappetizing tasks. This creates a model of frustration tolerance that will influence a youngster's behavior not only now, on mornings when he would rather stay in bed than go to day care or nursery school, but also at twenty, when he would rather stay in the cafeteria talking to friends than go back to his room to study for a biology test.

3. *Interweave the good with the bad.* This strategy is designed to create a third kind of model. In order to adjust easily and comfortably to the combination of the sad and the happy, the pleasant and the unpleasant, the things we want and don't want to do, which is the fundamental rhythm of life, a child must be flexible. This is especially true if he lives in a working family because he is going to be introduced to this life rhythm earlier. For everyone's sake, he has to learn how to deal with events that may be temporarily sad or upsetting — a scolding from a nursery school teacher, for example — without becoming stuck on them.

Modeling, in the form of seeing you maintain a cheerful demeanor as you go about difficult tasks, is only one way of emphasizing the importance of flexibility. Another way is by occasionally interlacing happy with sad moments. Sabine Miller, one of our REAP mothers, has found the end of shared times a good occasion for teaching her three-year-old, Samantha, about the way the good and bad are often twinned in life. "I usually plan our shared times so that there is one last activity we can't finish that night. Sam is in a very happy mood by this point," says Sabine, "so the prospect of delaying the finish of a game or book until morning doesn't upset her. And I think the interruption teaches her something important about how even very enjoyable times can contain moments of disappointment."

Barbara Cole, another REAP mother, uses breakfast to teach her four-year-old, Harry, about the way the sad and the happy inter-mix. "At first," Barbara told me, "I was reluctant to bring up the subject of our separation at breakfast. It is the high point of the morning for Harry and me, and I was afraid that saying something like 'Oh dear, we won't see one another again until tonight,' would ruin the meal for both of us. I was surprised by Harry's response, though, when one morning, I finally did point out to him that we were going to be separating for the day. Instead of becoming weepy as I expected, Harry looked thoughtful for a moment, then began to talk about our separations in a very ma-ture way.

"He said it upset him sometimes that we had to be away from one another all day. Sometimes, he said, it even made him angry. But he also said he knew that my work was important 'because it gives us all money,' and then with a big smile he told me I was 'the best mommy in the whole world.' "

I told Barbara what had produced Harry's thougtfulness is the setting she had chosen for the introduction of her sad note. The same was true for Samantha Miller's ability to accept gracefully Sabine's announcement that "we will finish reading this story in the morning." A young child finds it much easier to tolerate — and learn from — sad moments if they occur in a setting that makes him feel relaxed and comfortable. I also told Barbara that, over time, her twinning of the good and bad will have an impor-tant effect on Harry's outlook. He will come to see life as a process — something that is to be lived one day at a time and is interlaced with happy and sad moments, disappointments and triumphs. And, I added, the youngster who understands this is going to be much more resilient in his encounters with disap-pointments and upsets, because he will understand that they do not represent the end of the world but only a passing moment in time.

Forty-eight to Sixty Months

Sometime around the forty-eighth month, the question that comes to preoccupy a child is "How does the world work and what is my place in it?" Having gotten his personal developmental agenda in order, the four-year-old increasingly will focus his attention outward. Behaviorally, the most notable sign of this shift is the fondness the four-year-old shows for making discriminations. Understanding why A is different from B, and B from C, suddenly is very important to him because the more refined and precise his knowledge, the more effectively he will be able to operate in the larger world, which is increasingly absorbing his attention. His newly developed fascination with "bad guys" and "good guys" is an example of this drive to discriminate right from wrong. So is his new interest in his and your personal history. Knowing what he was like at two, what you were like at four, and how big Daddy was at seven provides a context in which he can begin to identify how he is the same as and how he is different from others.

The four-year-old's more adultlike interest in mother's work also grows out of the quest for more worldly kinds of knowledge. Thus, while work as an emotional phenomenon — something that takes mother away — remains of interest, it also begins to become the source of a more objective, almost scientific curiosity. Concrete details are suddenly important. The four-year-old wants to know exactly where your office is located, what it looks like, where you put your chair, and what you do there.

This new interest in what you do when you are away from him is why four is a critical year in terms of a child's feeling toward and perceptions about maternal employment. The four-year-old is now sophisticated enough to make comparisons. By this point, for example, he has noticed and taken into account the fact that although you work, his friend Michael's mother doesn't — and also sophisticated enough to think things through on his own. He will be full of new questions and new concerns about the reasons for your work and, even more, about what that work says about your feelings toward him. Here are some of the ways you can deal positively with his new concerns.

• *Emphasize reality attunement.* Four-year-olds spend a great deal of their time fantasizing. Part of their special magic — and four is a magical year — is their ability to take a simple object and conjure up an entire world around it. There are, however, dangers as well as charms to this trait, and it is important to be aware of them. Imagine, for example, what a mind that is able to transform something as uninspiring as a pencil into a superhero's sword can do with a subject as potentially rich as your work. The point of reality attunement isn't to dampen your youngster's flights of fantasy but to prevent him and you from becoming victims of them. The best way to do this is through the use of what I call at the center "what if" scenarios.

These scenarios take, as their starting point, your four-year-old's fantasy of you as an at-home mother. But they are designed to show him how this fantasy changes when certain pertinent facts, which can be relied on to have left out, are introduced into it. Beatrice Tate, one of our REAP mothers, has been particularly imaginative about creating "what if" scenarios for her four-year-old, Benjamin. Whenever he asks Beatrice why she can't stay home like his friend Michael's mother, Beatrice brings up one of the two scenarios she has devised just for such moments. The first one centers on how she and Benjamin would spend their days together.

"You would still be in nursery school with Michael, so we wouldn't be together in the morning," Beatrice points out. "And since Millie [Benjamin's caregiver] wouldn't be here to clean the floors, or make the beds, or do the shopping, or start dinner, I'd have to spend my afternoons doing those things myself. You know, I don't think we'd really have much more time together than we have now."

Benjamin always looks pensive when Beatrice says this. But her second "what if" scenario is the one that makes him think that maybe, after all, he is better off than Michael. It involves all the things the Tates wouldn't be able to do or buy if they didn't have the money Beatrice's job provides. Four-year-olds have enough understanding of basic economics to know that the things they want cost money. So when Beatrice points out that they wouldn't have been able to afford the trip the family took to Disney World last winter if she didn't work, or that Benjamin would have fewer toys if Mommy also didn't have a job that brought in money,

Benjamin usually drops his questions about Michael and why his mother stays home.

Such facts don't entirely stop a four-year-old like Benjamin from fantasizing that he can have everything, but they do take some of the gold lining out of his fantasies. Just as important, they make him aware that the life of his friend Michael, whose mother doesn't work, really isn't too different from his own.

• *Define your meanings more precisely.* One way you can help a four-year-old understand more clearly why A is different from B, and B from C, is through the use of adjective ladders. Instead of describing a person as simply sad or happy, or describing a bump on the knee as hurting or not hurting, always *grade* for a child. Using qualifiers like "a little," "a lot," or "less" shows him how words can be used to define more precisely. This will enable him to be more accurate in his explanations to you, to his caregiver, and to his day-care worker.

Instead of saying that this year's nursery school teacher is "different" from last year's, for example, he will be able to put that difference into words. He will be able to tell you she is "not as happy" as last year's teacher, or "more fun" or "less fun" than last year's teacher. An understanding of adjective ladders and how to use them will allow the four-year-old to provide you with the kind of detail every working mother needs to oversee the care of her child effectively.

Precision in language also is important in talking about your work. Statements such as, "I had a very depressing day at the office," or "I am so exhausted I feel like staying home," don't pass by a four-year-old the way they do a two-year-old. He understands what these words mean, and not only do they puzzle him — why, he wonders, if it makes you unhappy, do you go to work — they also can undermine your right to work, since in his mind, they raise the possibility that "well, now that Mommy doesn't like work, maybe she will stay home."

This train of thought is why, when the subject is work, you should be careful to put your occasional outbursts (which you have a perfect right to) into context. The best way to do this is through analogy. Point out to the four-year-old that even though he sometimes has difficult days, overall he likes going to the center because his friends are there and he enjoys himself. This makes it easier for him to understand why, although you also sometimes have a bad day, overall your work makes you very happy.

• *Encourage self-sufficiency.* In the course of this book, we have talked a great deal about self-sufficiency. But it has been within the context of an attuned environment that understands the child's individual needs in the individual ways attuned environments do and so is able to subtly support him as he takes his first tentative steps toward independence. In the fifth year, with full-time school approaching, more and more the child is going to be expected — by his teachers, by his baby-sitters, and by you — to be able to cope on his own when he is distressed, bored, or uncertain. The best way to prepare him for the challenge this change represents is by gradually beginning to remove some of the subtle supports you have been using to aid him.

Thus, in the fifth year, your reliance on distracting strategies such as channeling should decrease. At this age, a child should be encouraged to learn how to channel himself. When he gets upset or angry now, don't immediately try to distract him. Wait and see how he responds on his own. If he moves to an activity that lifts him out of his upset, join him in it. If he doesn't, then make some suggestions. But as much as possible, limit your role to that of facilitator. Let the child make the decisions about how to divert himself; helping him to implement his diversion should be your role.

Also important now is to change to more verbal forms of comforting. In the first three years your hugging, kissing, and other forms of physical soothing were echoed by the caregiver or day-care worker. Once the child begins school, however, that is going to change. Increasingly, the five- or six-year-old is going to find that his teachers, while solicitous, are not going to wrap him in their arms each time he is upset. They will expect him to be mature enough to be comforted by their words alone. And the youngster who will make the best adjustment to this change is the youngster who has already learned at home how to use solicitous words, instead of hugs, to soothe himself.

This last point touches on a thought that may have occurred to you as you read through our guide: that having been in the real world for most of his first five years, your child is better prepared for the major transition that occurs at six with the start of formal schooling. You are right; those years do. The follow-up studies we have done on our REAP youngsters indicate that the child of a working mother often makes the transition to traditional schooling more easily. Your life may create some special challenges, but it also creates special rewards for you and for your child. This is one of them.

14

A Final Word

HAVING READ THIS BOOK, you now understand the new developmental world in which you, as a working mother, are raising your child. You've learned the rules that govern this world, and you've learned how to create the secure attachment that will enable your child to feel your strong presence all day long, in the form of an evoked companion. It is this presence, you now understand, that lets your child have all of the benefits of this rich new world while avoiding the risks.

You've learned, in short, how to become the constant heart in your child's daily life. With this achievement comes an almost indescribable feeling—part triumph, part relief, mostly joy— that only another working mother can truly understand.

To the shame of our corporations and our national policy-makers, life is not made easy for the working mothers of young children in America today (and today there are more working than nonworking mothers of such children). Things are changing, but the limits of a still mostly inflexible workplace put the task, once taken for granted, of forging a deep mother-child bond squarely on the working mother's shoulders. Those shoulders are strong enough. And so are the shoulders of your child. As much as any book can try to tell you this, it is only when you experience it for yourself that the struggle with the responsibility, the guilt, the ambivalence, and the exhaustion seems worth it.

Not long ago, I arrived on a Saturday morning with a cardboard cup of coffee and the *New York Times* to meet one of my REAP mothers at a Central Park playground. I was early, so I settled in with the newspaper while I waited. But the sixth sense I've developed kept prodding my attention to a scene several yards away. Three four-year-olds had devised their own game at the swings, a game that seemed to feature tummy-flopping over the swing's canvas seat, shaking the swing chain, and jumping. The children clearly seemed elated at having usurped the equipment to their own original ends; still, their game could easily get in the way of any other potential swingers. Considering both of these facts was a woman who followed the scene from the sidelines with a twinkle in her eye, a slightly forward chin, and a mouth that was on the verge of opening and speaking. I realized I had met her once before, but then she had had her briefcase. Here her earnest monitoring — her combination of pride and anxiety — told me that she was a working mother relishing this full day with her child too much to want to dampen the fun, unless, as now, it was necessary.

Another mother and child made their way to the swing beside the one on which the four-year-olds were playing. This new mother looked around to locate the adult in charge and asked the woman, "Are these yours?"

"No; not them — just me," one child, a boy, suddenly asserted as he straightened up from the swing seat. There was something more than just a four-year-old's obstinate literalness in his voice — something more tender. "I'm *hers*," he said.

As his mother stood up to tell her son and his friends to please restrain their playing, she glanced sharply down to the ground for a moment.

I will never in my life forget the wonderful smile I saw on her face just then.

Index

Achievements (child's)
  children's pride in, 44–46
  mother's observance of, 178
  emphasis on, 153–158, 168
  unstructured, 51–52
Achiever maternal style, 136, 151–159
  advantages of, 155
  characteristics of, 155
  essential elements of, 156–159
  potential risks of, 155–156
Active guidance, 89, 90–117
Activities (child's). *See also* Play
  forbidden, 123–124
  as maternal symbols, 103
  pace of, 70–71, 81–83
  repeating favorite, 99–100
  sharing, after day care, 79–80
Activity-rest cycle, 82
Advice, acceptance of, maternal style
  and, 137–138
Ainsworth, Dr. Mary, 21–22, 23
"All-and-all" judgments, 109
Anger (child's)
  day care and, 60–61
  dealing with, 47
Anxieties. *See* Distress (child's); Stress
At-home mothers
  maternal sensitivity of, 38
  time spent with children by, 37, 182
Attachment
  building, 23
  caregiver and, 63

defined, 18
developmental sensitivity and, 92
evaluation of, 92–93
insecure, 22–23
maternal sensitivity and, 20–22, 25
maternal style and, 141–142, 148, 155
object constancy and, 109
promoting, 27–41, 63
Attachment disruption, 22, 56–57
Attentiveness, ensuring in child, 124–126
Authoritarianism, in caregivers, 209–210

Bath time, 83, 87
Bedtime, 83, 87
Behavior. *See* Child's behavior
Beingness, 51
Biller, Dr. W., 167
Body language (child's), reading, 43–44, 143–144
Bonding, parent-child. *See* Attachment
Boredom (in child), alleviating, 58
Boys. *See also* Children
  "feminine" traits in, 16–18
  importance of male authority figure for, 166–167
  learning problems in, 31, 167
Brazelton, Dr. T. Berry, 82
Bronfenbrenner, Dr. Urie, 5
Brooks-Gunn, Dr. Jeanne, 15–16

Business trips, child's anxieties related
    to, 132–133

Career goals, role satisfaction and,
    34–35. *See also* Work
Caregivers, 208–216. *See also* Day
    care; Day-care workers
    authoritarian, 209–210
    authority of, 213
    briefing about child, 211–212
    check-in calls and, 76–77
    competence of, 183–185, 210–211
    complaints about, 63–64
    as evoked companion, 179–180
    maternal style and, 137, 142, 146,
        149, 151–152, 156
    mentors for, 212–213
    problems with, 213–216
    reassuring child about, 73–74
    selecting, 208–211
    sensitivity of, 80
    themes related to, 62–65
Central nervous system (CNS)
    growth, 181
Channeling, as means of discipline,
    119–123, 127
Check-in calls, to caregiver, 76–77
Children. *See also* Boys; Girls; Infants;
    Toddlers; Preschoolers
    adjustment problems in, 25–27,
        70–71
    anger in, 47
    anxiety in, 19–20, 36, 49, 53–54
    desire for interaction by, 46
    differentiation of mother by, 80
    effect of day care on, 6
    expectations of adult knowledge
        about, 61–62
    individuality of, 93–101
    lying by, 63–64
    masculine and feminine traits in,
        12–13, 16–18
    mother's work and, 5, 15, 230, 231
    need to feel linked with mother, 51–
        52
    need to feel part of family, 52–53
    percent in day care, 4
    role model for, 227–230
    reading signals of, 21, 43–44, 115,
        143–144, 168
    reassuring, 73–74
    rejection of mother by, 56–58,
        111–112
    resilience of, 183
    security in, 18–20, 48
    self-absorption in, 48–49
    self-control in, 49–50

self-reliance in, 16, 62
sense of self in, 54–56
sick, 178–180
Child's development
    guide to, 217–235
    guilt about imagined lags in, 181
    guilt about missing, 178
    infants, 218–222
    preschoolers, 227–235
    returning to work and, 187–188
    toddlers, 222–227
Child's behavior
    following parent around, 122–123
    forbidden activities, 123–124
    guilt about not understanding, 180
    interpreting, 41, 42–65
    maternal style and, 139–142, 153–158
    paying attention, 124–126
    resistance, 126–131
    single mothers and, 161–162,
        167–171
    sleeping in parent's bed, 121–122
Child's preferences
    developing, 98–101
    encouraging decision-making with,
        101
    informing others about, 100–101
    using to soothe, 100, 101
Clinging, 50, 74, 132
Cognitive development, maternal
    style and, 155
Cohen, Dr. Sarale, 29, 30
Communication, distal, 143–144, 221
Companions, evoked. *See* Evoked
    companions
Competence
    of caregiver vs. mother, 183–185,
        210–211
    child's sense of, 30
    father's sense of, 200–206
Conflicted mothers, 35–36
Consistency, development of
    symbolic thinking and, 107
Creative uncertainty, 38–41, 44

Day care. *See also* Caregivers
    adjusting to pace of, 70–71
    difficult day at, 59–60
    discipline and, 133–134
    effect on children, 6
    percentage of children in, 4
    picking child up at, 77–81
    resistance to, 129–130
    rivalry for child's love and, 13–14
    single mothers' needs and, 164–165
    social skills and, 14–15
    stranger anxiety and, 15

Day-care workers. *See also* Caregivers
  leave-taking and, 74–76
  sensitivity of, 80
  themes related to, 59–62
Decision-making
  encouraging, in child, 101
  parental sharing of, 194–196
Departure themes, 48–51. *See also*
    Leave-taking
Developmental sensitivity, 23, 88, 89,
    92
Dinner time, social nature of, 82, 84
Directive maternal style, 29–31
Disappearance fantasies, 97
Discipline, 88, 118–134
  by caregivers, 213
  channeling as means of, 119–123
  at day care, 133–134
  identification method of, 129–131
  maternal absences and, 132–133
  multiple sources of, 133
  play acting as, 123–126
  resistance to, 126–129
  rolling-through technique for,
    126–129
  uncertainty about, 118–119
Distal communication, 143–144, 221
Distress (child's). *See also* Stress
  check-in calls and, 77
  at leave-taking, 36, 49, 71–72, 74–76
  mother's soothing of, 115–116
  upsetting experiences and, 53–54

Early Care Center, 7
Early education, emphasis on, 155, 157,
    168
Eating, resistance to, 70
Egalitarian attitudes, 13
Ellison, Dr. Ralph, 162, 167, 169
Evening, touch-points in, 81–88
Evoked companions, 19–20, 27, 236
  departures and, 48
  self-comforting and, 91
  when child is sick, 179–180
Exhaustion, 38
  dealing with, 81

Facial expressions, reading, 143–144
Facilitators, mothers as, 220–221
Family, child's desire to feel part of,
    52–53
Fatherhood Project, Boston Univer-
    sity, 203, 205–206
Fathers, 190–207
  assistance in night awakenings, 88
  enlisting help of, 196–197

feelings of incompetency by,
    200–206
  interactions with children, 204–206
  at leave-taking, 75–76
  maternal style and, 142, 148–149, 156
  mechanistic cognitive style of,
    200–201, 204–205
  nurturing by, 198–199
  problems sharing parental authority
    with, 193–195
  reluctant, 192, 199–207
  support by, 33–34, 191–192
  willing, 192–199
Feiring, Dr. Candice, 34
Feminine traits, in boys and girls,
    12–13, 16–18
Fields, Dr. Tiffany, 75
Flat-out maternal style, 37–38
Flexibility, promoting, in child,
    228–230
Focusing (by child)
  capacity to, 22
  difficulty in, 57
  overstimulation and, 31
Forbidden activities, disciplining for,
    123–124
Frustration
  avoiding overreaction to, 225–226
  teaching child to deal with, 224,
    228–230

Girls, "masculine" traits in, 16–18.
    See also Children
Goals
  career, 34–35
  maternal, 35–37
Gold, Dr. Dolores, 14, 16–17
Greene, Bob, 203
Group activities, child's noninvolve-
    ment in, 94–95
Guidance, active. *See* Active guidance
Guilt, 3
  case against, 177–189
  about competence of caregiver vs.
    self, 183–185
  about depriving child, 182
  discipline and, 118
  about having other interests, 185
  over imagined developmental
    failures, 181
  at leave-taking, 72, 74–75
  about leaving a sick child, 178–
    180
  about leaving child for vacation,
    188–189
  about maternal errors, 182–183
  maternal style and, 147, 148

Guilt *(continued)*
    about missing child's best years, 188
    about missing child's "firsts," 178
    for not being a superwoman,
       177–178, 180
    about not understanding child, 180
    about returning to work too soon,
       185–188
    at reunions, 78
    sources of, 174–176
    unrealistic goals and, 35–36

Habits, regularity of, in mother,
    113–114
Handover, reassuring child about,
    73–74. *See also* Leave-taking
Hewett, Sylvia, 177
Hock, Dr. Ellen, 35, 36
Hoffman, Dr. Lois, 175
Homecomings, 44–48
Household chores, division of, 33–34
Husbands. *See* Fathers

Identification, as method of disci-
    pline, 129–131
Independence (in child)
    enjoyment of, 62
    maternal style and, 141
Individuality (of child), 91, 93–101
    age-appropriate interests and, 97–99
    building blocks of, 97–101
    encouraging decision-making, 101
    informing others about, 100–101
    maternal style and, 148
    repetition and, 99–100
Individualizing, with caregivers,
    213–216
Infants. *See also* Children; Toddlers
    developmental stages of, 218–222
    individuality expressed by, 93–94
    interests of, 98
    leave-taking stress, 110–111
    memory training in, 105–107
    understanding of maternal
      departures by, 110–111
    understanding of maternal
      permanence by, 110–114
Insecure attachment, 22–23. *See* also
    Attachment
Interaction, 46, 219
Interests. *See also* Individuality
    of infants, 98, 219
    preferences, 94–97
    of toddlers, 98–99

Johns Hopkins University, 92

Kaye, Dr. Kenneth, 82
Knowledge gaps, in mothers, 38–41

Lamb, Dr. Michael, 22, 161
Language development, encouraging,
    225, 233–234
Learning problems
    in boys, 31, 167
    directive maternal style and, 31
Leave-taking
    child's awareness of likes and
      dislikes and, 94–97
    departure themes, 48–51
    fathers' attitude and, 75–76
    maternal distress at, 74–76
    maternal style and, 138
    mother and child, 71–72
    mother, child, and caregiver/
      teacher, 73–76
    reassuring child about, 73–74
    self-comforting and, 91–92
    stress of, 36, 71–72, 96–97, 110–111
*Lesser Life, A: The Myth of Women's
    Liberation* (Hewett), 177
Levant, Dr. Ron, 203, 205
Leveling, 39
Lewis, Dr. Michael, 73
Limiting, 27, 31–32, 56, 86
Limit setting, 88, 119. *See also*
    Discipline
Loomis, Dr. Susan, 70
Lying, dealing with, 64

MacKinnon, Dr. Carol E., 17
Male authority figures, single-mother
    households and, 166–167, 171
Masculine traits, in boys and girls, 12–
    13, 16–18
Maternal employment. *See* Work
Maternal goals, 35–37
Maternal sensitivity, 21–22
    attachment and, 22–23
    child's appreciation of, 109
    to child's complaints about work,
      116–117
    to child's need for soothing, 115–116
    to child's world, 114–115
    creative uncertainty and, 38–41
    after day care, 79–80
    defined, 25
    guilt and, 177–178
    maternal style and, 136–137,
      142–143, 145–146, 156–158
    role satisfaction and, 32
    of single mothers, 164, 168
    time pressures and, 27–32
    work pressures and, 25–27

Maternal styles
    achiever, 151–159
    directive, 29–31
    flat-out, 37–38
    optimist, 137–144
    types of, 135–137
    worrier, 144–151, 193
Maternity leave, 185–186, 219
Memory training, for infants, 105–107
Menu offering, 97–99
Minivacations, 38. *See also* Vacations
Mood, regularity of, in mother, 113
Moore, Dr. T. W., 175
Morning activities, child's resistance
    to, 68–71
Mothers. *See also* At-home mothers;
        Single mothers
    conflicted, 35–36
    as fallible, 227–228
    goals evaluation by, 36–37
    helping child to feel understood,
        114–117
    jealousy about sharing parental
        authority by, 193–195
    leave-taking distress in, 74–76
    prolonged absence of, 132–133
    rejection of, by child, 56–58, 111–112
    as role models, 227–230
    role satisfaction in, 32–38
    as superwoman, 174–176, 177–178,
        180
    symbols of, 102–105
"Mr. Rogers' Neighborhood," 61
Multimodal memory making, 106–107

Night waking, 88
Noninvolvement, of child, in group
    activities, 94–95
Nursery school, leave-taking and,
    74–76
Nurturing, satisfaction in, 198–199

Object constancy, 91–92, 109–117
    building blocks of, 113–117
    positive, 111, 114–117
Optimist maternal style, 135–144
    advantages of, 141
    characteristics of, 141
    essential elements of, 142–144
    potential risks of, 141–142
Organization (self), defined, 54
Osherson, Samuel, 201
Overcompensation, discipline and, 118
Overintensity, in single mothers, 161,
    164

Overinvestment
    signs of, 170–171
    in single mothers, 161–162, 167
Overprotectiveness
    in caregivers, 209
    signs of, 170–171
    single mothers and, 162, 169
Overreaction, discipline and, 118
Overstimulation (in child)
    day-care centers and, 60–61
    dealing with, 60–61
    directive maternal style and, 31

Pacing, 27, 32, 56
Parental nights out, child's reaction
    to, 58–59
Physical play, maternal style and, 144
Physical punishment, 126, 128
Play. *See also* Toys
    by infants, 218–221
    morning, 69–70
    physical, 144
    pleasure in, 28–30
    safety of, 123–124
    spontaneity in, 28–29, 31–32
    themes, 56–59
Play acting, as discipline, 123–126
Positive object constancy, 111, 114–117
Power struggles, discipline and,
    119–121
Praise
    discriminating use of, 226–227
    for initiative, 62
    using to enlist husband's help,
        196–197
Preschoolers. *See also* Children;
        Toddlers
    attitudes toward mother's work,
        231–233
    developmental stages of, 227–235
Pruett, Dr. Kyle, 13, 15, 16

Quality time, 27–28
    directive maternal style and, 29
    vs. shared time, 86
Quiet time, 60–61

Reading, interaction through, 46
Reading a child, 21, 115
    body language and, 43–44,
        143–144
    single mothers' ability to, 168
Reality Attuned Parenting (REAP),
    7–9
Reassurance, about strangers,
    caregivers, 73–74
Recall capacity, improving, 105–106

Regression, in child, 53–54, 59–60
Regularity, development of, in
    mother, 113–114
Reluctant fathers, 192, 199–207
Repetition, 99–100
Rescue fantasizing, in caregivers, 209,
    211
Resistance
    to being corrected, 130–131
    to day care, 129–130
    to discipline, 126–129
    dealing with, 120–121
    to eating, 70
    to finishing tasks, 131
    maternal style and, 156
    to morning activities, 68–71
Reunion, 77–81
Rituals, importance of, 113–114
Rivalry, for child's love, 13–14
Rogers, Fred, 61
Role satisfaction, 32–38
    career goals and, 34–35
    husband's support and, 32–34
    time constraints and, 32, 37–38
Rolling through, as discipline
    technique, 126–129
Routine, regularity of, in mother, 114

Safety
    dramatizing importance of, 124–126
    forbidden activities and, 123–124
Saturday mornings, themes, 51–54
Schedules, maternal style and, 139–140
Security
    in children, 18–20, 48
    self-comfort and, 89
Self
    formation of, in preschool years,
        227–230
    organization and, 54
    sense of, 54–56
Self-absorption, by child, at depar-
    tures, 48–49
Self-assertion, by child, 42–43
Self-care, maternal style and, 158
Self-comforting (in children), 89, 91–
    92
    capacity to define feelings and, 226
    self-knowledge and, 95–97
    symbolic thinking and, 104–105
Self-control
    child's struggle for, 49–50
    developing, in child, 223–226
Self-discipline, 88
Self-knowledge (individuality)
    development of, 93–94
    group activities and, 94–95

    ill-defined, 94–95
    self-comforting and, 95–97
Self-reliance
    in children of working mothers, 16
    encouraging, 234
Sensitivity. *See also* Maternal sensitivity
    developmental, 23, 88, 89, 92
    situational, 23, 88
Sequencing, 106
Sexual stereotypes
    avoiding, 12–13
    maternal employment and, 16–18
Shared time
    after dinner, 82–83, 85–87
    avoiding distractions during, 143
    open-endedness of, 86
    spent by working mothers vs.
        at-home mothers, 37, 182
    spontaneity in, 85–86
    themes, 56–59
Sick child, guilt about leaving, 178–180
Siegal, Dr. William, 162, 167, 169
Single mothers, 160–173
    day-care needs, 164–165
    guilt and, 177
    isolation and, 161–162, 164
    male authority figures and, 166–
        167, 171
    maternal sensitivity of, 164
    overintensity and, 161
    overinvestment and, 161–162
    over protectiveness and, 162
    return to work after birth by, 186
    support groups for, 171
Situational sensitivity, 23, 88
Skill development, maternal style
    and, 142, 155. *See also* Child's de-
    velopment
Sleeping in parent's bed, 121
Social skills
    day care and, 14–15
    dinnertime and, 82, 84
    maternal style and, 141
    REAP strategies and, 9–10
Spontaneity
    in children's play, 31–32
    maternal style and, 138–139
    need for, in children's play, 28–29
    in shared time, 85–86
Stalling tactics, at departure time, 50
Start-up activities, 69
Stern, Dr. Daniel, 19, 27, 179
Stimulation, child's need for, 63
Stranger anxiety
    day care and, 15
    returning to work and, 185
Strange Situation Test, 92–93

Stress. *See also* Distress
   avoiding overreaction to, 225–226
   benefits of, 175
   teaching child to deal with, 224
Stretchability, 18–19
Structure, maternal style and, 139–140
Structuring, 103, 131
Sunday nights, themes, 54–56
Superhero toys, 165
Supervised multimodal exploration, 107
Superwoman, guilt at not being, 177–178, 180
Support systems
   breakdown in, 33–34
   role satisfaction and, 32–34
   for single mothers, 171
Symbolic objects, use of, 107–109
Symbolic thinking, 91, 101–109
   building blocks of, 105–109
   consistency and, 107
   development of, 102
   memory training for, 105–107
   use of symbolic objects to develop, 107–109

Tantrums, 63
Television, caregiver's use of, 63
Themes, 41, 44
   caregivers, 62–65
   day-care workers, 59–62
   departure-time, 48–51
   homecomings, 44–48
   playtime, 56–59
   Saturday mornings, 51–54
   shared time, 56–59
   Sunday nights, 54–56
Thinking, symbolic. *See* Symbolic thinking
Time. *See also* Shared time
   for oneself, 146
   pressures, maternal sensitivity and, 27–32
   spent with child, 37, 182
   structuring, 37–38
Toddlers
   developmental stages of, 222–227
   development of symbolic thinking in, 102–105
   encouraging decision-making in, 101
   interests of, 98–99
   object constancy in, 111–112
   perception of mother by, 114–117
   terrible twos, 222–227
Tolerance, promoting, in child, 228–230

Touch-points
   coming home, 77–81
   dinner, 83–85
   evening, 81–83
   leave-taking, 71–76
   mid-morning check-in call, 76–77
   shared time, 85–88
   wake-up, 67–71
   waking up in middle of the night, 88–89
Toys. *See also* Play
   age-appropriate, 98–99
   reducing distress with, 57
   superhero, 165
Tracking ability, 168
Transitional objects, 104
   encouraging use of, 108–109

Vacations
   guilt at leaving child behind, 188–189
   minivacations, 38
Vulnerability
   maternal style and, 156–157
   single mothers and, 162

Waking up
   children's needs, 68–71
   mother's responsibilities, 67–68
   at night, 88–89
Weekends, themes, 51–56
Willing fathers, 192–199
Withdrawal, in children, 47
Work
   attachment disruption and, 22–23
   career goals, 34–35
   child's reactions to, 230, 231
   child's sexual stereotypes and, 16–18
   effects of, 5–6
   guilt about enjoying, 185
   guilt about returning to too soon, 185–188
   legitimacy of child's feelings toward, 116–117
   presenting a positive image of, 72, 84–85
Working mothers. *See* Mothers
Worrier maternal style, 136, 144–151, 193
   advantages of, 148
   characteristics of, 147
   essential elements of, 149–151
   potential risks of, 148–149
Worrying, keeping perspective in, 149–151